The Future of Preaching

The Future of Preaching

Edited by

Geoffrey Stevenson

scm press

© The Editor and Contributors 2010

Published in 2010 by SCM Press
Editorial office
13–17 Long Lane,
London, EC1A 9PN, UK

SCM Press is an imprint of Hymns Ancient and Modern Ltd
(a registered charity)
13A Hellesdon Park Road
Norwich NR6 5DR, UK
www.scm-canterburypress.co.uk

British Library Cataloguing in Publication data

A catalogue record for this book is available
from the British Library

978-0-334-04362-1

Originated by The Manila Typesetting Company
Printed in the UK by
CPI William Clowes Beccles NR34 7TL

Contents

Part Three   People

Foreword

LESLIE GRIFFITHS

In the course of an eventful life, I seem to have become a snapper-up of ill-considered titles. Those who have invited me to preach or speak at some event or other often ask me how I'd like to be described. They are not easily fobbed off with my standard reply that I'd like to be simply 'Leslie Griffiths'. They seem keen to impress their public with the full panoply of my honorifics. If they persist, I send them the whole list in alphabetical order and invite them to do whatever they like with them. One title is invariably missing from such a list, yet it's the one I'd give up all the others for; indeed it's the one I have chosen for my epitaph when that final day comes. On Welsh slate, affixed to the wall of the memorial garden at Wesley's Chapel, and above the spot where my ashes will be interred, the announcement will be made to all passers-by that here lies 'Leslie Griffiths, one of Mr Wesley's preaches'.

It is as a preacher that I most want to be remembered. Not as a teacher or lecturer, not a broadcaster or writer, but as a preacher. It is to this work that I was called, and I can think of no vocation more noble, no art more intricate, no cause more necessary than that of declaring the good news which God has made known to us through the person and ministry, the life and death, the resurrection and ascension of our Lord Jesus Christ.

The pages that follow make a serious attempt to re-imagine the role of preaching for our day. A brilliant essay on the Bible asks us to move beyond seeing it merely as *text* towards understanding it as *message*. And that must surely be the supreme challenge in an age where the world's agenda is relentlessly driven forward by breaking news, reality television, the cult of celebrity and the latest sales wheeze of those who want to sell us something. The Bible undergirds the work of every preacher, but no one should be left thinking of our holy book merely as a tidy arrangement of pages held firmly within unyielding (or even floppy) covers. This book has done sterling service but it ceases to be useful if it comes to entomb the lively, life-giving story to which it bears witness. And if it becomes a kind of text book, pushing preaching remorselessly towards cerebral utterance, erudite exegesis and the careful language of lawyers, then we must surely work hard to release the message we preach from its bondage. And the internet (I never thought I'd be caught admitting this) is just the catalyzing force which might enable this to happen. It might just be for the twenty-first century what the printing press was to the sixteenth. It might be the tool which allows our story to take wings again.

Here are essays which view the art of preaching from a variety of standpoints – that of the listener, or of the herald commissioned to announce good news, or of the cultural context within which sermons are prepared and delivered. We are given pen pictures of the place of preaching in our varying church traditions. I especially liked the insight given of how the 'Black church' goes about it – all that interaction, those sighs and hallelujahs, the rhetorical 'tricks of the trace' and the heightened atmosphere where expectation features large, the sheer drama of it all.

I have already referred to the *art* of preaching, and that is an appropriate way of describing it. In the Middle Ages, the three strands of the *ars preadicandi* laid it upon the preacher to persuade, instruct and delight his hearers in equal measure. And there's much in what follows that addresses one or more of these lines of thought, although I personally might have wanted a little more attention given to the way 'delight' might be created in the hearts of those listening to sermons.

I was sure there would be a reference within these pages to the classical definition of preaching given by Phillips Brooks in his 1877 *Lectures on Preaching* given at Yale. There invariably is, but I didn't expect it to appear quite as late in the book as it does. 'Truth through personality' remains as good a starting point for understanding the essence of preaching as any. I've used it often enough myself. But how I wish someone would amplify that definition with just a little more reference to what Brooks wrote just a few sentences later. This how he went on:

> The truth [proclaimed] must come really through the person, not merely over his lips, not merely into his understanding and out through his pen. It must come through his character, his affections, his whole intellectual and moral being. It must come genuinely through him.

The gender-exclusive language employed by Brooks is, of course, of its time but our insistence on a literary style more generous to all its readers cannot prevent us from sensing and agreeing with the thrust of his argument. Nor from recognizing the distinction he makes between two different kinds of preacher. He writes how the Gospel has come *over* one of them and reaches us tinged and flavoured with his superficial characteristics, belittled with his littleness. The Gospel has come *through* the other, and we received it impressed and winged with all the earnestness and strength that there is in him.

Brooks brings his case to its conclusion with a graphic contrast. 'In the first case', he writes, 'the [preacher] has been but a printing machine or a trumpet. In the other case he has been a true [human being] and a real messenger of God.'

I and, I suspect, all of us who attempt the noble art of preaching, can easily acknowledge that we have gone down each of these paths from time to time. Preaching has been both an exercise emanating from our thinking selves, an exhortation lacking depth or subtlety, and also something altogether more profound. When our words are conceived in the deepest parts of our being, when they resonate with everything we try to do in the rest of our lives, when they are marked with the ring of sincerity and truth, it is not difficult to recognize the way our words acquire an energy and strength which is not of our own making. The God-given-ness, God-blessedness, of the humble work of ordinary men and women who endeavour to say something meaningful about the extraordinary generosity of their Maker, the unfathomable love of their Heavenly Father, is surely as much a miracle as any ever recorded. Here is the bread from heaven that feeds us and our listeners now and evermore – humble scraps which somehow nourish multitudes.

Those of us who preach know how passionate an exercise it all is. Those who listen deserve only the best fare, food which offers a foretaste of the heavenly banquet itself. And those who have put their heads together, given some serious thought to the preacher's task, and now offer their work to the public are to be commended for continuing the struggle to give preaching a future at least as significant and transformative as its past.

Leslie Griffiths, One of Mr Wesley's Preachers

Contributors

Ruthlyn Bradshaw has been in ministry for 37 years. A native of Montserrat, she migrated at an early age to Boston, USA, where she received most of her formal education and early theological training. After some years she returned to her homeland, Montserrat, and for several years served as pastor, until the volcanic eruption caused her to migrate in 1997 to England, where she currently serves as senior pastor for two branches of the New Life Assembly Fellowship of Churches. Her penchant for learning, culminating in a Master's degree in Applied Theology from Spurgeon's College in the UK, has added to her capacity to preach and counsel with uncommon insight. She is currently a doctoral student and faculty member in two theological institutions.

Susan Durber is a minister of the United Reformed Church, presently serving as Principal of Westminster College, Cambridge, where she is leading the college in its development from a traditional theological college to a resource centre for the whole of the URC. She has served churches in rural, inner city, suburban and city centre settings. She publishes prayers, books and articles on preaching, and contributes regularly to the URC's *Reform* magazine. She is also on the Standing Commission of the Faith and Order Commission of the World Council of Churches.

Leslie J. Francis is Professor of Religions and Education within the Warwick Religions and Education Research Unit, University of Warwick, England, and Canon Theologian at Bangor Cathedral, Wales. His research interests are in practical theology, empirical theology and the psychology of religion. In particular, he is interested in the ways in which research traditions within the field of 'personality and individual differences' may help to inform a 'theology of individual differences'. It is this theological approach that has given rise to the SIFT method of biblical hermeneutics and liturgical preaching.

Paul Johns is a Methodist Local Preacher and Director of the College of Preachers. He has spent most of his working life as a management consultant working in industries as diverse as food production, finance and football. As well as tutoring in preaching, he writes plays and stories and is a former contributor to BBC's *Thought for the Day*. He also works voluntarily for a small Christian–Muslim development agency promoting interfaith co-operation in Bosnia and visits that country frequently. He has Masters degrees in History from Oxford and in Theology (preaching) from the University of Wales.

Richard Littledale is the Minister of Teddington Baptist Church, in West London, and has always had an interest in innovative and creative communication. He has written books for the Baptist Union of Great Britain and the Saint Andrew Press on the subject. His first book with Saint Andrew Press, *Stale Bread*, is a guide to narrative preaching, and his second, the *Preacher's A to Z*, is a preacher's companion on the craft and practice of preaching. Richard is a regular contributor to *Pause for Thought* on BBC Radio 2 and a tutor with the College of Preachers.

Duncan Macpherson is a Roman Catholic Permanent Deacon in the Diocese of Westminster. He preaches regularly in several Catholic churches as well as in those of other Christian traditions. Retiring from lecturing in Theology and Religious Studies at Saint Mary's University College, Twickenham, in 2000, he obtained his D.Min. in Preaching from the Aquinas Institute in St Louis Missouri in 2003. He is a tutor and executive member of the College of Preachers and is the features editor of *The Preacher*. His publications include *Pilgrim Preacher: Palestine, Pilgrimage and Preaching* (foreword by Naim Ateek; 2004 and 2008). He belongs to the US-based Academy of Homiletics and the Catholic Association of Teachers of Homiletics. He is a research fellow at the University of Wales, Lampeter, and teaches the MA module on 'Proclamation and Preaching' at Saint Mary's University College.

Ian Paul is Dean of Studies at St John's, Nottingham, where he teaches New Testament, philosophy of language and homiletics. From a Roman Catholic background, he came to personal faith as a teenager and studied Pure Maths and Operational Research (logistics) and made chocolate before training for ordination in the Church of England at St John's. After completing a Ph.D. on metaphor and the book of Revelation, he was involved in church leadership in Poole, Dorset, for ten years before returning to join the staff in Nottingham. He is married to Maggie and they have three children.

Contributors

Trevor Pitt was ordained in 1970 to parish ministry in Sheffield, and worked in local radio. He moved to Kent in 1979, combining parish ministry with teaching in theological education, and served as a Six Preacher at Canterbury Cathedral. In 1991 he became Principal of the North East Oecumenical Course (NEOC) and Hon. Canon of Newcastle Cathedral. His primary academic interests, since postgraduate work in liturgy and philosophical theology, have been in liturgical theology, performance and practice, and in preaching, communication and understanding of the faith, and practical ecumenism.

David J. Schlafer is an Episcopal priest who has taught philosophy, theology and homiletics at a number of seminaries in different denominational traditions, and has served on the staff of the College of Preachers (USA). He currently focuses professional energy as a conference leader and preaching consultant. Author and editor of 18 books, he contributes regularly to professional journals in homiletics.

Roger Spiller was born in Birmingham where he was influenced by the preaching of Canon Bryan Green, a founder of the College of Preachers. After a brief period in industry Roger read theology at Durham and Cambridge and trained for ministry at Ridley Hall. He later qualified in adult education at Nottingham University. He ministered at Bradford Cathedral, Stratford-upon-Avon and Nuneaton, before becoming Principal of a national ministerial training scheme (Aston). He has been involved nationally in developing new patterns of ministerial education as well as in training and teaching. He is currently Director of Ministry and Ordinands in Coventry diocese and a Canon of Coventry Cathedral. He is secretary of the UK network of the Ecumenical Institute, Geneva, where he spent a semester, and is tutor and council member of the College of Preachers.

Ian Stackhouse is pastoral leader of Guildford Baptist Church. He has been preaching for over 20 years in a local church context but he has also preached quite extensively overseas. Ian has hosted Preachers' Breakfasts and Conferences over the years to encourage pastors and also those starting out in preaching for the first time. He has authored two books, of which the first, *The Gospel-Driven Church*, seeks to underline the importance of expository preaching.

Roger Standing is a Baptist minister and is presently the Director of Training at Spurgeon's College in London, where he teaches mission, evangelism and pioneer ministry. With over 30 years of experience in ministry he worked as an evangelist in Liverpool before pastoring churches in Leeds and South London. Prior to taking up his present position, he was the Regional Minister/Team Leader for the Southern Counties Baptist Association. His previous publications include *Preaching for the Unchurched in an Age of Entertainment* (2002) and *Finding the Plot: Preaching in a Narrative Style* (2004).

Geoffrey Stevenson is an adjunct lecturer in preaching, communication and media studies at New College, University of Edinburgh. He recently completed a Ph.D. in homiletics at Edinburgh, and before that he was Director of the Centre for Christian Communication at St John's College, Durham. Prior to that he worked for 20 years as an actor. A deviser and performer of his own mime theatre shows, he toured extensively throughout the UK and Europe both to churches and to small-scale theatres. He has published two books on mime theatre in the Church and two on preaching: *Pulpit Journeys* (2006) and *Preaching with Humanity* (2008), co-authored with Stephen Wright.

Margaret Withers taught music for the Open University and in several Inner London schools, before becoming Diocesan Children's Adviser for Rochester in 1989. Her interest in liturgy led her to provide training for clergy, Readers and ordinands on involving children in services, especially all-age worship. This led to the publication by BRF of the teaching programme *Welcome to the Lord's Table* in 1999, which was followed by *The Gifts of Baptism* in 2003. Margaret was the Archbishop's Officer for Evangelism among Children from 2001 to 2006. Her role included providing advice and establishing training for churches wishing to develop their outreach among children. In 'retirement' she maintains her interest in inclusive worship as a tutor for the College of Preachers, and through church music, and writing. Recent publications include *Creative Communion* (2008) and *Local Church, Local School* (2010).

Stephen Wright has been in the Anglican ministry since 1986. He served in parishes in the north of England before taking his Ph.D. in New Testament studies from the University of Durham in 1997. From 1998 to 2006 he was Director of the College of Preachers. He is now Tutor in Biblical Studies and Practical Theology at Spurgeon's College, London, where he continues to direct the Masters in Theology (Preaching) course. Among his publications are (with Geoffrey Stevenson) *Preaching with Humanity* (2008) and (with Peter Stevenson) *Preaching the Atonement* (2005) and *Preaching the Incarnation* (2010).

Introduction

GEOFFREY STEVENSON

What is the future of preaching? More pointedly, as many have asked, is there a future for preaching? I will not here rehearse the well-known tropes from harbingers of doom. Instead, consider what Dean Inge observed, not about preaching but about human nature: 'Any hopefulness for the future of civilization is based on the reasonable expectation that humanity is still only beginning its course.' This encourages me to ask, what if, far from fading away under the harsh light of European secularism, Christianity is still only beginning her course? What if she returns, as she has time and time again, to the resurrection form of her Lord? Would a resurrection in preaching be far behind? As Richard Lischer observed, 'most every reform movement in the church whether Franciscan, Dominican, Lollard, Brethren, Lutheran, Presbyterian, or Methodist, has meant not only a revival of preaching but a re-forming of its method of presentation' (2002, p. xvi). Rumours of preaching's demise may yet prove greatly exaggerated.

But who would be so foolish as to try to predict the future of preaching? Almost every form as practised in British churches today – from the three- to four-minute homily before Mass to the 50- to 60-minute thematic or expository sermon – is located in a culturally specific ecclesial context. Very few practices can claim an unbroken lineage of rhetorical form and liturgical meaning that goes back more than a couple of hundred years. Shifts happen over time. Not only do theologies but also fashion and sensibilities change, sometimes gradually, sometimes abruptly. You have to ask, will the preaching of our digitally immersed younger generations migrate online, becoming a welter of tweets and text messages launched into the 'blogosphere'? And can that still be called preaching? Time will tell. But preaching isn't standing still.

As indicated by many of the contributors to this book, there are historical givens, without which whatever is being done with words in an act of worship or evangelism can no longer be called preaching. There are also new insights and understandings about the preaching act that result from theology being done afresh in our time and culture. This can result in tension and uncertainty. Tension can of course be enormously creative, and uncertainty

I

is not always a bad thing for a pilgrim people. It also gives a real provisionality to predictions and prescriptions. At base, however, a discussion about the future of preaching is implicitly an invitation to engage in preaching that is 'forward-looking' even while it acknowledges its roots and respects its heritage. Taken together, I think the contributors to this volume strongly assert that forward-looking preaching will hang on to three things (there may be more). It will engage faithfully with the Bible, it will engage directly with its listeners, and it will engage prophetically with the world.[1]

Forward-looking preaching engages faithfully with the Bible (and, by extension, with church tradition, doctrine and practice), to present and explain Jesus, the 'hope that is set before us'. Forward-looking preaching engages directly with the congregation, to connect with their hopes and seeking persuasively to apply itself to the future corporate life and that of each listener. Forward-looking preaching engages prophetically with the world, bringing the liberating, releasing, healing word of God to a society so often bound by the chains of the past, too slow to challenge injustice, too blinded by wealth or by poverty to see a Saviour. We will look at these three areas in turn.

Forward-looking biblical preaching

Isn't the Bible fixed in its canonical form, a narrative of God's past dealings with his peoples? Isn't it, moreover, a culturally bound text, locked into primitive agricultural societies of the eastern Mediterranean basin? Tribal warfare, law codes, songs without the music, wandering Aramaeans and temple disputes, itinerant religious teachers and their disciples: it's hard enough bringing the Bible into the present, never mind applying it to the future. And yet it is, and claims to be, profoundly about the future, setting out God's plans and purposes beneath a grand meta-narrative. The various smaller narratives are parables and paradigms for us as individuals, as a Church and as a society. Its principal subject is the incarnate Word, Jesus Christ, who shares a nature that is time bound, earthly and human, with a nature that is timeless, transcendent and divine. This means our hermeneutical/interpretative task is never easy, of course, and many are the theological differences over the detail, but if we are not at a very deep level passionately fired by the divine salvation economy of creation, redemption, restoration and re-creation, then we will surely be unable to preach in a forward-looking way from the Bible. Our homiletical hermeneutic is never about settling on a meaning, fixed for all time, squeezed or distilled or gouged out of the text with the help of an army of scholars and commentators. Instead it involves prayerful, imaginative and faithful listening to catch and pass on, through the preacher, inspired by the Spirit, the meaning that the biblical text has to say to this particular congregation, in this particular place, at this particular time. And to say this is to take them on into their future.

Forward-looking congregational preaching

Every listener and every congregation has a future, and they invariably bring to the 'sermon listening event' their hopes and fears – whether latent or fully present – about their futures. Forward-looking preaching gently names those desires and terrors, compassionately holding up a mirror to allow recognition. It is personal, it is direct, sometimes uncomfortable, sometimes deeply reassuring, but never irrelevant and yawn inducing.

Forward-looking preaching places those hopes and fears into context, bringing God's perspective through appeal to Scripture, tradition, reason and experience (to invoke the Wesleyan Quadrilateral). Interpreting the present through these lenses from the past can reshape our hopes and reduce our fears as we go into the future.

Forward-looking prophetic preaching

Prophetic preaching would be ill advised to try to be predictive preaching. Remember the American TV-evangelist Pat Robertson. In 1981 he was asked, 'Does the Bible specifically tell us what is going to happen in the future?' His reply: 'It specifically clearly, unequivocally says that Russia and other countries will enter into war and God will destroy Russia through earthquakes, volcanoes.'[2] Well, perhaps time will prove him right (although the exegesis seems a little suspicious to me).

Nor is there much scope in forward-looking preaching for castigating society, Amos-like, with threats of divine wrath. The lambasting and criticizing of society from the pulpit is too easy and one suspects achieves very little but letting off steam. A preacher's fulminations may bind a group together in some ways, but do little to empower them to be God's agents of change. Such handwringing also allows Christianity's 'cultured despisers' to pigeonhole and sideline us once again as impotent moaning minnies.

Instead of predicting doom or thunderously complaining, prophetic preaching should be attempting to bring witness of God's word to the world. And even then only rarely do we see a prophet/witness in the line of a Mandela or a Martin Luther King. More commonly, but still with humility and baited breath, forward-looking preachers are called to represent to the surrounding culture both the standards of God and the merciful grace of God. Prophetic preaching tells it like it is, refusing to ignore the elephant in the corner that is our hoarded wealth, our dispirited apathy, our lack of compassion, our blind eye or our ability to walk by on the other side. But instead of reducing us to guilt-ridden wrecks, prophetic preaching also leads people, to use Walter Brueggemann's marvellous phrase, into an 'imaginative "or"'. This preaching tells new stories and recasts old narratives to help people to re-imagine the future as one that is suffused with God's grace in the midst of failure, and marked by redemptive purpose. Prophetic preaching does not claim that the Church is right and society is wrong, nor that faith has all the answers. Prophetic preaching questions and even challenges the world to bring all to God, to bring to God its questions, its sufferings, its lack of peace and its inability to heal itself. And these can be brought to God with the expectation that moving forward with hope in God's mercy is viable and altogether desirable through faith in Jesus Christ.

The shape of this book

The 15 contributors to this book have possibly 15 (or even more) different approaches to preaching, and they present a wide range of views of the future of preaching in the UK church. In editing this book, I have not sought, still less tried, to impose a uniformity of theology, doctrine or style. I did not ask the writers to strike a balance between predictive and prescriptive. They are united in a belief that preaching has a future, and have been both bold and gracious, in my view, in suggesting what that future may look like, or what needs to be understood in order for preaching to reach for the future. Their contributions are grouped into three sections. The first part, 'Contexts', examines the location of preaching from a range of angles. The authors work from the recognition that preaching is inextricably linked with – even as it seeks to change – the culture, both sacred and secular, in which it operates. The second part, 'Practices', considers homiletical futures, in other words, the classic concerns of the art and craft of preaching such as sermonic form and language, use and misuse of Scripture, and doing theology through preaching. The last part, 'People', discusses psychology, inner resources and life-long development.

Roger Standing begins Part One, 'Contexts', by examining the cultural context for preaching in the UK Church. His analysis is perceptive and wide ranging, and he names the significant cultural forces that act powerfully upon preachers and their listeners, such as entertainment, consumerism, the cult of celebrity, and the ethos and atmosphere of our societies.

This is important material to grapple with if we are to fulfil preaching's prophetic calling, and he lays important foundations for the writers of the next section. Similarly the next three writers present important historical and theoretical perspectives for understanding the future of preaching as located in specific denominations and traditions. In a sense, these writers have to stand in for a dozen more, at least, who could have been included (albeit in a much longer and different book). Duncan Macpherson reminds us of the historical trajectory of preaching in the Roman Catholic Church, while Roger Spiller tackles the same thing from an Anglican perspective. Ian Stackhouse explores what that part of the Church sometimes called 'charismatic' has to offer the rest of the Church in its view of preaching. He calls for preaching to be prophetic, without conflating preaching and prophecy, and for preaching to be understood and practised as a spiritual gift, truly charismatic. Finally, Ruthlyn Bradshaw engages us with the distinctive culture of black preaching, helping to ease open the door through which mutual and highly fulfilling interchanges can take place. Such dialogue will surely be a part of the future of preaching, and these authors are to be commended for showing us some of the different sides of what will undoubtedly be the multi-faceted jewel of preaching in the future.

Part Two, 'Practices', contains work on some of the classic subjects of homiletics, with authors painstakingly crafting visions of the future of preaching. Trevor Pitt asserts that preaching is a primary form of theological reflection, and challenges preachers of the future to be theologically rigorous and tough-minded about how they develop the content of their preaching. Stephen Wright focuses a lens on what it will mean to base preaching on scriptural texts when there are important challenges both to the authority of Scripture as well as to the very idea of what constitutes a text in the 'information age'. Paul Johns reminds us that a future world immersed in 24/7/52 news coverage will require theologically nimble and courageously prophetic preachers, but presents important opportunities to do theology, to echo Trevor Pitt, at the preaching interface between Church, world and Scripture. Returning to questions of culture and communication, Margaret Withers, writing on preaching to all ages, reminds us that every service presents a challenge to communicate with the wide range of backgrounds, personality types and, yes, ages present, not just when children are present. Ian Paul looks at the Church's cultural linguistic context, and urges a fresh understanding of persuasive, metaphorical speech based on biblical rhetoric, to enable preachers to connect with their heritage in order to preach in the future. Finally, Richard Littledale helpfully and practically tackles the form of preaching in the future as the Church come to grips with the communications revolution.

Introduction

The person of the preacher is the title and subject of the last section, 'People'. This begins with a kind of straddling chapter, since Leslie Francis's work on the SIFT method of preaching is concerned equally with reaching listeners and with understanding the psychological orientations of the preacher. It is based on psychological type theory, and I expect will be quite challenging, or frown inducing, for some readers, and tremendously liberating or energizing for others. A chapter on the preacher's inner life, by Susan Durber, might be expected to be about holiness and piety, and, while these will be a part of preaching's future as much as its past, she proposes an important and unorthodox way of integrating the God-given humanity of the preacher with the sermons she or he is called to preach. Finally, in a chapter on forming future preachers, I propose a model for understanding what it is to learn to preach. I consider a range of what I consider to be vital factors in the trajectory of life-long learning that comprises a preacher's walk with God in the awesome calling and unparalleled privilege that is preaching.

I am delighted that the esteemed American homiletician David Schlafer agreed to write the Afterword, for he brings to his task great wisdom and an infectious enthusiasm for preaching, based on a confidence that if God wants preaching to have a future, then it will be unstoppable, and as glorious as anything seen in the past.

So what is the future of preaching? I would not dare to predict but, to return to my theme, I want to suggest that the question of whether preaching even has a future will be decisively influenced by the extent to which preaching in our churches becomes forward-looking preaching. The Church and the world alike need preaching that looks to the future, proclaiming, to the glory of God and in the power of the spirit, Jesus Christ as Lord of all space and time. May we find the strength, vision and courage to undertake that charge now and on into the future.

Notes

1. This is taken from The College of Preacher's Commitment to Preaching in 2010, its Jubilee year.
2. Pat Robertson (1930–), *700 Club*, 2 December 1981.

Reference

Richard Lischer, 2002, *The Company of Preachers: Wisdom on Preaching, Augustine to the Present*, Grand Rapids, MI: Eerdmans.

PART ONE

Contexts

Mediated Preaching

Homiletics in Contemporary British Culture

ROGER STANDING

The Word became flesh and blood, and moved into the neighborhood.
We saw the glory with our own eyes, the one-of-a-kind glory, like
Father, like Son, Generous inside and out, true from start to finish.
(John 1.14, The Message)

As Eugene Peterson wrestles with the prologue of John's Gospel and
the mystery of the incarnation the mind-boggling reality that defines
the whole of the Christian faith tumbles out. The one through whom
everything was created became a flesh-and-blood person at a specific
place and time. There was a locality, a neighbourhood, which was his.
There were people that he lived next door to, a community that he
was a part of, events that he was caught up into – this is real life as we
know it.

Context has always affected preaching. It is no surprise that, when
Jesus preached he spoke about what people knew, and used that as a
means to open up the truth of God to his hearers. Scan the Gospels and
you will find Jesus deploying insights from agriculture (Matt. 9.35–8;
13.1–43), the countryside (Matt. 5.25–34), the construction industry
(Matt. 7.24–9) and familial rites of passage (Matt. 22.1–14) as he addresses those who have come to listen to him.

There is no pure, culture-free, gospel. The apostle Peter's encounter
with the Roman centurion Cornelius, with its accompanying heavenly
vision, had woken him up to the issue (Acts 10 and 11), while Paul was
clearly aware of it too as is evident from his time in Athens. Attracting
the curiosity of certain Epicurean and Stoic philosophers he was invited
to the Areopagus to give a full account of his 'new teaching'. Drawing
on the poetry of Epimenides, Aratus and Cleanthes his preaching takes
on a decidedly Greek feel, while the gospel themes of judgement and
resurrection are the focus of his message (Acts 17.16–34).

Writing later to the church at Corinth he explains this gospel principle that informs his whole life as a missionary disciple, not just his preaching. 'I have become all things to all people so that by all possible means I might save some' (1 Cor. 9.22b). This is more than an evangelist's strategy. When Jesus commanded the twelve to make disciples of all nations, he was thinking more of culturally distinct groups than nation states (Matt. 28.18). Similarly, on the day of Pentecost, the Holy Spirit affirmed the cultural diversity of the crowd as they each heard the 'wonders of God' in their own language (Acts 2.5–12). This reversal of Babel goes to the heart of cultural identity and expression. Indeed, the climax of John's vision of the heavenly city is of a place where ethnic distinctiveness is retained as 'the glory and honour of the nations' are brought into it (Rev. 21.26).

If this principle has been at the heart of God's self-revelation from the beginning, it poses a challenging question to every preacher. In what culture does the gospel we preach live? Is it held in a biblical time capsule? Is it embodied in the culture of a denominational tradition or the history and context of our own personal experience of faith? Or, following the incarnational example of the gospel itself, is it shaped by the culture and context of those who are to receive the message?

There are dangers here. To fail to clothe the gospel we preach in the culture of those who are to receive it is to risk it being heard as irrelevant. By contrast, culture cannot be embraced uncritically as that will only swiftly lead to a syncretistic compromise of the message itself. There are no easy answers and no simple shortcuts.

So, what are the elements of contemporary culture that the preacher must engage with in twenty-first-century Britain? What are the issues to be negotiated and the pitfalls to be avoided if the twin errors of dogmatic irrelevance and cultural surrender are to be avoided? In this regard ecclesial expectations and the homiletical objective will always need to interact with contemporary culture to establish an appropriate balance in the preaching task. A weekly sermon for a well-established and historic congregation will be shaped differently from an evangelistic preaching opportunity in a university mission. The task of this chapter is to map the current cultural landscape as it affects preaching, to note its implications and to look for signs that might help us shape the task to hand.

Contemporary British culture

What does it mean to be British? From Norman Tebbit's notorious 'cricket test' to determine immigrant integration into the UK to Gordon

Brown's call to celebrate national identity and embrace the Union flag in the wake of the 7 July bombing in London in 2005, there have been repeated attempts to define 'Britishness'. The difficulty of the task is cast in high relief by the lack of success of all those who have attempted it.

While many lament the passing of an overarching 'British culture' and the increasing fragmentation of wider society, it would be a mistake to assume that there was nothing to be said. There are a range of common themes that run through our shared life. They may not be of the quirky 'stiff-upper-lip' variety that was supposedly illustrative of our national stoicism, but they are integral components of our wider cultural experience. They may lack the ability to restore a substantive social cohesion, yet they form a part of the tapestry of our shared life that it is important for any preacher to have in view. More than that, they form the contours of the landscape we inhabit, the cultural environment in which we live.

There are any number of trends and observations that it would be interesting to explore, but outlined below are those which might be of particular concern to those charged with preaching God's Word.

Entertainment

Back in 1985 Neil Postman wrote his classic text, *Amusing Ourselves to Death: Public Discourse in the Age of Show Business*. In it he charts how the 'age of exposition' has given way to an 'age of entertainment'. Gone, now, are the days when public political debates could go on for hours in an orderly fashion as a series of speeches and rebuttals. Similarly, in the Church the day of the great revivalists like Jonathan Edwards and Charles Finney had passed. These were men of learning whose sermons were laced with theology and doctrine. Edwards, for example, read his tightly knit and closely reasoned expositions, not trusting himself to extemporaneous utterance. If his hearers were to be moved by what he said, they had to understand him first.

The developments in technology that led to the arrival of television overwhelmed the expositional age that was rooted in the printed word. Rationality and substance were supplanted by the seductive nature of visual images and thus the nature of public debate was redefined by the 'supra-ideology' of TV as entertainment. Indeed, communication and debate were now mediated by, and subject to, a technology defined by show business. As Postman shrewdly observed, if television is our culture's principle mode of knowing about itself, 'television is the command center of the new epistemology' (1985, p. 78).

It is sobering to realize that estimates indicate people between the ages of 30 and 50 have watched an average of 40–50,000 hours of TV and some 300,000 advertisements.

The advent of 24-hour television news is illustrative of the demands of communicating content within the constraints of a medium defined by entertainment. A story only lasts as long as it can remain interesting or evoke an emotional response on the part of the audience. New angles can be explored and the speculation by commentators and pundits that precedes, accompanies and follows after events is constantly refashioned to maintain interest. When interest wanes, stories are dropped before ratings fall. This bears no relation to the substance and significance of a story, only to its ability to keep the attention of the viewers (Davies, 2009; Rosenberg and Feldman, 2008).

Narrative

If television has been the dominating medium of the last generation and it has embedded entertainment as the key component of communicating ideas within contemporary western culture, then it needs to be remembered that the staple diet of TV is story, and the narrative form heavily influences the whole viewing experience.

Narratives are impossible to escape. Like the air we breathe they are all around us. Most obviously in novels, films and TV programmes narratives actually inhabit the full range of human experience from our historic myths and legends, through conversational anecdotes to our own personal histories with their dreams and nightmares. Some have argued that narrative is so widespread that it must be one of the 'deep structures' of our makeup, somehow genetically 'hard-wired' into our minds (Abbot, 2002, p. 3). Certainly the early indicators of narrative ability begin to appear in children in their third or fourth year. You only have to witness their sheer delight at having a story read to them or their appetite to watch and re-watch a favourite film or TV programme to appreciate that narrative is fundamental to our human makeup. Indeed, without the ability to construct and understand stories it would be very difficult to order and communicate our experience of time.

The power of storytelling is in the way that the unfolding plot of a story mimics our own experience of life and the way reality unfolds sequentially for us as people. As such, narrative produces the feeling of events happening in time and evokes a personal and often emotional response from those listening to it. Whether true or false in what it depicts, it appears to replicate life. This is the reason for its penetration of our collective imagination and its dominance as a means of communication over against more analytical approaches. For the journalist Robert Fulford this is *'the triumph of narrative'* (1999, pp. 15–16).

Narrative is so all-pervasive that it is impossible to ignore. Indeed, it would be unwise to do so.

Consumerism

It was the Christmas Eve edition of the *Chicago Tribune* in 1986 that provided the first recorded use of 'retail therapy'.

> We've become a nation measuring out our lives in shopping bags and nursing our psychic ills through retail therapy. Freely and enthusiastically embraced by shoppers around the world, it is the explanation of choice to account for the trip to the shopping centre to buy things we don't need with money we don't have. But it makes us feel better!

There can be no doubt that one of the most significant developments of the second half of the twentieth century, if not the most significant, was the rise of consumerism. Historically the patterns of consumption and commerce within the life of a culture were expressions of the core values of the society. At some point within living memory this relationship flipped. As Craig Bartholomew points out, the idea of consumerism points to a culture in which the core values of the culture derive from consumption rather than the other way around (Bartholomew and Moritz, 2000, p. 6).

The sociologist Zygmunt Bauman identifies three key elements in contemporary consumerism (2007b, pp. 82–116). The first has to do with identity. What we consume defines who we are by association with a particular reference group. It is a sobering exercise to sit down and ask ourselves what our clothes, our car, our house, the possessions that we value highly actually say about us. More telling are the things that other people see and associate us with. Bauman makes the point that consumer goods come with a 'built-in' identity, they are rarely value-free. Of course, the possibility of redefining ourselves and becoming someone else is always there. He sees this as a present-day substitute of the older ideas of salvation and redemption. Second, he observes that consumerism has increasingly built-in obsolescence to the products it sells. While this is clearly a requirement of keeping the marketplace alive, a consequence is to liberate the present from the past and the future 'that might have impeached the concentration and spoiled the exhilaration of free choice' (2007b, p. 84). Of course, the freedom to choose has increasingly become adopted as the defining characteristic of contemporary ethics. The third element of consumerism that he identifies flows on from this idea of free choice. In it he demonstrates how consumerism both appears to affirm choice while at the same time limiting it. Consumerism is a forced choice from the available options that have been provided. However, it is important to recognize that freedom is identified with choices made in private life.

> Choosing . . . is not at issue, since this is what you must do, and can resist and avoid doing only at peril of exclusion. Nor are you free to influence the set of options available to choose from: there are no other options left as all realistic and advisable possibilities have been already preselected, pre-scripted and prescribed. (2007b, pp. 84–5)

Ethos and atmosphere

Commentators often talk about 'the spirit of the age', the overarching 'feel' of a particular point in history. The importance of such observations is that they identify the broad themes and sensibilities of time and place. They are significant for preachers in that they indicate where the gospel message has deep resonances with the surrounding culture and where, by contrast, it is profoundly counter-cultural. Where there is commonality between Christian discipleship and the context it inhabits, clearly it is right for the Church in general, and preachers in particular, to embrace it fully. Indeed, where contemporary culture is genuinely indifferent to biblical teaching and neither affirms nor contradicts it, it is wholly appropriate for our proclamation to inhabit that world too. It is only those things that are inimical to Christian faith that should be resisted.

So, what are the elements of the ethos and atmosphere of contemporary Britain that preachers have to have in mind? What are the broader trends in attitudes that impact the homiletical task? Perhaps the most critical for the pulpit is the suspicion of motives of those in authority and a tendency to entertain the most damning interpretation. This has been fed in no little part by the sceptical interrogation of those in positions of responsibility by certain sections of the media and catastrophic breaches of trust in public and commercial life. The Christian community has not been beyond this with abuses of position that range from the scandalous financial dealings of televangelists to the predatory abuse of paedophile priests.

This has left those in leadership in a much weakened position. Trust has to be earned rather than just given as a mark of deference. Leaders have to prove themselves to those they lead through their practice of leadership. If it is seen as manipulative, bullying or self-serving, what trust there is will quickly evaporate. Christian leadership should be open in style, consultative in process, transparent in practice and accountable.

A second identifiable trend is the evolution of 'soft' levels of commitment. Membership of political parties, trades unions and churches are at an all-time low. Only the National Trust seems to buck the trend, but even there it can be argued that there is a consumer dimension as members flock to historic buildings on the basis of the 'free' admission that membership brings.

People want to be selective in their participation. If they feel motivated they will join a demonstration, sign a petition or put on an event to raise money for 'Children in Need'. However, they will not want to do it every week. Rather they choose to 'dip in' to things when they choose. Reality TV becomes the model of engagement, with a low-cost, low-commitment way to participate and play a part in influencing the outcome.

This 'soft' expression of commitment is also carried over to issues of social and political concern. There is no doubt that global warming, people trafficking, third world debt and issues of social justice register as high concerns in the public mind. However, the concern diminishes as it impacts personal preference and behaviour. BBC2's *Newsnight* explored issues of sustainable lifestyles through its 'Ethical Man' feature in 2007–8. One of the sobering observations was the reluctance of members of the public to consider dropping their overseas holiday, even when the impact of the accompanying air flight wiped out all their other attempts to reduce their carbon footprint for the rest of the year.

Virtual relationships

There can be no doubting the fact that recent years have seen an explosion of communications technology and, through the World Wide Web, the growth of social networking. We are more connected now than at any other time in history: Facebook, Bebo, Twitter, Second Life, internet gaming, email, texting, the impact of technology in shaping how we communicate together is breathtaking. Yet how far is the quantity of communication representative of a depth of relationship? Is it legitimate to call a social network a community?

If 'virtual reality' is a computer-simulated environment that gives the impression of actually being somewhere where we are not, then there are virtual dimensions in our technologically generated communications and networking realities. While we might have a large number of 'friends' on Facebook, the capacity of any of us to hold and maintain relationships of substance remains the same as it always did.[1] And face-to-face, real-time engagement is a non-negotiable part of that. Likewise, that Stephen Fry has 1.4 million followers on Twitter is merely confirmation of his popularity as a celebrity and his ability to maintain an interesting narrative in 140-character Tweets.

Of course, in so far as time is invested in maintaining our online presence and interaction, this erodes our available time for pursuing real-time relationships in real-time communities. Back in December 2009, the pop songstress Lily Allen spoke about her conversion to becoming a 'neo-Luddite'.

> So I put my BlackBerry, my laptop, my iPod in a box and that's the end. I won't use email, I play records on vinyl, I don't blog. I've got more time, more privacy. We've ended up in this world of unreal communications and I don't want that. I want real life back.[2]

Allen's observations are not unique and express the sentiments of other commentators like Steve Tuttle of *Newsweek* and Virginia Heffernan of the *New York Times*.[3]

The consequence of the growth of virtual relationships is almost inevitably going to result in social atrophy. Our ability to form and develop substantial friendships and build those friendships into communities will be diminished.

Celebrity

In many ways the growth of celebrity in western cultures is a direct corollary of the rise and rise of entertainment as the basis of contemporary media. While societies have always had heroes, the basis of their acclaim was in their heroic exploits on the battlefield or in some other distinguished service or accomplishment in the wider life of the country. It has only been relatively recently that popular mass celebrity in its present-day form has emerged. First with the music halls and then the movies, sport and the broadcast media celebrity has grown. Fuelling its reach and cultural impact has been the growing amount of available leisure time and disposable income of an ever-increasing proportion of the population to access and consume celebrity.

Thus the culture of celebrity was born and established itself among us. The success of publications like *Hello* and *OK* magazines along with the gossip columns and 24-hour TV following their every move is indicative of how deeply embedded this has become within our society. The power of celebrity endorsement is not lost on organizations like the United Nations as they appoint high-profile figures as 'Goodwill Ambassadors' to increase publicity and interest in their good causes. The role of Bono and other musicians in the Make Poverty History and Drop the Debt campaigns is further evidence of this phenomenon, as is the Alpha Course's endorsement by Bear Grylls.

To the identification of individuals as 'A list', 'B list' or minor celebs, relatively recent developments in Reality TV have brought a further category into play, namely, those who are famous for being famous. Such is the infamy and then tragedy of a character like Jade Goody, one-time anti-hero in the Big Brother house and then transformed by her battle with cancer into a national heroine: Reality TV brings celebrity within reach of ordinary people. The storming success of franchises like *Big Brother*, *The X Factor*, *Britain's Got Talent* and the rest are testimony of the significance of celebrity in validating reality. For all that most people happily live ordinary lives, the culture of celebrity constantly whispers a different story.

Liquid modernity

We live in changing times and the present looks very different from the past. In trying to understand the reality that confronts us and the future that lies ahead, many have turned to the conversation regarding postmodernism for help. Along the way almost every change and trend in contemporary life has been used as an illustration of the postmodern advance. For some this is a deeply unsettling dialogue as old certainties are swept away: others want to embrace this new context enthusiastically and so to enable the gospel to contextualize itself into the new cultural reality. Scholars like Stanley Grenz have attempted to sum up these influences and demonstrate that the future will be defined by the postmodern impetus to pessimism, holism, communitarianism, relativism, pluralism and subjectivism (1996, pp. 14–15). Other voices hold that the Christian community needs to take seriously the deconstruction of Derrida, Lyotard's 'incredulity towards metanarratives' and Foucault's work on the relationship between knowledge and power.

There is no doubt that these are important thinkers who have significantly influenced contemporary ideas. However, Christians often have either been overly fearful or, conversely, have over-interpreted this debate. James K. A. Smith in his *Who's Afraid of Postmodernism?* looks to exorcize the fear while giving a more accurate account of the ideas of postmodern theorists (Smith, 2006, see also White, 2006). For example, Smith outlines how Lyotard's 'incredulity towards metanarratives' addresses a distinctly modern phenomenon where the grand stories were legitimated by an appeal to universal reason. What he had in view were the scientific narratives told by modern rationalism, scientific naturalism and sociobiology insofar as they claimed to be demonstrable by reason alone. By contrast, while the biblical narrative is grand in scope, it does not make an appeal to a supposed universal, scientific reason. Rather, it is a pre-modern matter of proclamation and requires a response of faith. By Lyotard's definition, it is not a metanarrative (Smith, 2006, pp. 64–5).

While most commentators will make clear that in talking about postmodernism the subject of the conversation is about this time of transition and flux at the end of the modern era, the very term itself can be deceptive. It is often misunderstood as implying that the whole of life is now being lived after the modern era, which is patently not so. In many ways contemporary western society remains thoroughly modern as both our individualism and scientific rationalism clearly demonstrate.

An early writer on the advent of postmodernism, the sociologist Zygmunt Bauman began to publish his series of books on *liquid modernity* in the year 2000, seeking to reframe the conversation. In short, Bauman's thesis is that one of the most significant and formative dimensions of our late modern culture is the speed of change. It 'is a society in which the conditions under which its members act change faster than it takes the ways of acting to consolidate into habits and routines' (Bauman, 2005, p. 1). He goes on to observe that it is increasingly difficult for elements of culture to hold their shape or stay on course for long, and that predicting the future on an extrapolation of past events is an increasingly risky and potentially misleading thing to do. He charts the five key challenges of liquid modernity as:

1 The inability of social forms to keep their shape for long.
2 Power and politics separating as power flows beyond national boundaries in a globalized world.
3 The loss of community with the increase of a randomized network of relationships.

4 The collapse of long-term thinking, planning and acting.
5 The responsibility for resolving life's problems and challenges shifting onto the shoulders of individuals.

Christianity and British society

There is no escaping the fact that the place of Christianity significantly changed over the second half of the twentieth century. A seemingly inexorable decline in attendance at Sunday worship and increasingly strong calls for the secularization of public life and its implied demand for the disestablishment of the Church of England are all evidence of this trend.

Many writers have begun to explore the idea of a post-Christian Britain and have concluded that it might not be as bad a context in which to engage with the *missio Dei* as some might have feared. Stuart Murray defines this period of Post-Christendom as,

> the culture that emerges as the Christian faith loses coherence within a society that has been definitively shaped by the Christian story and as the institutions that have been developed to express Christian convictions decline in influence. (2004, p. 19)

Once again the designator 'post' can be deceptive by implying to the casual observer that Christendom has already been consigned to history. This would be a mistake as Murray himself points out, as he identifies a range of ecclesiastical and social vestiges of Christendom in the life of both the Church and wider society (pp. 189–93).

There can be no mistake that the place of Christianity in British society is changing. But what is its present form and what might the future hold? The best empirical data that is presently available indicates that on any given Sunday between 6 and 7 per cent of the population attend services of worship, rising to 15 per cent on any given month and 25 per cent, if it is once or more each year (Brierley, 2006, and Tear Fund, 2007). Indeed, if attendance at a Christian service for a christening, wedding or funeral is taken into account, it is 80 per cent. Or again, according to the 2001 census 71.75 per cent of people in England and Wales considered their faith identity to be Christian.

The uncoupling of the formal relationships between Church and state seems irreversible. While Rowan Williams may have admitted to the *New Statesman* in an interview on 18 December 2008 that he could 'see that it's by no means the end of the world if the Establishment disappears', he confessed to a 'bloody mindedness' that would resist a push to the privatization of faith by that route. While the old Christendom settlement may be passing, some have speculated on the arrival of a new expression of Christian social influence through the growth of Christianity in the global South. In Africa, Asia and Latin America the churches saw spectacular growth during the twentieth century. Many admit that the centre of gravity for Christianity has already shifted away from the West, and commentators like Philip Jenkins have observed that through social, economic and politically driven migration, not to mention missionary endeavour, the Church of the South will re-evangelize the first world. This is 'The Next Christendom' (Jenkins, 2007). With 44 per cent of worshippers in inner London being drawn from the black and ethnic minority communities, this is already a reality in the capital (Brierley, 2006, p. 99).

Mediated preaching

So, what does this all mean for the future of preaching? Some are convinced that it spells the end of an out-of-date, six-foot-above-contradiction monologue that is both educationally flawed and culturally anachronistic as a means of communication. Such critiques more often than not interact with exaggerated stereotypes that do not bear scrutiny, or they extrapolate from the experience of sub-standard preaching an overly pessimistic assessment of the whole. There is no doubt that bad preaching is boring and that cultural change has the potential to make a more traditional approach to preaching appear dated and out of touch. However, there is much more to be said.

It has always been true that preaching is a mediated discipline. Incarnational theology has taught us that the Word of God must always be clothed in the specific culture of place and time. In addition, as the Word of God is proclaimed it is not a pure distillation of divine revelation, but rather it has to take shape in the thoughts, words and ideas of the preacher and then be mediated through their experience, character and personality. Our contemporary context adds additional layers to a view of 'media-ted' preaching through both the all-pervasive nature of 'the media' alongside the ever-more sophisticated technological tools of communications multimedia.

If preaching must be mediated through its surrounding culture, and we live at a time of significant cultural change, it is inevitable that preaching will change too. Not to allow for this would place the proclamation of the word of God over against the surrounding culture and require it to take a step away from such a dangerous influence. Such a view might be admissible for those dimensions of culture that are antithetical to the gospel, but it would be a serious mistake to adopt with regard to preaching as a whole. Indeed, because of the mediated nature of preaching, it would only result in the continued embrace of the cultural embodiment of homiletics from another time and place.

Many of the voices calling for change in the practice of preaching, consciously or unconsciously draw on that movement in the second half of the twentieth century that became known as 'the new homiletic'. With Craddock's call for a move from deductive to inductive preaching (Craddock, 1978) and the work of others like Lowry with his advocacy of the narrative plot and his infamous graphic 'loop' (Lowry, 1980) the sermon was shifted towards the emerging cultural trends like the growing pervasiveness of storytelling in the entertainment industry and suspicion of the motives of those attempting to make authoritative pronouncements. McClure (1995, 2001), for example, argues for a collaborative approach that sees the preacher preparing in a 'roundtable' context with other members of the congregation, where shared insights and concerns are established to form the substance of the following week's sermon.

Underlining the importance of an inductive approach for postmodern people, Graham Johnston (2001) also stresses the significance of storytelling alongside the inclusion of drama, art, audiovisual aids and the use of humour. Appealing for a creative 'remixing' of preaching, Jonny Baker advocates a similar range of strategies that keeps the 'unleashing of the power of Scripture' in a sermon fresh. Team working ensures a mixture of ideas and styles that can be integrated into an inductive approach that surprises and, at times, 'pulls the rug out from underneath' the listeners' expectations (Baker, 2009, p. 86). In this way preaching is accommodated to contemporary culture that enables an expression of the gospel that connects and is accessible to its audience.

This, of course, is only part of the story of contemporary culture. Talk of the death of the 'monologue' is premature. In a number of significant contexts it is alive and well and continues to thrive. First there is the 'After Dinner Speaker' circuit. Bill Clinton reputedly earned £15 million in his first four years after leaving office, while in December 2007 Tony Blair was commanding up to £200 k for each speaking engagement.[4] Clearly Clinton and Blair are at the top end of this particular marketplace, but it is evidence of a thriving industry and of people's willingness to pay to hear a good speaker. JLA is the UK's largest agency for 'Keynote, motivational and after-dinner speakers'. Established in 1990 they carry a list of over 6,000 speakers. This is not a dying industry.

Second, the arrival of Barack Obama onto the American political scene when he spoke at the 2004 Democratic National Convention brought another dimension of public speaking into 'high relief': its power to inspire. Drawing on the classical skills of oratory Obama embodied the truth that personal, face-to-face, communication can have a quality and depth to touch the human heart and lift the human spirit. In a very different context on 19 March 2003, Colonel Tim Collins addressed the First Battalion of the Royal Irish Regiment as they prepared to enter Iraq from Kuwait,

> We go to liberate not to conquer. We will not fly our flags in their country. We are entering Iraq to free a people and the only flag which will be flown in that ancient land is their own. Show respect for them.[5]

These are high-profile examples of the power of inspirational addresses. In public and private spheres, in business and the voluntary sector, from campaigning organizations to sports teams, the ability of individuals to speak and inspire those around them has not been lost.

Third, and perhaps a little out of left field, is stand-up comedy. Theo Hobson, writing in *The Guardian*, makes the link between it and the 'essential performance-art of our Protestant past: preaching'.[6] One voice holds hundreds captive by the power of their speech and creates a sense of unity in the crowd by establishing common points of reference and insight. From the left-wing polemicists of the 1990s to the eclectic themed shows of the Edinburgh Fringe, these contemporary folk heroes among the young are compelling communicators. As Joe Moran observes, also in *The Guardian*, 'Great comedy clarifies reality in some way. It changes our perceptions rather than simply confirming them.'[7]

While there is a gulf between the proclamation of the gospel of Jesus Christ, the anecdotes of the after-dinner speaker and the ironies of life laid bare by the incisive wit of a comedian, the preaching of Christ fulfils that to which these contemporary expressions of communication aspire. Truth is expressed, the heart is inspired and the will is engaged.

Deploying technology and utilizing contemporary communications solutions are also increasingly popular in seeking to enable preaching to engage with its twenty-first-century context. From the introduction of the printing press the Church has always been an early adopter of such technology, seeking ways to deploy it in more effectively communicating the good news of Jesus.

From Microsoft's first offering of its new PowerPoint software that it acquired with its purchase of Forethought Inc. in the late 1980s, its use has burgeoned within the preaching community. While Jonny Baker astutely observes that most of this usage is about 'recreating the old world' by posting the three points or alliterated observations of the sermon on a screen behind the preacher, rather than exploiting the creative opportunities the medium offers, still it is evidence of the life and vitality within preaching as it struggles to engage with a changing context. Movie clips, locally produced 'vox pops' and illustrative graphics have all begun to play their part. It is interesting to note that evidence seems to suggest that in the experience of the listening congregation these developments were neither as radical nor as controversial as they were thought to be. Indeed, in rating a sermon, substance always triumphed over presentation and issues of spiritual growth over contemporary relevance (Standing, 2002, p. 58).

Others have begun to explore the possibilities of interactive preaching through texting, Twitter and email. While in some congregations live feeds display questions and comments, in others they are gathered for introduction following the conclusion of the sermon. Reactions are mixed and dilemmas arise. With live feeds, should they be moderated to ensure nothing inappropriate is projected for all to see? Others see it as a dynamic new departure that puts a preacher more fully in touch with their listeners. Then there are questions of inclusion and exclusion, with the 'techno-literate' gaining an advantage over against the 'techno-challenged' (Charles, 2010, pp. 39–40).

The internet is the other significant technological development of the last 15 years. Large numbers of church websites now routinely post each week's sermon for download, and many have experimented with live webcasts of their worship services. Mainly servicing their own members who are unable to be present in person, these developments fall into Baker's category of recreating the old world.

There are also rather more creative online experiments. The virtual congregations of Saint Pixels, Church of Fools, i-Church and the various Christian communities in the virtual world of Second Life all have to wrestle with whether to include a sermon in services and, if so, how. At Saint Pixels, during their real-time services, a separate window appears at sermon time providing a virtual pulpit.

The congregation can take part, and see others taking part, and heckling during the sermon is not unusual. At the same time, everyone can read what is being said 'from the front,' which helps to stop large meet-ings descending into anarchy. In terms of authority, the pulpit also confers a 'first among equals' status to the speaker, without in any way censoring other participants. (Howe, 2007, p. 15)

If traditional technology enables us to envisage 'broad-casting', the World Wide Web opens up the opportunity to 'narrow-cast', to grasp the opportunity to preach to a highly selective community. The Baptist Min-ister Peter Laws set up the website www.theflicksthatchurchforgot.com/. Using podcasts he has now produced two seasons of gospel presentations to fans of horror movies. His highly targeted preaching presentations in-clude a review and comment on a selected movie and an exploration of the theological themes that it raises. Forums and message boards then allow for interaction and an ongoing conversation. Ministering within a relatively small church, his online community has nearly 600 subscribers with the downloads and streams of his podcasts running into the thou-sands (Laws, 2010).

It is, in part, paradoxical that in embracing the best of present-day com-munications technology and therefore seeking what might be considered a more 'incarnational' approach to preaching, the preached Word of God loses rather than gains 'flesh'. The sermon augmented with PowerPoint and video clips reduces the real-life voice of the preacher by complement-ing it with audiovisual support, while, over the internet, the strength of preaching and worship to build relationships and a sense of community is diminished as they are, in both senses of the word, 'virtual'.

Yet preaching is more than just adapting to cultural style or tone, iden-tifying contemporary models of monologic communication to fight a re-arguard action that stands against the forces of change, or pressing into service the latest technology and gadgety gizmos to give our sermons a sense of pizzazz. If preaching is truly a mediated discipline, then what is conveyed through its mediation must not be lost sight of. It is the Word of God. In and of itself it is neither passive nor inert. Rather, as the writer of the letter to the Hebrews makes clear, it has a life and active vitality of its own. It is penetrative into the very essence of what it means to be human (Heb. 4.12–13).

Monologues may prove to be a poor method of conveying information and an even poorer strategy for delivering education. But it is a mistaken assumption to believe that preaching is primarily about either of these. Neither is it merely about the uplifting experience of spiritual inspira-tion. As Stephen Holmes observed in his 2009 George Beasley-Murray lecture, 'preaching that inspires is not enough: we need preaching that transforms, enlivens, converts' (Holmes, 2009, p. 7). This is the work of the Holy Spirit who took what even appeared to be foolishness in the apostolic era and through it was pleased to bring salvation to believers (1 Cor. 1.21). Yet the Holy Spirit does not work alone, and herein lies the mystery of preaching and the secret of its transformational power, the interplay between the human and the divine, between the sovereignty of God and human freedom. As Holmes so deftly observes, 'we must be careful to steer the right course: human acts do not cause divine action – of course not! – but nor are they irrelevant to it. God has chosen to use our words in his sovereign work of salvation' (2009, p. 7).

Conclusion

Preaching is a demanding discipline. The preacher is called not only to wrestle with the Scriptures so as to understand them more adequately but also to wrestle with their contemporary cultural context to determine how the gospel message is to be appropriately formed and communicated. None of this is simple, straightforward or static. Culture is continually shifting and presenting new faces to us, while our own theological perceptions are shaped and reshaped by our ongoing interaction with the Scriptures and the ever-unfolding narrative of our personal experience. It is truly mediated preaching, as it is within this dynamic, three-dimensional interaction between the preacher, their culture and the Bible, that God chooses to give life to his Word.

Notes

1. Anthropologists suggest that a healthy number is around 150 in concentric circles of closeness of 5, 10, 35 and 100. See Dunbar, 2010.
2. *Daily Telegraph*, 22 December 2009, 'Lily Allen describes quitting Facebook and Twitter'.
3. Steve Tuttle, 4 February 2009, 'You Can't Friend Me, I Quit! On Facebook's fifth anniversary, a not-so-fond farewell', *Newsweek*; Virginia Heffernan, 26 August 2009, 'Facebook Exodus', *New York Times*.
4. http://www.dailymail.co.uk/news/article-502649/Tony-Blair-makes-1m-month-private-speeches-offers-flood-PM.html.
5. http://thenightingaleinstitute.com.au/wpress/?p=1367.
6. http://www.guardian.co.uk/commentisfree/belief/2009/aug/10/religion-comedy.
7. http://www.guardian.co.uk/commentisfree/2009/aug/07/tv-comedy-humour-mockery.

References

Abbot, H. Porter, 2002, *Narrative*, Cambridge: Cambridge University Press.

Baker, Jonny, 2009, *Transforming Preaching: Communicating God's Word in a Postmodern World*, Grove Evangelism Series, 86, Cambridge: Grove.

Bartholomew, Craig, and Thorsten Moritz (eds), 2000, *Christ and Consumerism*, Carlisle: Paternoster.

Bauman, Zygmunt, 2000, *Liquid Modernity*, London: Polity.

_____ , 2003, *Liquid Love*, London: Polity.

_____ , 2005, *Liquid Life*, London: Polity.

_____ , 2006, *Liquid Fear*, London: Polity.

_____ , 2007a, *Liquid Times*, London: Polity.

_____ , 2007b, *Consuming Life*, Cambridge: Polity.

Brierley, Peter, 2006, *Pulling Out of the Nosedive*, London: Christian Research.

Charles, Tyler, 2010, 'Thumb Wars', *Leadership Journal* 31.1, *How Will They Hear?* pp. 39–40.

Craddock, Fred, 1978, *As One with Authority*, St Louis: Chalice Press.

Davies, Nick, 2009, *Flat Earth News*, London: Vintage.

Dunbar, Robert, 2010, *How Many Friends Does One Person Need?* London: Faber & Faber.

Fulford, Robert, 1999, *The Triumph of Narrative: Storytelling in the Age of Mass Culture*, New York: Broadway.

Grenz, Stanley, 1996, *A Primer in Postmodernism*, Grand Rapids: Eerdmans.

Holmes, Stephen, 2009, '"Living like Maggots": Is Preaching Still Relevant in the 21st Century', The George Beasley-Murray Memorial Lecture 2009, Unpublished.

Howe, Mark, 2007, *Online Church? First Steps towards Virtual Incarnation*, Grove Pastoral Series, 112, Cambridge: Grove.

Jenkins, Philip, 2007, *The Next Christendom*, 2nd edn, Oxford: Oxford University Press.

Johnston, Graham, 2001, *Preaching to a Postmodern World*, Grand Rapids: Baker.

Laws, Peter, 2010, 'Preaching in the Dark: The Homiletics and Hermeneutics of Horror', unpublished University of Wales M.Th. in Preaching dissertation.

Lowry, Eugene, 1980, *The Homiletical Plot*, Atlanta: John Knox.

McClure, John, 1995, *The Roundtable Pulpit*, Nashville: Abingdon.

_____ , 2001, *Other-wise Preaching: A Postmodern Ethic for Homiletics*, St Louis: Chalice.

Murray, Stuart, 2004, *Post Christendom*, Carlisle: Paternoster.

Postman, Neil, 1985, *Amusing Ourselves to Death: Public Discourse in the Age of Show Business*, New York: Penguin.

Rosenberg, Howard, and Charles Feldman, 2008, *No Time to Think*, London: Continuum.

Smith, James K. A., 2006, *Who's Afraid of Postmodernism?*, Grand Rapids: Baker.

Standing, Roger, 2002, *Preaching for the Unchurched in an Age of Entertainment*, Grove Evangelism Series, 58, Cambridge: Grove.

Tear Fund, 2007, *Churchgoing in the UK*, Teddington: Tear Fund.

White, Heath, 2006, *Postmodernism 101*, Grand Rapids: Brazos.

2

Preaching in the Roman Catholic Ecclesial Context

DUNCAN MACPHERSON

Preaching in the ecclesial context of the Roman Catholic Church falls into three broad categories already present in the early Church: proclamation, formation and instruction. In the modern context, preaching takes place most frequently within the context of the sacramental rites, including the Sunday Eucharist. Proclamation has become the primary aim of such preaching but formation and catechesis are also seen as important. Each of these three complements the others in the life of the Church and together all three seek to provide access to the truth by which the Christian can live and die.

Historical background

The sermons in the Acts of the Apostles provide examples of proclamation or kerygmatic preaching directed at the unbaptized but later directed sometimes at Church members needing to experience the conversion of life appropriate to their baptism. Formational or catechetical preaching in the early Church was concerned with preparing candidates for Baptism, Confirmation and first Holy Communion: the sacraments of initiation originally given together to mainly adult converts at the Easter liturgy. This formational preaching continued as 'mystagogical preaching' during the period after Easter when the newly baptized were instructed in the significance of the rites they had experienced. Overlapping with the third category of instructional preaching, mystagogical preaching included instruction on the Creed, the Lord's Prayer, the Commandments and the Sacraments.

From the fourth century onwards more and more Christians were baptized as infants with the result that mystagogical preaching largely disappeared. Meanwhile disputes about the nature of Christ necessitated

a greater emphasis upon preaching as a safeguard for doctrinal orthodoxy. For this reason liturgical preaching became the prerogative of the
bishop.[1]

During the early medieval period preaching largely fell into abey-
ance until it was revived in the eleventh century, first to promote the
crusades and then to combat the Albigensian and other heretical movements. Preaching during Mass fell into decline and preaching outside of
Mass became the business of the monastic orders and, more popularly, of
itinerant preachers, often belonging to the new orders of Franciscan and
Dominican friars. Some of this preaching took place not only outside the
context of liturgy but also outside the church building itself, in the public
square. In the first instance much of this preaching consisted in doctrinal
and moral instruction, but it also involved evangelistic proclamation directed both at combating heresy and at bringing about a revival in religious commitment among the populace.

The Protestant Reformation proved the catalyst for a greater emphasis
on preaching in the Catholic Church as part of the 'Catholic Reformation', sometimes called 'the Counter Reformation'. From the sixteenth
century onwards reforms associated with the Catholic Reformation included the education of the clergy, a new catechetical movement and the
requirement that a sermon should be given at every Sunday Mass. Consequent upon new geographical discoveries, the Catholic Reformation also
involved massive missionary expansion. New active religious orders, such
as the Jesuits, engaged in preaching. This embraced catechetical instruction (often polemically anti-Protestant) as well as preaching for primary
evangelization in newly discovered lands. In both kinds of preaching
there was a new emphasis on moving the will of the hearers to accept
God's grace offered in the sacraments of the Church and to embrace the
Christian virtues.

In the centuries that followed we find a similar pattern of preaching
by the religious orders, combining an emphasis on instruction in faith
and morals with affective proclamatory preaching not only in the new
areas of missionary expansion in Africa and Asia but also, in the Catholic
equivalent of revivalist preaching, in parish missions preached against the
background of the rising tide of anti-clerical secularism in Europe. At the
parish Sunday Mass, however, the sermon would be primarily doctrinal
and moral, with systematic instruction on the creed, the sacraments and
the commandments. Such sermons were usually quite unrelated to the
biblical readings provided for each Sunday, which were in any case only
accessible to the minority who used missals giving the translation of the
Latin texts of the Mass.[2]

Proclamation – the liturgical homily

The Second Vatican Council (1962–5) introduced liturgical reforms directed at bringing about a greater emphasis on Scripture and increased lay participation in the liturgy. In this new climate, the biblical homily was seen as 'a living commentary on the word' and as an integral part of the liturgical action (*SC* 56, 7, 33 and 52). Far from being an interruption in the celebration of Mass, the homily was now seen as a bridge between the liturgy of the word and the eucharistic liturgy, a Breaking of the Word that prepares the congregation to participate in the Breaking of Bread. Since Christ is both the living Word and the living Bread come down from heaven, the homily was now seen as the proclamation of the Word made flesh. In the Scripture readings, proclaimed by the preacher in the homily, God is speaking to his people, 'opening up to them the mystery of redemption and salvation, and nourishing their spirit' and 'Christ himself is present in the midst of the faithful through his word' (*GI* 55) and the homily 'must always lead the community of the faithful to celebrate the Eucharist wholeheartedly so that they may hold fast in their lives to what they have grasped by their faith' (*LM* 26).

Congregation, preacher and text

In this renewed understanding of liturgical preaching the preacher became a 'mediator of meaning' making effective links between the message of the text and the experience of the congregation, building up the faith of those present at the Sunday assembly, the people of God united by their faith and baptism. An important document on preaching from the American Catholic Bishops Conference stressed that, to be such a mediator, the preacher needs 'to be a listener before he is a speaker' (*FIYH* 10). Preachers were instructed to study the congregation as well as the text. This document identified three essential elements: the assembly, the preacher and the message itself, but it is the assembly which is given pride of place since 'only when preachers know what a congregation needs to hear will they be able to communicate what a congregation needs to hear' (*FIYH* 4). The same message was stressed 26 years later by the president of the US episcopal conference, urging that priests and deacons with their bishop should 'meet with the laity to listen to their struggles and to understand better how they might preach the Word in ways that relate to those struggles'.[3]

The understanding of the preacher moved from that of teacher of the doctrines of the faith to that of a herald, proclaiming the good news that in Christ God has entered history in a new and decisive way, reconciling humanity to himself. This model of the preacher as herald does not exclude catechetical instruction, but this becomes a secondary objective rather than the primary aim of the homily.

Desirable qualities for the preacher include competence in biblical and theological studies, a background in both classical and popular culture, and an understanding of the 'complex social, political and economic forces' shaping events. However preachers do not need to have all the answers to all the questions, and what was most required 'was simply to hear a person of faith preaching . . . As long as we carry the Word of God with us, a Word that we have allowed to touch on our lives in prayer and reflection, and as long as we speak that word in language and images that are familiar to the dwellers of the particular avenue we are travelling, the Word of God will be preached, and the possibility of faith and conversion will be present' (*FIYH* 14 and 15).

The content of this transforming message is always the Living Word of God, the second Person of the Holy Trinity revealing the Father and reconciling the world to God, and in the preaching of the message contained in the Scripture, 'Christ himself is present in the midst of the faithful through his word' (*GI* 55). Theology and biblical studies are crucial to the interpretation of the texts, but the preacher is less concerned with explaining the texts than with interpreting them as 'real words addressed to real people' (*FIYH* 21).

Formation – Christian initiation of adults

We have seen that in the renewed understanding of the function of the liturgical homily the proclamation of the good news is directed primarily to deepening the commitment of those who are already baptized members of the community. The post-Vatican II Church has also placed a new emphasis on formation, not only as a secondary objective of the Sunday homily but also in the revival of mystagogy.[4] Reflecting the wish to provide instruction for the adult convert within the framework of the Christian community, the Rite of Christian Initiation of Adults (RCIA) was revived in 1962. This was done both in response to the large numbers of adult converts in Africa and elsewhere and partly because of the need for a new evangelization in de-christianized parts of Europe where growing numbers of people had not been baptized as children. During a series of brief ceremonies candidates first express their desire to become Christians, are enrolled as catechumens and begin their instruction, usually coinciding with Lent. Baptism, Confirmation and first Holy

Communion take place at Easter, followed by a period of mystagogy taking place between Easter and Pentecost. This provides the opportunity for the developing formation of new Christians, enabling them to learn more about the sacraments that they have received within the framework of the eucharistic community. Mystagogical preaching accompanies these rites and can also serve to refer other members of the congregation back to their own Christian initiation.

Instruction – catechetical fruits

The usefulness of such reference back is evident from the fact that, for the majority of Catholics, involvement in the Church is limited to weekly – or sometimes less frequent – attendance at Mass. For these Catholics the Sunday homily becomes the only channel for adult religious education. This has led to demands that the teaching objective of preaching should come more to the fore. Pope John Paul II stressed the importance of the homily not only as liturgical and biblical and tailored to the needs of the congregation (the description favoured by Pope Paul VI) (*EN* 43) but also as bringing 'catechetical fruits' (*CT* 48). The Catechism, too, stresses the instructional value of the homily (1074), while at the same time defining the homily as an exhortation to accept the Word 'as what it truly is, the Word of God as put into practice' (*CCC* 1349).

In 2007, Pope Benedict emphasized the need for an improvement in the quality of preaching, stressing that the homily is 'part of the liturgical action'. It is meant to foster a deeper understanding of the word of God, so that it can bear fruit in the lives of the faithful and should be preached in such a way that it 'closely relates the proclamation of the word of God to the sacramental celebration and the life of the community, so that the word of God truly becomes the Church's vital nourishment and support'. He then goes on to urge that 'the catechetical and paraenetic aim of the homily should not be forgotten. During the course of the liturgical year it is appropriate to offer the faithful, prudently and on the basis of the three-year lectionary, "thematic" homilies treating the great themes of the Christian faith, on the basis of what has been authoritatively proposed by the Magisterium in the Catechism . . . four pillars namely the profession of faith, the celebration of the Christian mystery, life in Christ and Christian prayer' (*SAC* 138–42).

The future of preaching in the Roman Catholic Church will always involve seeking to find a balance between the three elements of proclamation, instruction and formation, with varying emphasis on each according to the changing circumstances of the times. Setting the direction for the immediate future Pope Benedict, like his predecessor, follows a path of recommending all three of the elements in the role of the preacher but restores emphasis on the need for doctrinal instruction. Before becoming pope, Cardinal Ratzinger spoke eloquently that the aim of preaching was 'to tell man who he is and what he must do to be himself. Its intention is to disclose to him the truth about himself, that is, what he can base his life on and what he can die for' (Ratzinger, 1995, pp. 62–3). It would be hard to think of a better aim for preaching in any ecclesial context!

Notes

1. In 529, Saint Caesarius of Arles persuaded the Council of Vaison to allow priests to preach at Mass and, in their absence, to allow deacons to read the homilies of the Fathers. Hendrie, 2005, p. 45. Today canon law restricts preaching to bishops, priests and deacons (Code of Canon Law 767). Suitably qualified laypersons can be asked to preach at Word services, at services of Holy Communion from the reserved Sacrament outside of Mass and at funeral services where there is no ordained minister to officiate. Pastors sometimes get around the restriction by inviting laypeople to offer 'reflections' rather than homilies, often after Communion.
2. From the sixteenth century onwards the Gospel (and sometimes the Epistle) texts were read in the vernacular after they had been read in Latin. This practice became widespread during the years leading up to the Second Vatican Council (1962–5).
3. Bishop Gerald Kicanas of Tucson, at the 2008 synod of bishops, 'Ideas for Better Sermons Emerge at Synod: Guidelines and Year of the Homily Proposed' http://www.zenit.org/article-23849?l=english.
4. Mystagogy, or teaching about Christian sacraments and liturgical rites, comes from the Greek *mystagogia*, or 'interpreting of mystery', literally 'the leading of the initiated'.

References and further reading

Church documents with abbreviations used in this chapter

CCC   *The Catechism of the Catholic Church*, 2nd edn, English translation includes corrections promulgated by Pope John Paul II

on 8 September 1997. http://www.vatican.va/archive/catechism/
ccc_toc.htm

CT   Apostolic Exhortation, *Catechesi Tradendae* of Pope John Paul
II on 'Catechesis in Our Time' at http://www.vatican.va/holy_
father/john_paul_ii/apost_exhortations/documents/hf_jp-ii_
exh_16101979_catechesi-tradendae_en.html, para. 48.

EN   *Evangelii Nuntiandi*, 'On Evangelization in the Modern World',
Apostolic Exhortation of Pope Paul VI promulgated on 8 December 1975. http://www.papalencyclicals.net/Paul06/p6evan.htm

FIYH   Bishops Committee on Priestly Life and Ministry, *Fulfilled in
Your Hearing: The Homily in the Sunday Assembly*, United
States Conference of Catholic Bishops, Washington DC, 1982.

GI   *General Instruction on the Roman Missal*, http://www.usccb.
org/liturgy/current/revmissalisromanien.shtml

LM   *Lectionary for Mass*, London: Geoffrey Chapman, 1981.

SAC   *Sacramentum Caritatis*, Post-Synodal Apostolic Exhortation,
http://www.google.co.uk/search?sourceid=navclient&ie=UTF-
8&rlz=1T4GFRD_enGB212GB214&q=sacramentum+caritatis

SC   *Sacrosanctum Concilium* (Vatican II Constitution on the Sacred
Liturgy) http://www.ewtn.com/library/COUNCILS/v2litur.htm

Other texts referred to in this chapter

Hendrie, Robert, 2005, *Go Tell Them: Towards a Theology of Preaching*, London:
Saint Paul's.
Ratzinger, Joseph Cardinal, 1995, *The Nature and Mission of Theology*, trans.
Adrian Walker, San Francisco: Ignatius Press.

Further reading

De Bona, Guerric, OSB, 2007, *Fulfilled in Our Hearing: History and Method in
Christian Preaching*, Mahwah, NJ: Paulist Press.
Hilkert, M. C., 1997, *Naming Grace: Preaching and the Sacramental Imagination*,
New York: Continuum.
Janowiak, Paul, SJ, 2000, *The Holy Preaching: The Sacramentality of the Word in
the Liturgical Assembly*, Collegeville, MN: Pueblo.
Waznak, Robert P., 1988, *An Introduction to the Homily*, Collegeville, MN:
Liturgical Press.

3

Preaching and Liturgy

An Anglican Perspective

ROGER SPILLER

The primary ecclesial context of preaching in the Church of England is that of public worship, and 'a sermon should normally be preached at every liturgical celebration'.[1] Thus the pattern of worship influences and conditions the character and practice of preaching itself. In the last three decades or so the largely uniform and 'common' pattern of worship that could be found in every Anglican parish church, with minor variations, has been replaced by a wide diversity of worship and preaching styles. Cultural and aesthetic, as well as theological and liturgical, pressures in the 1960s ushered in a period of great liturgical creativity and experimentation that culminated in *Common Worship*, published in 2000. This prayer book authorizes alternative worship material and discretion in the use of local practice. *Common Worship* does not in practice, however, circumscribe the increasingly diverse patterns of worship that seek to match changing lifestyle patterns and especially the new initiatives that attempt to connect with the unchurched. It may be the destiny of liturgists to be latecomers, offering shape and coherence to local liturgical innovativeness that tries to respond to the fast-changing local missional landscape.

Since the 1960s, in the wake of the Parish Communion movement, the Eucharist has become the main Sunday act of worship in most churches, replacing the Prayer Book service of Matins. This has usually meant the reduction in the sermon time or, conversely in some churches, reducing the ministry of the sacrament to an addendum to the service. When, however, the dramatic character of the Eucharist is recognized and brought to life it reinforces the preaching through song and sign and action offering what Calvin called the visible preaching alongside the audible Eucharist. Typically the preaching is addressed to the Confirmed member and reflects the lectionary readings and church seasons. However, to provide greater accessibility for those who are unchurched, many churches now provide a Service of the Word in addition to, or instead of, the eucharistic worship. This gives scope for more extended and creative preaching. Typically in evangelical churches an extended, expository, propositional and 'teaching' sermon will be the centrepiece of the worship. It provides its hearers with a solid grounding in the biblical text, although it can be less willing to engage with the features of the human context that seem to defy the solution of the gospel. Churches that are clumsily regarded as 'middle of the road' usually take their preaching cue from the intractable issues that confront the human condition, but in trying to avoid any trivializing or triumphalist tendencies, they risk confining the gospel to what their hearers already experience and understand. Churches with a catholic character recognize the Word made flesh in the eucharistic celebration and the community which is re-membered around it. This can lead to an impatience with extended biblical exposition and explanation, and the marginalizing of preaching itself. This inevitably crude summation of Anglican preaching traditions is intended to suggest that for a future, healthy development of preaching, churches will benefit from engaging with the insights witnessed to by other preaching styles within the Anglican Communion.

Different preaching styles

Common Worship affirms that 'the "sermon" can be done in many different and adventurous ways' (2005, p. 21) and proposes that this 'includes less formal exposition, the use of drama, interviews, discussion, audio-visuals and the insertion of hymns or other sections of the service between parts of the sermon' (note 7, p. 27). This rubric will continue to remain largely overlooked, except by liturgical nerds, unless explicit attention is drawn to it by church leaders. Its significance is that it provides the mandate for the whole Church to be 'adventurous' in seeking to communicate the Christian gospel. It may include, as for some younger preachers, using lyrics, clips from films, sports events, soaps, adverts, phone-in discussions not merely to excite interest or to illustrate the gospel but as reference points of modern culture that force us to engage with fundamental theological questions (Lynch, 2008). *Common Worship*, too, characterizes preaching as 'story'. Few could doubt the reach, power and fascination of story. We relate to one another through story; we are transformed by story. Story, moreover, as Jesus demonstrated, is not merely the preferred vehicle but the intrinsic shape and content of the gospel. It enlists the primary religious faculty of the imagination, in order to access the alternative world of the gospel that God is creating, which cannot be accessed in any other way. Story, as we see in the dominical parables, creates space for hearers to be active, responsible participants as they locate themselves within the plots, trajectories and characters of the story. The future for preaching is likely to depend upon the rebirth of the story. It has the potential to capture the imagination of a generation who have been turned off by rarefied theological argument. Story, of course, may be augmented by sensory resources. One preacher, speaking on 'the bread of life', secreted a bread-making machine under the pews and an unsuspecting member of the congregation remarked that the preaching was so vivid that she could almost smell the bread. I myself was preaching on the theme of 'the great cloud of witness' while an over-zealous dry-ice machine operator allowed the entire chapel to be permeated by cloud so that the whole congregation disappeared from view. Preachers will need to be resourceful if they are to enable their hearers to inhabit the Gospel stories. Preaching as story is a model and catalyst to the hearers to rehearse the interweaving of their stories within the divine story of redemption and help the local church to be 'a storytelling community of imagination' (Wells and Coakley, 2008, pp. 81, 84). Preachers who know the power of story from its use in all-age and child-centred worship can still be reluctant to launch into the now respectable pedigree of story or narrative preaching, uncertain of the response they may receive. The future vitality of preaching is likely to be dependent upon a boldness to be 'adventurous' in the use of 'story' in order to connect with a generation who will hear the story with the surprise and newness as of the first hearers in first-century Palestine.

Opportunities for preaching

As 'the Church by Law established', it is estimated that the Church of England is in contact with some 85 per cent of the nation (Barley, 2006). The shape of the contact we have will often involve some form of preaching. At times of national significance or crisis, the Church will be expected not merely to articulate the public mood but to locate it within a transcendent frame of reference. Anniversaries of luminous figures, as diverse as Wilberforce, Handel, Milton, Darwin, and events that mark human achievement provide a 'secular' calendar that deserves, arguably, a recognition similar to that we give to the calendar of saints. The centenary of the discovery of the electron did not escape the vigilant eye of a cathedral dean, who saw the opportunity to engage with the physicists in the city.[2] This is but an example of the ingenuity that is required if the Church is to initiate a focused engagement with the 'secular' events, artefacts, activities and anniversaries that shape our corporate life. The Church of England is particularly well placed to occupy this contested ground in our national life.

Demands for the 'occasional offices', although reduced in number, are still significant. There is evidence from a study of church marriages that those for whom their marriage may be the only contact with the Church wish for a more extended relationship with the Church's worshipping community than clergy either expect or offer. [3] This intimates the need for a more extensive marking of the human lifestyle, and the great archetypal transitions, than the Church has traditionally provided. The future for preaching will reckon with what has been called 'inventive new personalised ritual' (MacCulloch, 2009, p. 1013). Wedding vow renewal services, Valentine's Day services on relationships and services of remembrance for the bereaved are only part of what could form an accessible and comprehensive liturgical cycle and the basis of an annual preaching curriculum on key issues of birth, identity, parenting, family, environment, loss, ageing and death (Barley, 2006, p. 51). Intrinsic to many family celebrations is the annual contact with the Church through the Christmas services. The preaching requires huge sensitivity if it is to strengthen the mystery, intrigue and awe of the story, juxtaposed against the grim reality of the world, and tell the difference that is made by this small child so that the hearers will be urged to 'turn the page' and let the wonder linger in them. At the same time, Christingle, crib and Christmas tree festivals are forerunners of new and local liturgies that are making imaginative ways of reconnecting with the traditional story. As the future of preaching will respond to new liturgical opportunities, so also it will respond to different ways of being and doing 'church'. Mid-week, after-school and Saturday afternoon services are likely to fit better into emerging lifestyle preferences, while hundreds of 'Fresh Expressions' and church plants require an informal and interactive style of preaching typified by testimony, story and the discussion of questions within the context of a minimal and creative liturgy.

Issues for preachers

There are particular issues and challenges for preaching within the framework of the 'established church'. The Church of England has provided the 'sacred canopy' over English life and has historically, and perhaps inevitably, been over-identified with western and establishment culture.

This appears not to have inhibited the Church's prophetic challenge of social and ethical issues, and, sometimes, of government policy, at least since the early twentieth century. What is less sure, however, is the extent to which preaching on public concerns contents itself with appealing to the broad support of supposedly universal values and reasoning rather than to the distinctive character of God's history in Jesus of Nazareth. The comment that 'There continues to be a surprising dearth of arguments that are rooted in theological or biblical perspectives' (Partington and Bickley, 2007) does identify the collusive temptation to which the national church is particularly prone. Preachers are likely to find that an appeal to shared values and beliefs ceases to be as obvious as it once seemed. The values of freedom and equality, for example, are not self-explanatory; they will be shown by our public preaching to arise from a vision of human flourishing that is inseparable from the image of God in Christ. Conversely, preaching will meticulously expose the 'black hole' in the nation's life which it believed to be the ultimate cause of the pervasive collapse of trust and social disease. This concerted campaign of attrition will enlist the artistic idiom of story, song, praise as well as satire and mockery as deployed by the ancient prophets, in order to wear down and undermine the prevailing worldview (Brueggemann, 1989).

The Anglican tradition has sought to focus on the wider community rather than merely the congregation and to address through its preaching issues of wider cultural and community interests rather than being over-absorbed with the narrow and particular interests of the faithful Christians. This perspective needs careful nurture at a time of institutional decline when pressure on the local church for the survival of its ministry can lead to an unhealthy parochialism and inwardness. In the manner of the major prophets who were preachers to the nations, not simply to their own constituency, it is to be hoped that the preaching ministry of the 'national church' will address the whole creation (Croft, 1999, pp. 115–17).

The preaching in parish churches in England has been shaped by pastoral, rather than missionary, assumptions and has sought to maintain the reassuring continuities of faith and culture and the latent faith of the nation.

Some find new reassurance for this traditional position from the burgeoning interest in spirituality. However, the default character of much contemporary spirituality when divorced from its religious framework renders it impotent, while Gracie Davie's latest analysis of religion points to the vocation of believers acting in proxy, and by consent, for society as a whole (see also Wells and Coakley, 2008, pp. 147–69). The shrinking of the believing community, however, dilutes the Christian witness, and this points to the need for preaching to assume an intentionally educative role. The postmodern insight that we live in different 'worlds' created by language and that experience, including of course religious experience, is linguistically structured should give new confidence to preaching as the means by which people may be transported to and inhabit an explicitly Christian story-centred 'world'.

Arising, again, from an inherently pastoral model, the preacher has been inclined to maintain a conspiracy with biblical scholarship that evades the voicing of problems presented by the text. The faith of the preacher can thus be different in kind from that of the congregation (Fenton, 1975). An Advent sermon I recently heard, on Luke 21.25–36, unusually began with the candid acknowledgement by the preacher that 'I don't understand this Gospel' and went on to spell out the difficulties he encountered in the text. I suspect that the thoughtful hearer would be conscripted to their own intense engagement with the text and the shattering of some of the superficial comforts that resulted from the honest exposition of the problems it presents as a result of this approach. In doing so it gave permission for the honest voicing of intractable problems whether with the interpretation of the text or with our own personal issues.

The preachers and their authorization

As well as clergy, lay people who become Readers in the Church of England are licensed by their bishop to preach and to perform liturgical functions. The demanding training equips them to be authoritative interpreters of Scripture, while they are particularly well placed through their rootedness in the world of work to act as 'street theologians' and to equip members of congregations to connect theologically with their own working lives. Their role is particularly crucial because the local church can often seem uncomfortable with the world of work and fails to equip its members to mount a reasoned defence against the fierce challenges they are likely to face. Congregations may, for their part, be thankful not to be reminded of or bring their working life into church, and Readers may find it more rewarding to ape their clergy colleagues in theological erudition than draw on their own unique experience and insight from their rich and diverse working lives. The ministry of Readers is the primary lay ministry and its members, whose numbers outweigh those of clergy, have been vital to the continuance of the preaching and liturgical ministry. However, the age profile of Readers remains high and the recruitment of younger members has not been encouraging. Reader ministry may be caught in a generational trap. It is generally recognized that with the growth in opportunities for lay members to preach on an occasional basis, there is little incentive to undertake a three-year intensive course to become a Reader.

The burgeoning numbers of those preaching on an occasional basis in many of our churches has brought vitality into worship and has been the catalyst for many once-hesitant lay people to discover their gifts and exercise a valued ministry, often going on to full-time ministry. If, as seems likely, a local lay preaching ministry will continue alongside that of Readers for some time to come, this presents important questions about the assessment of gifts, the supervision and training that is required, the frequency with which an 'occasional' preacher is expected to preach in relation to their Reader counterparts and the level of authorization and accountability that is felt appropriate. This has to be managed in a way that affirms and liberates, rather than controls, while also ensuring the quality and theological consistency of preaching for the edification of the congregation.

This can be no more than a brief and personal snapshot on the fast-changing preaching landscape in the Church of England.

In future we can expect to see an expansion in the number, age and background of those being given the opportunity to preach. Informal non-church settings will be usual settings for preaching, while preachers will employ testimony, story, conversation and dialogue and licensed clergy will discover the power of the narrative shaping of preaching, whether as story, as argument or as images. More will be invested by colleges and dioceses in resourcing people on a continuous basis for their preaching ministry. The decline of preaching is, as they say, greatly exaggerated and will remain so while people continue to discover that the young man who hung to death on a cross one dark Friday afternoon is the Father's way of restoring the whole inhabited world.

Notes

1. Canon B5.
2. Held at Birmingham Cathedral, 13 June 1997, and addressed by Professor Sir John Polkinghorne.
3. Weddings Project of the Church of England. See weddings.project@ c-of-e.org.uk.

References

Barley, Lynda, 2006, *Christian Roots, Contemporary Spirituality*, London: Church House Publishing.

Brueggemann, Walter, 1989, *Finally Comes the Poet*, Minneapolis, MN: Fortress.

Common Worship: Daily Prayer, 2005, London: Church House Publishing.

Croft, S., 1999, *Ministry in Three Dimensions*, London: Darton, Longman and Todd.

Fenton, J. C., 1975, 'The preacher and the biblical critic', in *What about the New Testament? Essays in Honour of Christopher Evans*, ed. Morna Hooker and Colin Hickling, London: SCM Press, pp. 178–86.

Lynch, Gordon, 2008, 'The preacher as cultural critic: possibilities and pitfalls', *The Preacher* 129, April, pp. 7–9.

MacCulloch, D, 2009, *A History of Christianity*, London: Allen Lane.

Partington, Andrew, and Paul Bickley, 2007, *Coming off the Bench: The Past, Present and Future Representation in the House of Lords*, London: Theos.

Wells, S., and S. Coakley (eds), 2008, *Praying for England*, London: Continuum.

4

Charismatic Utterance

Preaching as Prophecy

IAN STACKHOUSE

Historically, charismatic renewal has had an ambivalent relationship to preaching. Even though it has produced some outstanding preachers, at other times it has ended up ignoring preaching altogether. For instance, the other day I heard of a church service where, instead of preaching the sermon he had prepared, the preacher announced to the congregation that the Spirit had led him to abandon the sermon in favour of a time of prayer and healing. And thus ensued what can only be described as 'a holy carnage', as people came out in their droves to be prayed for.

To one who has hung around the charismatic wing of the Church for the best part of nearly 30 years there is nothing particularly unusual about this nor particularly wrong with it. Whatever else the charismatic movement has contributed to the wider body of Christ, it is surely this: that ability to suspend the liturgy out of an instinct of 'Behold, I am doing a new thing.' And maybe we should leave it there. Our preacher was simply acting out of his very best instincts for the new wine of the Spirit.

But why we cannot leave this unchallenged is because such times often bequeath something of a mixed blessing to the Church. What so often communicates to the congregation as a result of such a decision on the part of the preacher, sometimes inadvertently and other times deliberately, is that the essence of the charismatic life of the Church is by definition non-kerygmatic or, worse still, irrational. A consequence of such a move on the part of the preacher, or sometimes the worship leader, to abandon the sermon for 'just worship', is that Paul's desire in 1 Thessalonians 1.5 for preaching that is 'not in word only but with the Holy Spirit and with deep conviction' is misunderstood as a desire for no word at all. In other words, abandonment of preaching, in the way described, sends its own message to the congregation that the deeper one goes into the things of the Spirit the less textual we need to be.

It is this false dualism that I want to correct here. Preaching, I want to argue, is *the* charismatic event. The Pentecostal experience of the early chapters of Acts issues forth not only in strange tongues but also in preaching in the Spirit. As has often been pointed out, the same Spirit that gave utterance to the disciples in Acts 2.4 to praise God in foreign languages is the same Spirit that enables Peter to open his mouth in Acts 2.14 in a sermon. 'The holy wind at Pentecost is power unto speech', as William Willimon puts it (2005, p. 25). Clearly there are times when the Spirit's activity may well relativize the importance, and even the length, of the sermon (the homily remains largely unexplored by Baptist preachers!). Furthermore, we must be careful not to read back our own sermonic forms into the pages of the New Testament. The fact of the matter is: we don't really know how the early Church did their preaching. Even so, we must be careful that in our pursuit of charismatic experience we do not miss the essentially charismatic nature of preaching. Preaching is not something to satisfy the rationality of our faith – as it is often regarded even in Reformed charismatic circles – so that we can then attend to the non-rational work of the Spirit.[1] That way lies Gnosticism. Rather, the combination of text, congregation and preacher ought to be understood as replete with charismatic possibilities. Indeed, in so far as the Scriptures are themselves prophetic, as Walter Brueggemann has been at pains to point out throughout his writings (Brueggemann, 1989, p. 4), then, strange as it may sound, expository preaching ought to be as momentous an event as the giving of an oracle of God (1 Peter 4.11). That it so often isn't is the fault not of preaching *per se* but of low expectations on the part of the preacher and the congregation.

We can perhaps see this coming together of Spirit, text and preacher most clearly in the letter to the Hebrews. Despite attempts by David Norrington and others to deride sermons and to question their existence in the New Testament, it turns out that one of the reasons we can't find sermons is because, like searching for the hippo in the river, we are standing on it: Hebrews is a rhetorical and homiletical master class. Described by the writer himself as 'a word of exhortation', Hebrews does what we see Paul and his companions doing in the synagogue in Acts 13.15: namely, expounding from the law and the prophets as they are read to the congregation (Long, 1997, p. 2). Indeed it may well be that Hebrews is one long (as opposed to short!) sermon, in which the preacher expounds and exhorts, in equal measure, the deep truths arising from his initial reading of Psalm 110.

What is important to note, however, and why we mention it here, is the role of the Spirit in all of this; because, as far as this preacher is concerned, it is the Spirit who brings home to the congregation the immediacy of the Scripture. Arriving at one of the many exhortatory breaks in the letter, following three chapters of text upon text, one can almost see the preacher point his finger at the congregation as he announces, 'So, as the Holy Spirit says, "Today, if you hear his voice, do not harden your hearts"' (Heb. 3.7). In fact, it is the Spirit who for this preacher provides the hermeneutical key to unlock Scripture. Disregarding the historical-grammatical method, the Spirit instead guides us into all truth, and enables this congregation at least to see the new covenant not simply emerging from the words of Jesus but going all the way back to the Psalms and the prophets. Theologians speak about Spirit hermeneutics; this is Spirit hermeneutics at its best: taking the text of Scripture and, by the Spirit, driving it home to the hearts of the listening congregation.

Again, it is important to repeat that this celebration of charismatic preaching should in no way minimize the importance of other charismatic gifts, nor to conflate preaching completely with prophecy. It is important we recognize the place for the whole panoply of charismatic gifts, including healing and miracles. This has been one of the important legacies of the charismatic renewal. Indeed, for all of our commitment to the text in preaching, there is a very real sense in which Paul admits a certain irrationality about particular charismatic gifts. What is the phenomenon of speaking in tongues, as it is commonly referred to, but a by-passing of the mind (1 Cor. 14.14)? But what is often overlooked in Paul's adumbration of gift is not only the pastoral importance of limiting the public manifestation of ecstatic irrationality but, more importantly, the inclusion of what we might understand as preaching within this list of graces. As scholars point out, and as practitioners need increasingly to realize, the word of wisdom in that infamous list of gifts in 1 Corinthians 13 is not that specific ability to know the mind of Christ for a specific situation, any more than a word of knowledge is a specific message for the lady on the third row in a red jumper. Not withstanding God's ability to act in such ways, it is clearly not what is being referred to. Rather, the word of wisdom in the context of 1 Corinthians 2, in particular where Paul expounds on the wisdom of the cross, is first and foremost 'to be found among those who give spiritual utterances that proclaim Christ crucified in this highly "wisdom" conscious community' (Fee, 1987, p. 592). In other words, at the heart of a church in pursuit of spiritual gifts is a celebration of the scandalous particularity of gospel speech. The word of knowledge that Paul places alongside the word of wisdom is not, we suggest, some esoteric gnosis but rather a fresh articulation of the grace that has freely been given to us in the gospel.

How this is done, and in what context, is a matter for debate. Again, we must be careful not to reify a particular style of preaching. But in so far as early Christianity is to some extent a spill over from the synagogue, then it is no surprise that the new wine of the Spirit manifests, to some extent, in lection, text and word. Far from being an antipathy to the charismatic, preaching ought more readily to be understood as its adjunct.

Conclusion

Just recently, on a trip home from West Wales, I happened to drive through the small town of Newcastle Emlyn. Recalling that the famous Welsh preacher Martyn Lloyd-Jones was buried there, I decided to look up his grave, and sure enough, after searching for about twenty minutes, I found a very modest, inconspicuous tombstone with a simple Scripture text: 'For I resolved to know nothing while I was with you except Jesus Christ and him crucified.' Anyone who knows anything about this celebrated preacher will know that this text was his watchword; whatever else the Doctor's ministry at Westminster Chapel represented it was the recovery of this Pauline gospel and, alongside it, the recovery of the pulpit.

What is less well known, however, is that towards the end of his life, as he came to reflect on preaching, he began to speculate as to whether preaching was in fact what the Bible understood as prophecy. For sure, we must guard against mere pulpiteering. Lloyd-Jones was aware, more than anyone, of the temptation to mere oratory (1971, pp. 13–14). But in the end, what we do in the pulpit is not unlike what the prophets did in the Old Testament: calling the people of God back to the grand themes of covenant and obedience. As P. T. Forsyth put it: 'The Christian preacher is not the successor of the Greek orator, but of the Hebrew prophet' (1907, p. 1). Furthermore, Lloyd-Jones foresaw that for preaching to be effective it must carry the same unction as the prophetic word. To be sure, we need to guard against mere emotionalism in the pulpit; as a Welshman, Lloyd-Jones was more aware than most of the dangers of the hywl. But that aside, for preaching to be truly gospel speech it must carry unction – the divine *afflatus*, to use his words (1971, pp. 304–25). And if charismatic renewal is to continue to make a contribution to the wider body of Christ it is important, it seems to me, to recapture not just the ebullience of praise but the essentially charismatic nature of the preaching ministry of the Church. Unlike other traditions in the Christian Church, charismatic renewal has the potential to espouse not only a rich doctrine of the Spirit but also a high view of the Word. But in order to do that, the notion that the Word and the Spirit are deemed to be antithetical to one another needs finally to be dispelled.

Note

1. See Deere (1996) for a good example of this odd dualism in popular charismatic understanding of preaching.

References

Brueggemann, W., 1989, *Finally Comes the Poet*, Minneapolis: Fortress Press.
Deere, J., 1996, *Surprised by the Voice of God*, Eastbourne: Kingsway.
Fee, G. D., 1987, *The First Epistle to the Corinthians*, Grand Rapids: Eerdmans.
Forsyth, P. T., 1907, *Positive Preaching and the Modern Mind*, London: Independent.
Lloyd-Jones, D. Martyn, 1971, *Preaching and Preachers*, London: Hodder and Stoughton.
Long, T. G., 1997, *Hebrews*, Interpretation, Louisville: John Knox.
Norrington, D., 1996, *To Preach or Not to Preach?* Carlisle: Paternoster.
Willimon, W., 2005, *Proclamation and Theology*, Nashville: Abingdon Press.

5

Preaching in the Black Church

RUTHLYN BRADSHAW

God's *ecclesia* does not come in colours and tribes. However, for analytical purposes, it is necessary that one recognizes the role of culture and ethnicity and their impact on certain activities – in this case preaching.

In addressing Muslims in Egypt recently (June 2009), US President Barack Obama drew on his Muslim connections and African-American heritage to more effectively connect with his audience. His use of phrases in the language of the people added authenticity and richness to his speech. Ethnicity and culture help to define us and what we do and how we do it.

Africans, for instance, have an innate love of rhythm, and this is evident in their worship style, which is a dramatic contrast to the style in an Anglo-Saxon congregation. Thus preaching style and content cannot be separated from the culture of a people. While there is no inherent difference in the essence of Christianity there is a difference in how it is expressed.

The black church defined

Definition is one of the main difficulties when talking about the black church, as there is no simple undisputed definition for this term. Definitions vary depending on the context. Formulating a term acceptable to all that captures the full meaning and essence of the black church is nigh impossible. Over the years several labels have been used to define or describe churches with a black majority following and just as many objections have been lodged to disqualify using them. At present, the term 'Black Majority Churches' originating in the UK seems to have superseded all other terminologies and is widely used as an acceptable description.[1]

The term black church, as used in this chapter, refers to those churches in the UK that are led by black leaders, with a majority of the congregation being Africans, African-Caribbean and people from other countries who define themselves as being black.

History of the black church in the UK

The history and uniqueness of the black church in the UK and the associated black preaching emanated from the predicament in which post-Second World War African migrants found themselves. Many of them encountered imperialism, colonialism and racism. Blacks were dehumanized and excluded from meaningful participation in British society. The development of the black church could be summarized thus: enslavement in the Caribbean to emancipation; post-Second World War mass migration and the current migration trends; permanent residence in the UK, with the task to craft a livelihood in a country established on the premise that 'all men are equal until they are seen to be darker than me'.

The first stage began with the Africans enslaved in the Caribbean up until emancipation. In this context the Anglo-Saxon Church fully supported plantation slavery. Preaching was geared towards maintenance of the status quo despite the obvious inconsistency with the Christian message represented in the brutal dehumanization of the African. The Church actively engaged in teaching the enslaved to be good servants, obedient and submissive, in spite of the inhumane treatment being meted out to them.

Although forced to worship in the church of their masters, amid grave contradictions and a theology of oppression, being deeply religious the Africans did not relinquish their religiosity. 'To be without religion amounts to a self excommunication from the entire life of society and African peoples do not know how to exist without religion' (Mbiti, 1989, p. 2). Recognizing the futility of the situation, the Africans voted with their feet and, notwithstanding the inevitable consequences, established their own brand of churches, similar to those established by their brothers and sisters in North America.[2] Their actions in defying their oppressors and establishing ecclesiastical spaces demonstrated the extent to which they esteemed religion and the role it played in shaping and defining their lives.

In addressing the overwhelming challenges facing them at the time, the Church became the vehicle for their total expression and development. It functioned as a one-stop shop focusing on the 'whole person' and served as their school, parliament, hospital, place of refuge and solace. The Church also became their economic and spiritual warehouse and inevitably propelled their emancipation as it became the forum for plotting escape and political uprising in the name of equality.

The second stage of development of the black church in the UK concerns the post-Second World War mass migration from the Caribbean in response to the call from the colonial power for assistance in rebuilding a devastated Britain. The arrival of hundreds of descendants of enslaved Africans from the Caribbean on the SS *Empire Windrush* in 1948 has been referenced and acknowledged by historians and theologians as a focal point in the emergence of the black church in Britain (see Phillips and Phillips, 1998; Sturge, 2005, p. 82).

The African migrants from the Caribbean were treated in ways not dissimilar to the treatment which they received when enslaved. Alongside this was the brutally cold climate and the hostile welcome. Confronted with the harsh realities of colonial racism, they turned to the Church in hopes of finding spiritual refuge, consolation and support. In the absence of black churches in the UK, they initially attended the same denominations as the ones transplanted by Britain to their home country. Their hopes quickly dissipated as they discovered that the hostile climate, permeating the society, was equally present in many of the churches. Instead of receiving a Christian welcome they were rejected and dissuaded from attending church. One of the many disheartening reports is that of a man being told by the vicar following a church service, 'Thank you for coming, but I would be delighted if you didn't come back . . . my congregation is uncomfortable in the company of black people' (Phillips and Phillips, 1998, p. 149). Judging from the treatment received, they came to realize that the oneness and inclusiveness expressed in the Church's liturgy did not include blacks in many of the main churches in the UK.

It is noteworthy to mention that not all the churches in Britain responded in this way. Some black Christians found a degree of acceptance in churches and, regardless of the shortcomings, defied the odds and remained. Their presence in these churches eventually helped to transform them. However, for the majority, racism, coupled with rejection and the absence of their familiar brand of churches, forced them to resort to the methods of their forefathers. Borrowing from the traditions of the black churches established in the Caribbean and in Africa, they initiated churches in Britain that were nonexistent before. In recent times it has been argued that it was not solely as a result of racism that black churches came into existence in Britain, but they were raised up to fulfil spiritual, social and cultural needs which would otherwise have been left unmet (Sturge, 2005, p. 87). The Church was at that stage primarily a spiritual warehouse and the preaching was similarly crafted.

The third stage of development is characterized by the black migrants permanently remaining in the UK, striving to obtain a livelihood as independent men and women. The migrants at first had no intention of permanently residing in the UK. Intending their stay in Britain to be temporary, they busied themselves with becoming economically secure, hoping to return home in better financial positions. In their quest for survival, accommodation and employment, church attendance was jeopardized and in some cases completely sacrificed. When dreams of returning home did not materialize, many reconnected with the Church. With the influx of new attendees, the emerging churches quickly outgrew the bedrooms and sitting rooms in which they had begun, so it became necessary to hire halls and acquire buildings in which to accommodate the fast-growing congregations. 'These are the independent "black-majority" churches which have become such a marking feature of present-day British Christianity' (Wilkinson, 1993, p. vi).

Emerging black churches and leaders

Faced with the complex and compelling needs of their main constituents, the emerging black churches became centres of social significance, implementing various strategies and techniques for survival. In the early beginnings, the Church was the only place where the suppressed emotions of black people could have been released. Subsequently, the churches in this dispensation continued to provide non-threatening safe environments in which to meet, worship, share and deal with their problems together. It appears that if black people in the African diaspora were not clever enough to have formed churches and made spaces for themselves, they would not have survived (Reddie, 2008, p. 115).

Early pioneer leaders in the black churches served as bedrocks to the new settlers. They were highly respected, admired and accepted as the instruments and oracles of God. These leaders, as representatives in a common struggle and carrying the burden of the slavery experience, understood the plight of the people they shepherded. They 'lived in their skin'; hence they faced the same predicaments, trying to exist in an environment that was not conducive to their survival. Nevertheless, they managed to offer a quality of pastoral care that was adequate for the spiritual, social and emotional needs of their congregants. Functioning as advocates, confidants and advisors they represented the claims and frustrations of blacks.

Most black preachers in the earlier years were limited in education and training. Yet, they preached sermons that uplifted and inspired people who were beaten down and dealing with life's contradictions and challenges. Conscious that social context plays an important part in shaping one's biblical understanding, these preachers crafted sermons that were instrumental in helping powerless people connect with a powerful God. Generally speaking, it was in a socio-cultural context of marginalization and injustice that black people's understanding of God was forged. Through theologies expressed and messages preached black churchgoers saw that the God of the Bible was not indifferent to their sufferings. Aided by the Scriptures they comprehended that God was not their enemy but, instead, their ally.

Preaching in the black church

It is not trite to say that the black church and its preaching have kept black folks going. Church services are times of retreat from the surrounding pressures. Whatever else happens in the worship service, embedded deeply in the hearts of many is the question, 'Is there a word from the Lord?' In the black church, preaching is taken very seriously and is the focal point in the service. As a matter of fact, preaching is considered to be much more than an act of worship. It is an event integral to worship and not merely adjunct to it. There is a eucharistic aspect about the sermon. Unlike the more traditional churches where all aspects of the worship, including the preaching, lead up to the Eucharist, in the black church, every activity in the worship is geared towards the sermon; feasting on and embedding something of the Living Word.[3]

The sermon, usually 40 to 60 minutes long, is often introduced as being 'the most important part of the service' or 'the moment which we have all been waiting for'. 'Thus saith the Lord' and 'I have a word from the Lord' are statements used to indicate that the text was provided by divine inspiration. The congregation, having a vested interest in the delivery of the word, helps the preachers by urging, groaning, praying and encouraging them.

Drawing on inherent ability and acquired skills, black preachers have developed an idiosyncratic approach to preaching. There are several distinctive qualities, which, although not exclusive to blacks, undergird and make black preaching unique.[4]

To begin with, black preaching is rooted in Scripture. The Bible is key in black people's struggle for freedom and is unquestionably the main source for preaching and teaching in the black church. Unlike today, where consulting various resources in sermon preparation is not only acceptable but also encouraged, years ago the Bible was the only book black preachers used in preparing sermons. It would have been inconceivable or even deemed sacrilegious in the past for the black preacher to have consulted any other source.

The Scriptures helped black people affirm a view of God that differed radically from the distorted version offered them by their white slave masters (Cone, 1997, p. 29). Reading Scripture through the lens of their experiences of powerlessness and struggle, they came to understand God to be almighty, all-powerful and forever championing the cause of the oppressed. The awareness of God being actively involved with them in their struggles, and engaged in facilitating their liberation, intuitively caused them to realize they were much more than what the white society had defined them to be. They learned from Scripture that they too were made in the image of God, and this knowledge enabled them to interpret their condition from a different perspective.

It was also through the Scriptures that black people learned to assimilate the truths of Jesus Christ. The 'Jesus of the black experience is the Jesus of Scripture' (Cone, 1997, p. 103). He came into human existence, in human flesh and dwelt among the poor and downtrodden of earth. He was rejected, scorned, despised, ridiculed and crucified, yet he rose from the dead to a position of exaltation, high above everyone else. The unwanted Stone, cast aside by the builders, became the head of the corner, the liberator of captive humanity and the helper of people struggling with the inconsistencies of life. Black people, living in the context of discrimination, injustice and deprivation, identify with Jesus and see in his experiences similarities to their own. His final victory gives rise to hope and the possibility of a new way of living. In black churches, as well as in Christianity in general, Jesus is recognized as the central figure and hope of humanity.

Second, coming from an oral culture, many black preachers have maintained the traditional spontaneous style of delivery, which incidentally appears to have been the style practised by Jesus. The black church tends to be characterized by spontaneity in both worship and preaching, but perhaps less so now as training including homiletics has brought changes. There is still a certain amount of seemingly extemporary preaching, but this is often underpinned by preparation. Even so, perhaps in the black church more than in others, preachers often feel 'led' to depart from their elaborate notes and take direction in their sermon 'as the Spirit leads'. Typically, in the black church, there is stated openness to the intervention of the Holy Spirit in preaching. Allowance is always made for divine intervention.

However, this discussion about spontaneity, flexibility and prepared sermons is not meant to be dichotomous. Preparation is perhaps the best grounding for inspiration and oracular utterances. It is accepted that preparation is the best guarantee against foolish preaching.

Third, storytelling is linked to a rich African heritage that has translated over into black preaching. The preacher's skilful and creative usage of words invokes the listeners' imagination to the point where they not only understand the story but also live the story. Although entertaining, the goal is not to entertain. The preacher seeks to engage effectively and connect the hearers with the story and make the Bible story become their story. The story speaks to the hearers about what God has done in the past and also speaks of what God is doing for them in the here and now. By aligning themselves with the heroes in the story, victims envision themselves becoming victors, disinherited people see themselves reinstated and the downtrodden see themselves rising up. Simply stated, the Word of God, made current, allows for a creative encounter with God to take place.

Fourth, preaching in the black church is mostly dialogical. Preaching is never the sole right of the clergy. Provision is made in the black worship service to facilitate interaction between the listeners and the preacher. The use of repetition, prevalent in black preaching, is not a time-filler, rather it is a technique used to ensure assimilation and to elicit response. Indeed repetition is used to generate an atmosphere for congregants to experience the word.

The call-and-response interaction is an integral part of the black preaching style. Phrases such as 'Do I have a witness,' 'Can I get an amen,' 'Are you with me' and 'You're coming through, preacher' lace black preaching. Defining statements, assertions, affirmation and encouragement, punctuated by a chorus of response, are also associated. This kind of interaction is beneficial to both preacher and listeners. It connects and narrows the distance between the pulpit and the pew. Preaching is made a corporate event and at the same time encourages and inspires the preacher.

While there is much value in this interactive event between preacher and listeners, there is merit in the arguments put forward against it. For instance: the congregation could overly participate; listeners at times do make automatic non-thinking responses no matter what is being said; other listeners may have difficulty hearing and miss central points in the sermon. Besides, visitors not accustomed to this 'freestyle' preaching may become confused by or uncomfortable with it. Preachers also, rightly or wrongly, may evaluate their performance on the basis of the listeners' responses. Nonetheless, call-and-response interaction, ingrained in the black church, plays an integral part in the preaching event.

Fifth, combining other characteristics, black preaching is prophetic, passionate, enthusiastic, energetic and expressive. Preachers in the black church feel free to be themselves, bringing to the pulpit a variety of personal styles, mannerisms and gestures which contributes to the effectiveness of the preaching. The black congregation celebrates the preacher's ability and uniqueness and is often tolerant of his or her expressions, as long as they are not overbearing. In addition, black preaching is rhythmic, poetic, marked with linguistic flexibility and rhetorical embellishment. The musical tones, modulation of the voice, the hum, the moan, the stammering are all mechanisms used by the black preacher in conveying a message that is both emotive and cerebral.

On the subject of emotions, black preaching is sometimes described as appealing more to the emotion than to the intellect. There is no antithesis between a more emotive sermon and one that is delivered more calmly with less feeling as far as intellectual content is concerned. Black preachers who deliver dramatic and emotion-packed sermons are also mindful of intellectual and theological content. Black preaching is geared to stirring the mind as well as the emotions.

Finally, black preaching is a journey towards celebration, often culminating in a celebrative tone. Celebration is a response to the sermon. As the preaching progresses and increases in volume and intensity, the worshippers are jubilant, uplifted, encouraged and rejuvenated. 'The remembrance of a redemptive past and/or the conviction of a liberated future transform the events immediately experienced' (Thomas, 1997, p. 52). Worshippers, accepting the prophetic word preached as being already fulfilled, celebrate and rejoice. A good example of this is Dr Martin Luther King Jr, who ended his 'I Have a Dream' speech with the glorious celebration, 'Free at last, free at last, thank God Almighty, I am free at last.'

Black preaching encompasses a wide variety of styles. Therefore, this is not an exhaustive list of its distinctive features. The diversities and uniqueness of this tradition are much broader than what have been implied or conveyed here. Further, there are different styles and characteristics of black preaching manifested in differing denominations as well as in individual churches. Despite its diversities, black preaching is always an expression of hope, survival and liberation.

Growth of black churches in the UK

Black churches in the UK are growing at phenomenal rates. It is estimated that there are over 500,000 black Christians in over 4,000 local congregations in the United Kingdom.[5] Furthermore, church plants from Africa are ongoing and occurring rapidly. Judging from these figures and the rising trend, it is apparent that church remains an integral part of the life of black people in the UK. Today's black generation are in need of a word from God as were their black ancestors decades ago. Every generation has their battles to fight and issues with which to contend. Undoubtedly, some of the issues have changed in appearances and positions, but the essence of them remains the same. No generation has yet emerged that is not affected by the experience of Transatlantic slavery or by the colour of their skin (Bailey and Wiersbe, 2003, p. 11).

In contradiction, the dreams and hopes of the black community and individuals are gradually gaining visibility. Africans are rising in prominence all over the world and in all segments of society. In the United States of America, the highest elected position is currently held by a black man. Notable social, economic and political improvements are seen in the UK. There are now policies and legislation that support ideas of a more tolerant UK, which is now considered a multicultural society. However, old racist habits still abound, and so too does discrimination. Black people within UK society are seen and treated in ways that still present major obstacles to their livelihoods. In the light of ongoing pressure and discrimination, church intervention and preaching 'suited to Black temperaments and culture' (Mitchell, 1990, p. 24) remain vital as a way of maintaining their roots and cultural identity in their quest to achieve equity in British society.

New challenges

History has proven that black churches 'are enormously resourceful and potent agents of social reform' (Billingsley, 2003, p. 185). Surprisingly today, it appears as if the black church has lost its zest and has become passively subdued in dealing with certain issues and making representation. There are numerous compounding and demoralizing issues plaguing, crippling and oppressing humankind, which the black church cannot afford to ignore – issues such as poverty, homelessness, hunger, injustice, racism, immigration laws, human trafficking, unequal distribution of wealth, mental health, drug abuse, sexual issues, crime, unemployment and gang violence.

Of equal importance are incarceration and HIV/AIDS. A significant number of the black community, particularly men, are represented in the prison population. This holds significance for the stability of families and the vulnerability of children. HIV/AIDS is a menace to the black population worldwide with the highest prevalence in Sub-Saharan Africa. Alongside these issues are existing laws and policies in the UK and those currently being debated, which have direct bearing on the fundamentals of the Christian faith. Churches and ministers may well be called upon to obey laws that are against conscience and the adherence to Scripture. The black church, arguably one of the most dominant forces in the black community, must find intelligent and creative ways to tackle these realities.

In response to some of the challenges facing black people in the UK, some black churches have formulated strategies for social intervention. Drawing from within the churches themselves, they have initiated and developed projects such as: Families for Peace,[6] RAFFA International Development Agency,[7] Street Pastors UK[8] and The Family & Relationship Crises Centre.[9] Also, after-school programmes, Saturday schools to help under-achievers, elderly day care centres, mentors and a variety of other initiatives. As trend-setters, these churches have given an indication as to where the black church is going.

Crucial to the future of preaching in the black church

In recent conversations with black religious leaders,[10] relevance, being prophetic, training and eschatology are some of the elements identified as being crucial to the future of preaching in the black churches in the UK.

Remaining relevant and consistent with its tradition of being at the forefront of the struggle for human rights is essential. It is a matter of concern that black preachers are apt when addressing spiritual matters but seem not as effective when addressing social ones. They appear at times to be out of date with the issues that the congregation and community are facing. Being attuned to social, economic and political issues is a must. The Church again has to champion the cause of its constituents and rise to current challenges which pose as hindrances to people attaining their God-given potential. The context in which the Church operates as well as the circumstances confronting black people and the society as a whole are factors which gave and should continue to give direction to preaching. Both the biblical text and the contemporary context have to contribute to the theological and sociological elements of sermons aiming to speak relevantly to the needs of oppressed people. Culturally relevant sermons rise out of the totality of people's existence and address all aspects of the person, spiritually, socially, intellectually, psychologically and economically.

Conscious effort to embrace change should be a critical part of black preaching. Change should be embraced strategically to preserve its uniqueness and identity. The black church must never think that there is no need for its preaching to be updated and kept in touch with reality. It is vital that preaching steps up and moves with the times, not reverting to the sixties. Its preachers and pastors must connect with lived experiences of all ages, sorts and conditions of men, women and children, if they are to inspire, challenge and hold their interest.

Prophetic preaching is also indispensable. It was the prophetic preaching of black ministers, denouncing sin, speaking up against the wrongs in society and the awful predicaments in which humans found themselves, that helped to revitalize the ailing Church in Britain. Preachers speaking out on God's behalf instructed the Church on issues of righteousness, justice and mercy. At present, fundamental secularism seems to be successfully displacing Christian influence. Preaching in the black church cannot be neutral. Its position must be clearly stated as it addresses the moral and spiritual values influencing the life of the UK, bringing Christianity back from the margins to the centre of public life. Prophetic preaching is important in restoring Christians as believing groups possessing the power to impact society at large. The power of the gospel and a transforming encounter with Jesus Christ will save individuals and eventually the society. Prophetically, the black church has always proclaimed that Jesus Christ's death, resurrection and ultimate authority generate hope and salvation.

It is a misconception to think that prophetic preaching always means foretelling future events. Prophetic preaching tells forth more than it foretells. It speaks for God, providing guidance, direction and vision of a better world and hopeful possibilities for the future. As long as people are struggling for life and wholeness, there is need for a voice with a prophetic word to emancipate, uplift and equip. 'Thus saith the Lord,' proclaimed with conviction under the inspiration of the Holy Spirit will touch people's lives, articulate their concerns and liberate the oppressed.

Additionally, training is paramount. Unfortunately, some have held and still hold the notion that training robs preachers of the anointing and the ability to deliver relevant heart-reaching sermons. This thinking is perhaps due to the fact that in early years black preachers were trained in white theological institutions which neither catered for nor celebrated black culture. This resulted in black preachers losing some of their identity; the loss came across to the black congregation as loss of anointing rather than loss of self-identity. However, black preachers who have been professionally trained admit that training, rather than taking away from, adds richness to what they present and communicate. An elderly black minister I know in counselling the young ministers he mentored often said to them, 'a dull axe with the anointing will cut, but a sharp axe with the anointing will give the cut a cleaner finish'.

The wave of modernization has brought about an enhanced intelligence that has increased both the complexity and complications of today's life. The makeup of the congregations in black churches has changed remarkably over the years and people ranging from the top to the bottom of the academic and professional ladder are occupying the pews. Sermons need to be better structured and more methodological in their presentation as this affects how they are listened to and viewed. Regrettably, lack of structure has made it difficult to keep up with the preacher's thoughts and has turned off congregations and other people seeking to learn from black preaching.

As one generation of preachers succeeds the other, training at different levels has been introduced and black preachers are becoming increasingly better equipped. Pulpits today are being filled by highly educated black preachers, many of whom, especially in the USA, have earned doctorates and other academic achievements. Black leaders who still oppose training are failing to realize the large intellectual gaps that are being created between the pulpit and pew, as well as the importance of being trained and equipped to speak skilfully into contemporary society.

Finally, in dealing with the here and now, black preaching cannot afford to lose the eschatological aspect of the message. Earlier preaching focused greatly on the hereafter and the imminent return of the Lord Jesus. The black congregation expects to be given something to look forward to that would transform their despair into hope. In the modern Church, the Lord's return must still be preached with conviction and urgency. Also, the unity of the Christian faith and Church must remain the central thrust in its eschatological message.

Lessons to be learned

Black preaching is inadvertently influencing culture and the perception of the black church and preaching, as black televangelists, radio preachers and literature expose the black preaching style and methodology to the world. There is no particular reason why black preaching, however defined, should remain the preserve of black pulpits. Black preaching has principles that can be generalized to all preaching to good effect. For instance, it can help more effectively to engage congregations, increase church attendance and enhance church growth. If this propagation of principles is to happen, literature should play a part. Black preachers and others can reflect on, analyse and write about black preaching. In other words, a body of theory emanating from practice can be built up to inform both scholarship and preaching.

Knowledge of the context from which black preaching comes will hopefully lessen the misunderstanding and misconceptions that have overshadowed the black preaching tradition for decades. Anyone wanting to gain an understanding of this unique style of preaching has to familiarize him- or herself with black culture and the concerns of black people. Dialoguing, discussing and genuine listening are all steps in the right direction in dismissing the myths and biases that people of different cultures hold regarding each other.

Pulpit swapping could be an enriching and enlightening experience for all. There are white ministers who have never listened to a black preacher. Black and white preachers need to learn to read and understand Scripture from each other's point of view. It is to their credit that some religious training institutes in the UK are now introducing black preaching to students doing preaching modules. Others need to take this on board, as there are students being trained who might eventually be called to lead black majority congregations or congregations with black members.

Unfortunately the standard of preaching in the UK has not quite reached that of its American counterpart in its breadth and scope. Unlike in the UK, the black American preachers are given the necessary setting, training and exposure, and these have allowed them to excel tremendously. In the beginning the black church in the USA served as inspiration for the development of the black church in the Caribbean and now the UK. Once again an analysis of the practices and institutions that have developed as part of the black church in the USA could be used to good effect to inform and enhance the role of the black preacher and in turn broaden the scope of the black church in the UK in attending to the contemporary challenges of their constituents.

Sermon forms and delivery styles in the future

Preaching is an intensely creative event. To avoid the possibility of it becoming stale, predictable and stereotypical, new and fresh approaches are necessary. Openness to new ideas could enhance the form and delivery of sermons. New approaches might challenge both the preacher's and the listener's comfort zones. The following ideas are intended to provoke thought or simply speculate about sermon forms and deliveries in the future.

Multimedia and a vast range of technological aids offers numerous and creative approaches to preaching. Sermons could be projected or animated and can incorporate snippets from movies or songs. The hustle and bustle of life, along with the iPod and mp3 era, would mean that the parishioners would be able to download the sermons they have missed or would like to hear again while they are on the move. Virtual preaching through web links allow ill parishioners to be in the service without leaving their houses.

We must become eleventh-hour harvesters and capture the hearts of the youth. Interjecting a bit of rapping or rock into the sermon would surely delight the youth. They would be impressed with the preacher's effort in trying to engage with their culture and be more apt to listen to the sermon.

People like stories. The story in the sermon could be dramatized by a drama group while being preached. Whatever method or technique is used to package the sermon, every effort must be made to ensure that the content remains the same. The central message of liberation and salvation procured by Jesus Christ must always be kept intact.

Conclusion

'The days of coming to church for personal salvation alone are over, the time has come, or come again, for changing the community' (Billingsley, 2003, p. 186). Jesus did not only come to save souls, he came to give life a more abundant dimension. Black preachers and black majority churches are positioned in the UK to make a difference. The black pulpit is strongly influential and is a great place from which to initiate action. Preaching must reflect that while it is imperative that black churches look after their own needs, they are engaging with the broader issues and not remaining internalized or focusing only on institutional maintenance and organizational concerns. The churches' programmes may need to be re-examined. If the church is inundated with activities and not engaging with the issues of human need, then it is a far cry from its mandate and call to serve Christ's interest.

People are driven to the UK for many reasons, but they have the same spiritual and social needs. Black people ought to remember that they too were strangers in the UK and offer worship spaces and preaching that are inclusive. The lessons learnt from the past should elicit an empathic response. Diversities are to be respected, celebrated and affirmed and every human given the opportunity to fulfil his or her God-given destiny.

The future of black preaching depends on it retaining its ethos, essence and role. Black preaching, born in the context of struggle and marginalization, must seek to be relevant in the same context today. The black church and its preaching helped black people to survive the vicissitudes of dehumanization and the many attempts at breaking their body, mind and soul. People in the pews, whose circumstances and experiences daily militate against them, want to know that the preacher has heard from God and will deliver a life-changing word. Black preaching, fearlessly proclaiming the liberating truths of God to a sinful and unjust world, will efficiently serve the future.

Notes

1. The use of this term was instigated by the African Caribbean Evangelical Association (ACEA). See Sturge, 2005, p. 29.
2. The black churches referred to are those that were transplanted from America, started by slaves in response to oppression, and resonated with the Africans in the Caribbean whose circumstances were near identical to their brothers and sisters in America.
3. A conversation with Dr Joe Aldred, pastor and published theologian, on the role of preaching in the black church.
4. See LaRue, 2000, p. 14.
5. See online Directory of Black Majority Churches UK, http://www. bmcdirectory.co.uk/, welcome page. Available also is the listing of Black Majority Churches.
6. Families for Peace is an organization campaigning against gun crime and gang violence. It was started in Birmingham in 2001 by founder and director Gleen Reid, whose son was a victim of a gun crime. She is a member of the Church of God of Prophecy, which offers support.
7. Launched by the Church of God of Prophecy, London, November 2006. Primary interests are in development research, environmental sustainability, community health and social care, social enterprise development and learning and skills.
8. Pioneered in London in January 2003 by Les Isaac, Director of the Ascension Trust. Results include drops in crime in areas where teams have been working. There are now over 100 teams around the United Kingdom.

9. Located in Luton and part of the Church of God of Prophecy, founded 12 years ago and providing intervention activities that target domestic abuse within the community, as well as other activities.
10. Lovel Bent, senior pastor of New Life Assembly Fellowship of Churches; Bishop Wilton Powell, Church of God of Prophecy; Dr Joe Aldred, pastor and published theologian; Lloyd Crossfield, pastor of Church of God Pentecostal.

References

Bailey, E. K., and Warren W. Wiersbe, 2003, *Preaching in Black and White: What We Can Learn from Each Other*, Grand Rapids, MI: Zondervan.

Billingsley, Andrew, 2003, *Mighty like a River: The Black Church and Social Reform*, Oxford: Oxford University Press.

Cone, James H., 1997, *God of the Oppressed*, Maryknoll, NY: Orbis Books.

LaRue, Cleophus J., 2000, *The Heart of Black Preaching*, Louisville: Westminster John Knox.

Mbiti, John, 1989, *African Religions and Philosophy*, London: Heinemann.

Mitchell, Henry H., 1990, *Black Preaching: The Recovery of a Powerful Art*, Nashville: Abingdon Press.

Phillips, M., and T. Phillips, 1998, *Windrush: The Irresistible Rise of Multi-racial Britain*, London: HarperCollins.

Reddie, Anthony G., 2008, *Working against the Grain: Re-imaging Black Theology in the 21st Century*, London: Equinox.

Sturge, Mark, 2005, *Look What the Lord Has Done: An Exploration of Black Christian Faith in Britain*, Milton Keynes: Scripture Union.

Thomas, Frank A., 1997, *They Like to Never Quit Praisin' God: The Role of Celebration in Preaching*, Cleveland, OH: Pilgrim Press.

Wilkinson, John L., 1993, *Church in Black and White*, Edinburgh: Saint Andrew Press.

PART TWO

Practices

6

The Conversation of Preaching and Theology

TREVOR PITT

The view from here

'He charged nothing for his preaching – and it was worth it too', was the way Mark Twain once described a preacher he knew. Preaching has long had a poor press, and that alone can subtly disable preachers in their task. Preaching must be able to sustain itself, but only preachers committed to their proper task can guarantee its future.

Such commitment becomes harder and harder, not least in a practical sense, 'on the ground'. In most British churches, diminishing numbers of ordained ministers are expected to 'manage' groups of parishes or local churches on commercial/business models, with the attendant stretching of the fundamentally necessary bond between pastor and preacher to breaking-point. It is a common experience to hear Sunday sermons that are little more than hastily assembled comments on one or more of the Sunday readings. Expectations are low, and it is far from easy to discern when and how the tide might turn. Clearly, hard-pressed clergy will not be able to effect the required sea-change alone. There is a forgotten truth here. The appointment and authorization of persons with a special responsibility for preaching does not take away from all the baptized their responsibility for proclaiming and witnessing to the gospel. It is evident that lay preaching still has a long way to go in terms of the resources available. Only the provision of better theological education for clergy and laity alike – and preferably together – will make any difference. So the future will not be guaranteed by better organization in any of our churches. As Douglas John Hall's analysis suggests: 'Our churches do not need managers, they need thinkers! They need people whose knowledge of the Scriptures, tradition and contemporary Christian scholarship is more developed than has been required in the past' (1998, p. 195).

A tension still exists in every denomination between 'progressive' and 'traditionalist' factions, between those concerned for relevance in the modern world and those concerned with maintaining a clear Christian tradition (famously characterized by Jürgen Moltmann as a 'crisis of relevance and identity' [1974], p. 7). But this is not all. Every local church continues to struggle for clarity in determining its current purpose, and still expends time and effort in meeting the secondary question of whether it is, in the current jargon, 'fit for purpose'. This managerial tendency unfortunately leads to an inordinate self-concern ('how are we doing?') or merely a concentration on institutional survival. In all this the essential factor is too often missing, a concentration on the 'poetic' theological task of contextual reading and interpretation of Scripture, of preaching and sharing a 'living word'.

Better theological education is obviously necessary during a time when books such as Hawkins's *A Brief History of Time* and Richard Dawkins's *The God Delusion* enjoy such massive sales. Their influence extends far beyond their actual readership, and many have come to feel that theism is no longer plausible as organized religion rapidly loses its credibility. Many believe that science has somehow 'disproved' religion, and extreme religious fundamentalisms, both American, Islamic and (latterly) Israeli, seem to have intensified the nature and extent of global violence. The context in which the future of preaching must be set is a difficult one indeed. Searching questions will need to be asked, questions that go beyond methods and techniques of preaching. Indeed, the central question is surely 'How dare we speak of God today?' It is a pity that the North American preference for 'Homiletics' as a discrete theological discipline tends to separate both the sermon from the worship in which it is set and the preacher from the pastoral work of ministry.[1] Not only so, the American Mid-West displays a more fundamental separation, where Christian beliefs can be cultivated and sustained within close, religiously bounded communities. British and many European Christians inhabit very different cultures in which many competing beliefs coexist in unfenced religious worlds. The art of preaching must always be set in the wider framework of the world in which priest and people, preacher and congregation alike, live together. Walter Brueggemann suggests that the world we live in must be 're-imagined' and that 'daring speech' will be required:

> Poetic speech is the only proclamation worth doing in a situation of reductionism. Such preaching . . . is the ready, steady, surprising proposal that the real world in which God invites us to live is not the one made available by the rulers of this age. (1989, p. 3)

For a disintegrating culture in a transitional phase, when so many yearn and long for a new world order that as yet can only struggle painfully to birth, the proper and authentic task of preachers is to communicate meaning that connects with people's often troubled life experience so directly that the possibility of transformation becomes real. The speech required to transform our hearing will be not only daring but also artistic, prophetic and poetic. T. S. Eliot once remarked that the poet's task is the painful one of 'turning blood into ink' (Eliot, 1933). I warm to the suggestion that the preacher's supreme responsibility is the no less painful one of turning ink back into blood (Bartow, 1995, p. 15), by the oral interpretation of Scripture through the medium of theology. It is no longer enough to distil relatively harmless, insipid, topical lessons from biblical texts – the task is a much more demanding one in every sense. One of the greatest preachers of the twentieth century, Harry Emerson Fosdick, spoke of preaching as drenching the congregation in one's life-blood (Killinger, 1985, p. 205). That level of personal demand is no less true now, but our world has changed. Those who still hear sermons regularly are fully aware of the real challenges to faith and the slow crumbling of ancient religious institutions. The Bible is no longer unquestionably looked on as an authoritative source of truth, and preaching with honesty and intellectual integrity demands that proper attention be given to contemporary scientific, historical and moral understanding, including, of course, the consequences of the sexual revolution. That this last, conflated with issues of biblical authority, has become the touchstone by which Anglicans have come to judge one another indicates some kind of paralysis in that church's intellectual life. Such a bleak situation arguably needs theologians with personal identities beyond denominations and fixed doctrinal positions who are still able to cross these contextual boundaries, and who will refuse to avoid the difficulties inherent in finding a renewed truthfulness at the heart of the Church's life.

Not all theologians are great preachers (there are exceptions – Tillich, Barth, Schillebeeckx, for example), because preaching is not providing information about the gospel, preaching *is* the gospel.[2] Of course, the reverse surely ought to be true: all great preachers should be theologians. What we say, sing and do in our liturgies should contribute to the making of theology.

A closer look

The practice of theological preaching ought to be an exciting process of discovery as the Christian tradition is reinterpreted and reapplied within contemporary social contexts and human experience. Real theology is neither a remote specialism best left to academic experts nor a shallow ignoring of the tradition in the desperate attempt to be relevant. Theological preaching requires the ability to think theologically in and from contemporary contexts. There is no simple equation between theology and preaching, but as Geoffrey Wainwright put it:

> Obviously Christian preaching should be true to the discernible revelation of God in Jesus Christ; it should be . . . a legitimate development of its implications. Second, [it] should be both intelligible and pertinent to its present audience; these two qualities are demanded by the claim that the Christian message is indeed a 'revelation'. (1980, p. 178).

Whether or how far this is true in current practice remains an open question.

The accelerating indifference towards preaching during the latter half of the last century led to its increasing trivialization. Often seen (sometimes accurately) as facile, pompous or just plain boring, attempts were made to broaden its appeal by introducing discussion, group preparation, drama and so on, seeking to help congregations give serious attention to its rationale and actively to participate. More recently, some have argued for mutual or conversational styles that seek to minimize the perceived gap between preacher and congregation (such as Rose, 1997). Preaching is fundamentally concerned with the Christian formation of all those who share in it, with opening up fresh worlds through insight and imagination, and with outworkings in transformative personal change and communal action. In other words, preaching is not simply an educational tool. Perhaps it is precisely that category mistake which has enabled the easy dismissal of preaching as a supremely ineffective means of instruction, persuasion or inspiration – who is prepared nowadays to listen to a single speaker for any length of time?[3] The arrival of PowerPoint, however, dealt a deathblow to any attempt to distinguish between genuine preaching and teaching, and classroom methods have now deeply infiltrated all churches, certainly at the popular level. This has been accompanied by uncritical and widespread adoption of entertainment techniques in many places, which although sometimes capable of enlarging congregations will do little to stem the tide of popular secularism. These tendencies have unfortunately reinforced the efforts of some to promote unhealthy dependence on 'leaders' and to protect congregations from modern biblical scholarship rather than help them find a credible faith through biblical scholarship in mature, thoughtful interpretation. The fear of critical approaches to Christian thinking has certainly been a factor in the continuing shift to conservative positions in most churches. How much longer can those of a highly educated and highly skilled generation accept the sectarian naiveties of church leaders who are afraid to make intellectual demands of their members?

Another reason for the sidelining of preaching in recent years is that, seen only as monologue rather than conversation, it has been judged to be a poor means of effective communication. Communication theory calls attention to ways in which modern entertainment media impair our ability to listen and attend, and produce an audience capable only of short attention spans and passive reliance on visual stimuli and 'soundbites'. As a result the field of homiletics has seen a turn towards the hearer, not merely as a processor of information but as an active participant in a dialogue or conversation. A renewed interest in the techniques of rhetoric and the arts of persuasion suggests that the stage has also much to teach us in terms of congregational participation. There is a larger theological issue here, however, which takes us beyond the dynamics of communication. Preaching is also dramatic performance, if it is to echo, actualize or manifest the nature of God's self-communication in incarnation. In this sense a two-way process is always required, representing both the movement of God into the whole of human experience and the human response in worship and action through participation in the body of Christ. Theologically, sermons are never stand-alone events. All preaching is conceived as an essential part of the much wider purpose of liturgy that celebrates, energizes and enables God's mission in society.[4]

The yawning gap between academic theology and congregational preaching has been a subject of discussion for decades, certainly throughout the last century. An earlier question was *whether* academic scholarship should be kept separate from preaching on the grounds that the objective study of the Bible in secular universities is potentially damaging to the offering of worship, of which the sermon is an integral part. It is certainly true that much academic consensus runs counter to the common assumptions of many congregations, and the resulting conflicts are often exploited by commentators and television programmes. Some preachers have been at pains to ignore or soften the impact of the most contentious issues, no doubt for mainly pastoral or liturgical reasons; after all, Sunday worship is not the place for academic discourse, and in most churches the ability range is too great for high-level debate. On the other hand, the Church's role in leading and inspiring honest worship cannot exclude any path towards truth. My own experience has been that most congregations contain a majority who really do want to know what and how 'their' preacher thinks, and certainly do not prefer a constant safe diet of comfortable reassurance. The pulpit, however, is not the place for teaching, and some better opportunities for theological education are now available as we move towards becoming a 'learning church'. Again, my own experience of adult discussion groups, Bible study courses, house groups and the like, has been the oft-repeated question, 'Why were we not told this before?' Those priests and pastors who are attentive to the questions people are asking will make certain that links are constantly built between the study and the sermon; it is an essential part of the conversation between those who preach and those who listen, between modern understanding and traditional believing. In recent years there has been a greater sense of accord between biblical exegetes and theologians, recognition that the practice of embodied discipleship cannot be separated from the practice of biblical interpretation. This is largely a result of the trend away from the dominance of modernist historical-critical methods. While attention to the text alone tended to produce a search for a singular, correct reading, a new attention to the community of readers introduces far more diversity in interpretation. One senses that a climate change is developing – all the more reason, therefore, that honest preaching should not leave theological rigour behind.

However, this still leaves the question of *how* this is best done. Some obvious principles are involved. Preaching is not simply a case of 'applied theology', a matter of passing on theoretical insights or concepts formed in the academy. More importantly, preaching is itself a theological enterprise, and speaks from and to the lived reality of practical Christianity.[5]

Preachers, arguably, have faced two problems. On the one hand biblical critics seemed to raise questions about the historicity of the tradition, hitherto thought to be the essential ground on which truth rested; on the other hand, historical enquiry led to a contextualizing of the historical Jesus that seemed to widen the discontinuity between a first-century Jew and the mindset of the modern (western) world. More recently, modern hermeneutic theory has at least enabled us to understand that just as the biblical texts are set in their own historical and social contexts, so also their readers and interpreters inevitably bring their own perspectives and presuppositions, conditioned as they also are by the times in which they live, to the task. Preaching is now better understood as assisting in this two-way interchange, facilitating a deepening conversation, which is surely how the 'doing' of theology must proceed.

A longer view

The essentials for future preachers, therefore, are twofold. First, a genuine discernment, exploration and authentic participation in the actual situations in which they and their congregations find themselves. Second, a familiarity with the current, if necessarily provisional, consensus of biblical scholarship about the intentions and situations of the biblical texts. The risk, of course, is of failing to sustain this balance, and shifting either towards the moral, social or political stance of the Christian or the Church on the one hand, or towards textual exposition *per se* on the other. Certainly there is a place for both specialities, but as these are merely preliminary concerns, that place is not the sermon.

In recent decades a paradigm-shift has occurred in biblical studies from the earlier historical-critical exegetical method to a more literary approach, with particular emphasis on the various genres of Scripture and a special focus on the place of narrative. The former has been widely rejected because it seemed to conflict with prior doctrinal commitments or fundamentalist attitudes, but today it is simply insufficient to pretend that the biblical authors all relate a consistent theological package reducible to any preaching occasion, especially when understood in propositional terms. Narrative preaching seeks to match the form of presentation to the form of the biblical text, and its purpose is not directive, dogmatic or educational, but integrative and participatory.

Narrative preaching has become widely fashionable in recent years, moving away from expository preaching rooted in the more didactic elements of Scripture, notably the Pauline epistles. Narrative, in the form of history, story or parable, is the most prevalent of all the biblical genres, and the one most suited to the merging of past and present horizons. It has a wide appeal beyond the mere retelling of Bible stories.[6] It is not simply a matter of recapitulating a biblical story and then drawing out its lessons for today, but rather of retelling 'the story' in such an open way that its contemporary meaning can be heard between the lines, so to speak. Such has been traditional in African American preaching.[7] Any story presents an alternative world to the reader or hearer in concrete terms, and its extraordinary power lies in its capacity to make us wonder whether it is a world we might, could or should live in ourselves. Musical and dramatic forms of worship can be equally effective as the spoken word in narrative presentation. Performing in this way a vivid invitation to live and understand our lives differently has been taken up in recent years by Godly Play, a Montessori-based initiative encouraging both children and adults to develop larger dimensions of faith and understanding through wondering and open-ended questions in response to simple forms of dramatization (see Berryman, 1991).

However, it is not enough that hearers are addressed personally within their own situations; when hearers begin to discover how to hear the biblical story as their own story, and find themselves living biblically in contemporary ways, personal integration can begin to spread over into active concern for social, political and global issues. This growing realization then leads back into fresh appreciation of the way in which Scripture operates in the life and worship of the churches. Many current controversies about the nature of biblical authority fail to recognize how much of our Bible arose from dialectic and polemic, and provided the religious community with an identity which then shaped its further literature and its ongoing interpretation. Earlier historical-critical methods concentrated on the process of how the biblical text reached its canonical form. More recent approaches concentrate on how the Bible functions in modern contexts. What do biblical texts mean, and are all interpretations valid? Although academic theology has become an amazingly diverse field, there remains a tacit consensus about what the major issues are – the fact that all human understanding has a context and a history means that theology can never be, and never has been, doctrinally static or contextually neutral, and that therefore contemporary theology must become more explicitly sociological and 'political'.

So unlike lecturing or discussion, preaching can never be a straightforward, risk-free enterprise. It is always a serious adventure into the unknown, confronting and addressing the matrix of uncertainties within which the life of faith is aroused and nurtured – the mysterious hiddenness of God that only faith can perceive, the eschatological hope that moves faith on beyond assurance, the everyday encounters with some transcendent dimension as reminders that God cannot be kept safely at a distance, and the sense of God's presence that always undermines our self-assurance and leaves everyone, and especially the preacher, vulnerable and at risk, but open to all those realities that allow words and their various contexts to mediate the Word.

Beginning with hearers

Writing as a liturgical theologian, a formal statement of conviction at this point may be useful! My own view is that all preaching begins within the liturgy, the *theologia prima*, in the sense that *lex orandi* precedes *lex credendi*.[8] By 'liturgy' I do not have in mind the Sunday service as an isolated activity, but rather the liturgy as it is lived, prayed, proclaimed and celebrated within the life of society (as I noted above) and which is then also manifested in church rituals and patterns of behaviour. Within this wider liturgy is set the Ministry of the Word, which occurs in many contexts beyond worship occasions: catechesis (teaching), paraclesis (pastoral care), social action and mission (the evangelization of culture). At a practical level, therefore, liturgy and theology are closely related, and come together formally in what is, or ought to be, the pinnacle of liturgical speech, the sermon.

It follows that preaching is a theological discipline rather than a communication technique. It is a primary form of theological reflection because it is done, here and now, in a specific time and place. Its fundamental purpose is to extend the mission of God within society through the Church. Theological preaching is not a matter of 'reciting doctrine' but of 'doing theology'. In this sense, academic theology is a secondary form and exists for preaching, because doctrine becomes gospel only if it is the appropriate speech or action for particular contexts or situations. In British culture, broadly speaking, there have always been two different approaches to the task of preaching: either taking the word of gospel to culture (the broadly evangelical model) or discerning the word of gospel already implicit in culture (the broadly Anglican model). These are not exclusive models, and both lead to practical or social action within the wider setting of the liturgy as defined above.

Our future preaching should therefore be understood as a classic case of practical theology, a practice-to-theory inductive method of doing theology. Simple applications of textual meanings to life in general will no longer be sufficient. Beginning from the lived practice of faith and always rooted in concrete situations in the life of the world, it goes without saying that the ministry of any preacher will be integrated within the life of the Church *as it exists in the world*. This echoes the familiar model of the Anglican parson, who was priest, pastor and preacher integrated in one person. Such local, parochial integration is now lost and cannot be recaptured in our more global, interconnected world. Nevertheless, before anyone stands up in the Christian assembly to speak, the ability to listen to the world in which the assembly is situated remains the crucial component of authentic preaching. The question remains: how do preachers now listen to church and world in order to validate their preaching authority?

Every preacher wishes to speak in ways the world understands, but this can easily lead us astray. More attentive listening to the world would save us from captivation by 'relevance', which can be a dangerously reactionary trap. Relevant to what? Fashion? Opinion? Social analysis? Seeking to respond to trends and cultural shifts on their own terms by adopting current cultural norms ultimately leads nowhere. Making worship more accessible is a widely adopted aim, but it usually implies dumbed-down populism and is likely to prevent serious engagement with theology and deny access to credible Christianity just at the point where we seek to reopen it. Far too many of us still imagine that 'theology' belongs only in the study, and needs reworking if anything is to be 'heard', so it is little wonder that light entertainment becomes the main result. Charles Bartow comments:

> If preaching today seems tepid . . . it may not be so because preachers have failed to match the entertainment value of televised discourse. Perhaps it is because they have succeeded! (1997, p. 134)

A constructive dialogue with contemporary culture must surely be the true basis of any future theology of preaching. Theological intent naturally belongs at every level of the sermon-making process – exegesis, hermeneutic, style and delivery – but it is critical at the level of the hearers. For too long it has been assumed that theology is primary at the level of the exegete and interpreter, and secondary at the level of the hearer, but *it ought to be the other way round*. Biblical preaching is not a matter of applying some fixed text to some aspect of life or variety of circumstances, much less reiterating ready-made points of doctrine or ethics. Theology cannot begin from any top-down authority in deductive mode, and it cannot arise in a vacuum or be developed in the abstract: it can only begin from the sociological contexts and the human situations of its hearers.[9]

Rather than engage in constructive dialogue with the world, there are many who would still prefer the Church to have something definite, universal and unequivocal to bring to it, such as clear rulings on what are deemed to be orthodox fundamentals of faith and ethical absolutes. Their need for sharp boundaries between truth and falsehood tends to polarize every issue and reduce the opportunity for dialogue and that attentive listening I consider vital for genuine preaching. My position does not represent an uncritical, subjective, totally relativist or naively pluralist approach. I certainly think that all preachers should read more deeply in Church history and the development of ideas. An incarnational theological approach locates truth and meaning in human experience as a first step, so that the whole experience of being human is reflected in the historical presence of Jesus Christ. To begin Christology 'from below' avoids absolutist, authoritarian, single-track notions of God's Word simply given 'from above'. In this way, faith experience is never separated out from the whole of ordinary human experience, and centres on Jesus Christ as a living reality rather than a fixed object of prayer and worship. Such a living reality invites and embraces us through and from within the life of the world we inhabit. As one of us, Jesus Christ operates as the focus of God among us, a down-to-earth presence that makes all the difference.

This may seem too fluid amid ideological clamour for purity of doctrine, ecclesial urge to maintain church institutions in traditional forms and self-interested hankering after certainty, but in truth no interpretation, no preaching can ever be conclusive because the faith experience in a changing world must itself be a living, moving, changing thing. Every preacher knows that a sermon comes into its own because it lives only in the moment and dies by repetition. The real enemy is static thinking about issues, doctrines and identities, turning preaching into retailing products, hearers into consumers and churches into brand loyalties. Once meaning and truth become turned into fixed entities they become disconnected from any ongoing process of thinking or spiritual growth. When we fail to regard each other positively in our emerging differences we have already given up the task of building Christian communities. Beginning from the hearers means coming to terms with this postmodern diversity.

Beginning again: some characteristics of postmodern preaching

Postmodernism seems to many to rob Christianity of its traditional place in the scheme of things.[10] Instead what is offered is an open marketplace in which anyone can sell any set of values to anyone with all the means of persuasion at their disposal. A total relativism seems to destroy the permanence of everything, and we can make things mean whatever we want them to mean. While some Christians welcome such an ethos of free-for-all consumerism, making space for each new 'fresh expression' of church, others find only a new sectarianism, and fear the loss of a single cultural narrative or objective truth. When this concern comes to be portrayed as the complete loss of the biblical story as a totalizing grand narrative, the common solution is either 'shouting louder' in order somehow to get a hearing or radical adjustment to the style of the church showroom. But maybe the situation is not as critical or as novel as it is often represented. It is not really new, as most of us living today have grown up with a creeping postmodernism which has by now become almost second nature. Nevertheless it will be crucially important for preaching that seeks to begin from its hearers to adjust intelligently to postmodern outlooks and attitudes – it is simply not sufficient either to ignore them by simple derision or to baptize them by creating enough separate comfort zones for every lifestyle.

75

The world is different now. Postmodernism reflects the widespread appreciation of the vastness of physical reality and of biological and geological time opened up by scientific advance, and the consequent need finally to come to terms with the realization that *homo sapiens* is not at the centre of the physical universe. So many new possibilities, both inspiring and dreadful, open before us that all the old certainties, deemed to be the stock-in-trade of preachers, have disappeared without trace. Environmental disaster is alarmingly close, and the human future begins to look like a fight for survival. Neither historical grounding nor assured progress to future ideals seem to hold conviction, and the meaning and purpose of living can only be found in the unpredictable here and now. Unconditional absolutes are no longer available, and Christianity cannot claim any privileged access to truth. A new global reality of radical pluralism and cultural difference has left us without any common metanarrative beyond that of western capitalism. In societies across the world political systems are distrusted, and the enfeebling of democratic institutions leads to a weaker sense of the common good. Our world and our existence are no longer stable or coherent, even at the level of imagination, and it is not hard to see why frightened or bewildered Christians are tempted to turn away and find some kind of consolation in older frameworks. Brueggemann points us positively towards a necessary new integrity:

> Our circumstance permits and requires the preacher to do something we have not been permitted or required to do before. Ours is an awesome responsibility: to see whether this [biblical] text, with all of our interpretive inclinations, can voice and offer reality in a redescribed way that is credible and evocative of a new humanness, rooted in holiness and practised in neighbourliness. (Day, Astley and Francis, 2005, p. 25)

In other words, the churches need to be different now if they are to maintain a convincing mission in our world. So where can we begin? Despite what I have said so far about the importance of theology to good preaching, the starting-point for any good sermon will always be the ordinary concerns and everyday problems that beset us all in personal life and modern society. Certainly the preacher's task is to share the Church's theology rather than protect people from the issues theologians are addressing, for Christians need to be both deeply interested and well informed. The preacher's primary task is the theological one of doing theology contextually through the immediate and recognizable issues confronting preacher and hearer alike. This inevitably means that the preacher's task is a significantly larger one than preparing and delivering sermons! The substantive task is the redirection of the theological enterprise away from the narrow and select confines of self-referenced academic conversations to the larger learning contexts of church, community and society. This has become an essential corrective in a time when public discussion of religious issues has never before been so widespread and so passionate.[11]

So the postmodern task is a *theological* one. A sermon, as living speech in the contemporary world, is a necessary form of theological learning and teaching. Theology is primarily for worship and preaching, which is the lifeblood of the Church at work in the world, and not for the university or for the specialist alone. Like all worship, preaching is also a shared task. How do we do it together? Worship centres on the Bible. The Bible is primarily for worship, not for study. Study it we must, but preaching is not simply a matter of reconstructing its original settings, and much less pretending that we still inhabit any of those settings.[12] Much less is preaching merely the application of texts to contemporary situations, because the more we focus simply on applying one to the other, the more we are led to directives and imperatives that end up with our own thing rather than God's thing. Any biblical text stands before the preacher as a musical score stands before the conductor and performers, as 'arrested performance' (Long and Hopkins, 1982, p. 2), as an event waiting to happen again in a fresh way. The question is not a simple one of how the preacher will teach theology to others, but much more importantly of how preachers allow those they serve to teach them theology from their life experience and their sense of the presence and absence of God. This may mean that sermon technique needs to become more genuinely participative. Learning theology is surely never done by passive listening to speeches. Preachers and listeners together must find ways of becoming learners in new forms of dynamic conversation capable of shaping and reshaping active faith. In this way preaching could become a shared mode of doing theology by listening and paying attention, within our present experience, between the Bible we read and the world we inhabit. In both senses, because of what the Bible is, preaching begins with the human. Preaching is always an open response to the discovery of God in the midst of living, not a closed response in terms of preconceived ideas. Preaching should never be done to induce responses, for it belongs in worship, in the corporate celebration of God's presence and human activity and behaviour. What happens in people's minds and lives is not the preacher's business, except perhaps by invitation. It is the preacher's business to help everyone face their own and their society's question, of how God is claiming us, without providing ready-made answers from their own particular experience, background or training. Those who preach need to be aware of how much they too are being theologically shaped by the common ministry in which all are involved.

This means that the postmodern task is also an *experimental* one, creatively testing out what is as yet untried. In this sense too it is a shared task, for preaching has always claimed experimentation to be true of God. God is present in, and seeks us out from, the mundane, practical and social realities of life in the world. God invites our partnership in his purposes for creation. Sometimes when God emerges in our experience, the testing involved can be like Jacob's wrestling match, a risky business that nevertheless we cannot resist. Take, for example, the case of Jürgen Moltmann, whose own essential theological dialogue began in 1943 during the firestorm in his home city of Hamburg:

> During that night I cried out to God for the first time in my life . . .
> My question was not, 'Why does God allow this to happen?' but, 'My God, where are you?' . . . I felt the guilt of survival and searched for the meaning of continued life . . . During that night I became a seeker after God . . . one was alone and, like Jacob at the Brook Jabbok, exposed to the sinister powers and destructive forces of darkness. The one with whom I was struggling, and the one who was struggling with me, only became clear to me later. (2007, pp. 17, 26)

This powerful personal experience threw Moltmann into a lifetime of theological testing, as God was revealed to him in the human reality of the crucifixion, in Jesus' own abandonment by God. God became not an object for us to question but a subject who addresses us. Far from trying to work God out, theology became a matter of how we are claimed by God. If God is found in our world – on a cross – theology becomes a dialogue with the world. These, or something like them, are surely the fundamental human experiences from which our preaching grows and our theology is shaped. In the end, it all comes down to the urgent question: what sort of God have we got?

There is a God who is essentially removed from the human situation, a God expressed in so many traditional hymns, modern songs and liturgical texts, a God of dominance, order and control, even violence, and at some distance from human intimacy. Not the biblical God, but an 'almighty' mistake.[13]

There is a God who meets us from the future, an eschatological God who invites us to wait, and work, in the interim, resting secure in the fulfilment of the promise to redeem, to liberate, to make things new. I suspect that amid our doom-laden predictions of climate change and ecological catastrophe, our fondness for disaster movies and our anxiety about radical Islam, eschatology has become an alien dimension for most people.

There is a God who meets us in the depths of our being, intimately seeking out our inner selves, knowing us as a loving Father knows his only child, holding us in the arms of his constant loving provision. But we are all too prone to anxiety in a culture where trust has given way to suspicion for such an image to function beyond the private world of therapy and care for the individual.

So the shaping of our theology needs now to begin from the human world of real experience. God is different now. It seems obvious to me that the only possible starting-place for preaching theology is our own sense of solidarity with one another as members of one human race and citizens of one planet, living as we do in a radically plural world in which there is so much cultural and religious difference, and among so many fellow human beings who are marginalized, persecuted or forgotten. Our ongoing engagement in this human story will unfold as the continuing story of God. The God who is with us and for us is the God who suffers with us and who from that fellow suffering invites us to share his purpose. The heart of such a theology can only be inclusive, not exclusive, and within rather than over against the evolution of all things. Only the God who meets us within our own experience of the world can address us in ways that enable us to name God, speak of God, tell God's story as a human story, and find in that human sharing a communion with God. In the end, of course, the whole story is God's. It is a God who does not wait to be invited into my life, for the story is not about me. It is a God who is always inviting me into his life, so that my life, like God's, can be a moving part of the same reality.

The genuine human context from which we begin has become within our own lifetime essentially pluralist. The Christian faith is one of many. Postmodernity brings a fundamental untidiness to the way life is lived and found meaningful; consumerism and a 'freedom-of-choice' mentality has a profound effect on the way people respond to the claims of any religious system. We live in a climate of suspicion, and those who preach need to discover a fresh sensitivity in the way they make clear their own insights and convictions. Theology cannot live or develop in a world of its own. Theology has to declare and defend Christian truth in an authentic public discourse, articulating the criteria by which it is expressed, acknowledging the historical pluralism and syncretism already present in the Christian doctrinal tradition, and respecting the genuine differences of other faith traditions as an essential aspect of a forward-looking and enriching future. David Brown, in a series of major writings, has made a powerful plea for widening our perspectives of Christian faith beyond traditional biblical interpretation. He shows how biblical stories may be read in ever-new ways with significant fresh insights for engaging with, rather than opposing, changing cultures and environments. This approach clearly shifts the art of preaching decisively from monologue to dialogue. He uses reader-response theory to suggest how listeners may be invited to play a full part in engaging with the spoken word, and so contribute to the inevitably various layers of meaning. Meanings are not the property of the preacher, but emerge in the interaction between preacher, listener and the wider tradition or interpretative community of which both preacher and listener are part.[14] The biblical text does not present simple or single meanings, but does invite both response and dialogue that will change with each generation. The main point here is that the preacher is surely a key player in that critical process. The process must involve much more than dialogue within Christian communities. Preacher and hearer alike belong to many other communities which do not all overlap with the churches, and so must also be able to dialogue beyond their worshipping communities in language forms capable of common understanding. The Church's major concerns with apologetics, evangelism and, in the wider sense, mission, while distinguished from the task of preaching, will need routinely to inform it.

It follows from all this that there will always be some level of ambiguity or tension in any preaching occasion, not only between preacher and hearers, or between different parts of a congregation, but also between different generations of hearers, and so potentially between the sermon and other parts of the liturgy. Nevertheless, preaching can be genuinely inclusive because it is a truly collaborative exercise, recognizing and allowing that its hearers will occupy a variety of different places. As each hearer and each community is enabled to find in their own context an alternative world that begins to make more sense of the actual world they inhabit, some authentic new theology is being formed.

The world, if not the Church, is always assessing the adequacy of our theological preaching, and often finding it wanting. In a critical time such as ours, the churches urgently need this turn to theology in order not only to provide some remedy for theological incomprehension in the churches but also to help people more generally form some coherent sense of how it might be possible to frame a holistic interpretation of human life from a theistic perspective. This will not happen if theology remains largely tacit and unspoken in our churches and therefore not adequately reflected upon nor implemented in practice.[15]

Notes

1. In my former course, North East Oecumenical Course (NEOC), the preaching programme of study always formed part of a larger module, 'Worship and Preaching'.
2. In Greek the phrase 'to preach the gospel' is rendered by a single word, indicating a single dynamic concept.
3. Stand-up comics seem to manage it!
4. I am drawing here on the original Greek concept of *leitourgia*, meaning a public work of any kind. See, for example, Susan Holman, 2001, who considers the relationship of the poor in the early Christian world to the *leitourgia* of religious and civic practice. She shows how early Christian responses to help the poor drew heavily from the general cultural concept of liturgy in late antiquity.
5. Thomas Long prefaces his book on the practicalities of preaching with this fundamental axiom, that preachers do not come *to* their hearers from outside, but *from within* the shared life of the congregation and its place in the world (see Long, 1989, p. 10).
6. I recently arranged a large-scale act of worship for the theological course of which I had been principal, which included a tenor solo from Handel's *Solomon*. Many wondered about its suitability in that context, but it should be remembered that Handel's oratorios were supreme presentations of story as theology in an age prone to dismiss biblical narrative as lacking doctrinal purity. Handel 'took incidents from the past and so shaped their telling that audiences should perceive a pattern in the action that touched their own lives' (Swanston, 1990, p. 10).
7. 'To preach the gospel is to take the baton of an old story and run with it for a while as it transforms and remakes itself in your hand and heart, even as you run with it. I love preaching, but it is the story as opposed to preaching that keeps me preaching . . . Knowing the story is an unsung homiletical attribute. It is possible to overfocus on method and technique. Know the story and keep knowing it, and you'll find a way to tell it' (Jones, 2004, pp. 37–8).
8. I am aware, of course, that the precise meaning of this Latin tag attributed to Prosper of Aquitaine, *lex orandi legem statuat credendi* (let the law of prayer establish the law of belief) is much disputed and

can be differently applied (see Spinks, 2007, pp. 378–9). Nevertheless it has a rich Anglican usage, especially in the seventeenth century, which seeks to integrate worship and doctrine.

9. As a good example, I recently heard a sermon on Mark 10.2–16 (Trinity 17 Year B Proper 22). Instead of leading with a traditional reading, 'Jesus' clear denunciation of divorce', the preacher began with his own experience with 'Relate' before examining the context of this 'hard saying' in relation to the question of women's rights in ancient Judaism.

10. See for example Carey, 1989.

11. It is surely unnecessary to place the word 'contextual' in front of 'theology' since all theology takes place in a context, each one demanding its own particular rigour.

12. It is always, in my opinion, salutary for preachers to accept the routine discipline of a lectionary, preferably the one prescribed ecumenically and globally. For an alternative view, see Hedahl, 1996, p. 84.

13. See, for example, MacLeod, 2005.

14. See Fish, 1980, and Iser, 1978, and discussed by Dickinson, 2000, Barton, 2002, and Dunn, 2003.

15. See Allen, 2002, p. 18.

References

Allen, R., 2002, *Preaching Is Believing*, Louisville: Westminster John Knox Press.

Barton, J., 2002, 'Thinking about Reader-Response Criticism', *Expository Times* (February), pp. 147–51.

Bartow, C. L., 1995, *The Preaching Moment,* Kendal: Hunt.

____, 1997, *God's Human Speech*, Cambridge: Eerdmans.

Berryman, J.W., 1991, *Godly Play*, Minneapolis: Augsburg.

Brown, D., 1999, *Tradition and Imagination*, Oxford: Oxford University Press.

____, 2000, *Discipleship and Imagination*, Oxford: Oxford University Press.

____, 2004, *God and Enchantment of Place*, Oxford: Oxford University Press.

____, 2007, *God and Grace of Body*, Oxford: Oxford University Press.

____, 2008, *God and Mystery in Words*, Oxford: Oxford University Press.

Brueggemann, W., 1989, *Finally Comes the Poet*, Minneapolis: Augsburg Fortress Press.

____, 1995, 'Preaching as reimagination', *Theology Today* 52.3, pp. 313–29.

Carey, G., 1989, *The Great God Robbery*, London: Collins.

Day, D. V., Jeff Astley and Leslie Francis (eds), 2005, *Making the Connections: A Reader on Preaching*, Aldershot: Ashgate.

Dickinson, D., 2000, '"In Honesty of Preaching" 4. The Insights Offered by Literary Theory', *Expository Times* (July), pp. 328–32.

Dunn, J. D. G., 2003, 'What Makes a Good Exposition?' *Expository Times* (February), pp. 147–57.

Eliot, T. S., 1933, *The Use of Poetry and the Use of Criticism*, Cambridge, MA: Harvard University Press.

Fish, S., 1980, *Is There a Text in This Class? The Authority of Interpretive Communities*, Cambridge, MA: Harvard University Press.

Hall, D. J., 1998, *Professing the Faith,* Minneapolis: Fortress Press.

Hedahl, S. K., 1996, ' All the King's Men', in T. G. Long and E. Farley (eds), *Preaching as a Theological Task*, Louisville: John Knox Press, pp. 82–90.

Holman, Susan, 2001, *The Hungry Are Dying*, Oxford: Oxford University Press.

Iser, W., 1978, *The Act of Reading*, Baltimore: Johns Hopkins University Press.

Jones, K. B., 2004, *The Jazz of Preaching*, Nashville: Abingdon.

Killinger, J., 1985, *Fundamentals of Preaching*, London: SCM Press.

Long, B. W., and M. F. Hopkins, 1982, *Performing Literature: An Introduction to Oral Interpretation*, Englewood Cliffs: Prentice-Hall.

Long, T. G., 1989, *The Witness of Preaching*, Nashville: Abingdon.

Long, T. G., and E. Farley (eds), 1996, *Preaching as a Theological Task*, Louisville: John Knox Press.

MacLeod, J., 2005, 'Almighty Mistake', *Theology* (March/April), pp. 91–9.

Moltmann, J., 1974, *The Crucified God*, London: SCM Press.

____, 2007, *A Broad Place*, London: SCM Press.

Rose, L. A., 1997, *Sharing the Word: Preaching in the Roundtable Church*, Louisville: John Knox Press.

Spinks, B., 2007, 'Worship', in John Bainbridge Webster, Kathryn Tanner and Iain Torrance (eds), *The Oxford Handbook of Systematic Theology*, Oxford: Oxford University Press, pp. 378–93.

Swanston, H., 1990, *Handel*, London: Geoffrey Chapman.

Wainwright, G. 1980, *Doxology*, London: Epworth.

7

The Future Use of the Bible in Preaching

STEPHEN WRIGHT

In the preaching of the future, the Bible will surely continue to occupy a crucial place. As witness to the unique revelatory and redemptive acts of God, it is irreplaceable, and will continue to be so throughout this present age of gospel proclamation, until God's kingdom is consummated. The way that the preacher *uses* the Bible, however, will naturally and rightly be responsive to specific cultural developments. I will consider three such developments here, relating to the format of the Bible, the conception of the Bible and the life of the Bible in the congregation.

From codex to computer

It is easy to forget that 'the Bible' has not always had its familiar format as a modern book. Recollecting this may keep us alert to the fact that its format in fact continues to evolve, and prompt us to enquire about the implications of this for preaching.

The Bible arose largely from oral traditions. Even once those traditions had become 'fixed' in writing, there was a continuing element of fluidity in the way in which they were handed down. This applies to both Old and New Testaments, and then to the way in which both Testaments together were transmitted as Christian Scripture. In early Christianity, it was natural that the traditions and testimonies inscribed in Scripture should have a dynamic relationship with the continuing proclamation of the Church. Literacy was low, production of manuscripts was expensive and time-consuming, and for many Christians (as well as non-Christians) it was through the 'live' preaching and informal testimony of the Church, far more than through the written Scriptures, that the message of Christ would have been heard.

The Scriptures were not all handed down in one physical book even by the time a 'canon' was more or less agreed. Augustine, in his account of his conversion in the late fourth century, mentions taking up the 'book containing Paul's epistles'.[1] The two earliest codices (books) containing roughly what we know as the canon of Scripture, Codex

Sinaiticus and Codex Vaticanus, date only from the fourth century. The significance of the technological ability demonstrated by these codices is expressed on the website of the remarkable Codex Sinaiticus Project: 'The ability to place these "canonical books" in a single codex itself influenced the way Christians thought about their books, and this is directly dependent upon the technological advances seen in Codex Sinaiticus.'[2] It is useful to be reminded that the notion of a single-volume 'Bible' is as recent as that, and that it owes as much to technology as to theology. (The fact that a facsimile of a fourth-century book can be freely consulted on the internet is also a fascinating phenomenon in its own right, and provokes thought about the complex way in which we can now 'read' the Bible.)

The text of modern Bibles depends on the painstaking work of scholars over a couple of centuries, weighing up the evidence of manuscript traditions which converge and diverge in complex ways. There is continued (though eirenic) disagreement about which books should actually be in 'the Bible': the most well-known instance in the UK is the 'scriptural' status accorded the so-called 'apocryphal' books in the Roman Catholic Church but not in the Protestant Churches.

This complex process of development tends to be masked by the apparent uniformity bequeathed to us by the invention of printing, coinciding as it did with a Reformation intent upon the restoration of 'the Bible' to a place of commanding authority in the Church. Protestants, especially, tend to regard 'the Bible' as a fixed entity, and to think of the variety between translations as cosmetic and pragmatic, aiding comprehension of a single accessible 'meaning'. Some Reformation traditions give 'the Book' a highly symbolic place in worship, placed on the centre of the holy table, or opened on a carved eagle. This also masks the origin of the notion of 'Bible' in the Greek plural *biblia*, that is 'books'. There may be copies of 'the Book' for members of the congregation, and the preacher may defer very explicitly to it, sticking to it for the content of the sermon and inviting the congregation to check out the validity of the sermon with reference to it.

The content of the Bible has indeed remained remarkably stable down the centuries, and the varieties in canons and translations should certainly not be exaggerated. Yet the facts are that the presence or absence of certain books in the canon adjusts our view of the whole, and that translation is never merely 'neutral', but is always an act of interpretation. It is therefore good that simplistic appeals in preaching to 'what the Bible says' are perhaps heard less frequently now, since they tend to obscure the inevitable necessity of interpretation. At the same time, however, we can continue to rejoice in the considerable clarity of the Bible's central messages, above all its testimony to Jesus Christ. The Bible remains the preacher's indispensable companion.

But we should also reckon with the quite bewildering range of Bibles now published in various formats. The need obviously continues to be felt for Bibles which (like the *Glossa Ordinaria* and *Glossa Interlinearis* of mediaeval times) give not only the text but also interpretations of the text. We are used now to study Bibles, application Bibles, Bibles for women, men, young people and children. There is a Poverty and Justice Bible (2008), highlighting texts on those themes. It is interesting to read the publisher's blurb: 'A groundbreaking Bible that megaphones what God has to say about poverty and injustice . . . To engage compassionate young adults . . . This new Bible highlights more than 2,000 verses, revealing God's heart for the poor and oppressed . . . Builds on issues raised by influential Christians and public figures including *Bono, Rob Bell, Jim Wallis and Tony Campolo*' (their italics).[3] Such a sales pitch reveals an urgent sense that the Bible on its own is not likely to be enough to disclose the nature of God's 'heart', and that trusted interpreters need to be called on as additional witnesses.

The question that inevitably arises from such a phenomenon is whether, in practice, the interpretations offered are accorded the same authority as the text (by readers, if not by publishers). The array of Bibles on offer certainly bears witness to the fact that the Bible *does* continue to need interpreting. There is an instinctive lack of contentment with the 'text itself'. Such interpretation surely remains one of the preacher's central tasks; but preachers should realize that, in a literate society, those who want can find their interpretations in many other places.

They should also consider the implications of the fact that for the first time in five hundred years the *medium* of Scripture is changing. Increasingly it is possible to read and study it in digital format. There are Bible study packages for scholars, websites where different translations can be compared, programmes which allow the Bible to be read – in modern or ancient languages – on hand-held electronic devices. The consequences of this development for the use of the Bible in the Church, not least in preaching, could be far-reaching.

At first glance, we might think this statement is exaggerated. The physical 'pew Bible' is likely to remain more popular than electronic devices for everyone, certainly as long as it remains cheaper! Many (including myself!) will continue to find reading a book more congenial than reading a screen. And if the importance of the live physical presence of a preacher is assumed, it may seem a matter of comparative indifference whether he/she and the hearers prepare for or follow up the sermon by consulting a digital book rather than a printed one.

A more subtle shift, however, may be under way.[4] As soon as the idea of 'the Bible' or 'the Scriptures' loses its essential association with the image of a single tangible volume, it is likely that its 'authority' will become a more nebulous concept. After all, text on screen can be manipulated with great ease. For example, a preacher might copy and paste verses from different Bible versions into a sermon, and then forget which versions (or even Bible books!) they were from. He or she might even copy and paste someone else's sermon, without being too aware of which parts were biblical quotations or allusions. Students of the Bible may be bowled over with the wealth of interpretative material to be found on certain websites, and the boundaries between text and interpretation will get blurred: colourful maps and charts, as well as readings with particular doctrinal axes to grind, can be very compelling – not least when they are free and easy to access.

One can foresee two possibilities arising from such a situation. One is that the Church will resist any re-imagination of the nature of the Bible arising out of the changing media in which it is encountered; it will seek to preserve a sense of unique significance in the *format* of the Bible as a printed book, a tangible benchmark for Christian belief and conduct, symbolic in its fixedness and solidity. The other is that the Church will be reminded by the evolving technology of the dynamism of its own message, the impossibility of *confining* it within the format of a book or collection of books, and while retaining and treasuring the book (whose popularity certainly shows no sign of waning)[5] will also embrace the potential opened up by the digital age.

Preachers taking this latter route will surely have many creative options for helping congregations engage with Scripture – not leaving behind the face-to-face sermon but developing its potential. This would be a continuation of the pattern seen in the fifth century, when Augustine's stenographers gave centuries' worth of new life to his sermons by writing them down; in the nineteenth, when C. H. Spurgeon's sermons achieved a vast circulation in print; or in the twentieth, when sermons began to be recorded on tape, and thus had a new life beyond the live event. The internet age offers many such possibilities. Many sermons are now available on the internet, in text form or as audio or video recordings. Those for whom the internet is *the* central medium for engaging with the wider world (not least those who have not experienced a pre-computer era) may much more readily compare an online sermon with online Bibles, study aids and so on, rather than depend on having the physical Book to hand all the time. Sermons on the web might indeed include specific links to online Bible texts and interpretative aids that the preacher thinks will be helpful. Preachers are already 'blogging' their sermon preparation,[6] and there is potential here for a new and dynamic engagement with Scripture by everyone. This can enhance the depth of communication in the sermon as the preacher has opportunity to listen to other responses to Scripture (and, indeed, to contemporary events) prior to speaking. Further fascinating possibilities – and questions! – are raised by the phenomenon of 'online churches' such as St Pixels (www.stpixels.com) where real-time services, on a range of patterns, and including preaching, take place in a 'virtual' setting (see Howe, 2007).

For some, all this might raise the spectre of that 'democracy of knowledge' hailed by Jean-François Lyotard, prophet of postmodernity,[7] and feared by those who regard such a thing as the death-knell of proper structures of authority. In *Wikipedia* we have 'the free encyclopaedia that anyone can edit':[8] are we to have Bible commentaries and sermons posted and editable by anyone and everyone? To Christians who fear such an outcome, I would make two responses.

First, the internet *already* breathes an atmosphere of heady egalitarianism, and this affects religious material as much as, or more than, any other kind. The genie truly is out of the bottle, and there is no point trying to put him back. The networks are open, as desired by Lyotard, and there is no shutting them. Material of all kinds from the superb to the dreadful is available for 'consumption' at the click of a mouse. If Christians wishing to share the gospel with this generation ignore the arena altogether, they will simply leave the field to the cranks and the manipulators.

Second, it is a false assumption that this great freedom to share opinions and spread 'knowledge' of various kinds implies that we have dispensed with the need for sources of authority in our lives. Indeed, it has arguably increased it. We need to know which websites are reliable, and we seek out this information from others whom we trust – whether those 'others' are internet 'gateways' which have already done some sifting for us, or live individuals such as teachers, pastors or parents. In this light, the preacher may assume an even more important role than he or she already has. Certainly, preachers can (thankfully) no longer be regarded in the old paternalistic light as the main repository of 'knowledge', or understanding of the Bible, in a church or community. However, churches and communities still need people of wisdom, who will guide them through the maze of choices and possibilities with which the internet age presents us. And a vital part of that wisdom (as it always has been) concerns the way in which people use the Bible. The availability of almost infinite 'resources' on the web for understanding anything, including the Bible, is no guarantee that genuine understanding will occur. For that, the human race will continue to need trusted guides; and that is one role that preachers must surely continue to assume.

From text to story and image

In parallel with the developments I have just discussed, there have been two interesting conceptual shifts in thinking about the Bible, seen particularly in various recent projects and publications of the Bible Society. These are the move from a focus on the *text* to a focus on the *story*, and a new openness to *image* as a vehicle of biblical truth.[9] The latter especially is closely connected with the accessibility of the Bible in digital and multimedia forms, considered above. Both 'story' and 'image' are also important discussion-points in contemporary homiletics.[10]

Andrew Walker expounds the idea of the gospel as *story* (Walker, 1996). He argues that the invention of printing led to an over-emphasis in modernity on the nature of Scripture as 'text' and a loss of the sense that it embodied a community's story:

> Human skills, beliefs and stories could only be handed down by word-of-mouth and/or example. But with the invention of the printed word, that is typography, words are 'frozen' for all to see. Ideas can be wrenched out of their individual contexts, shared, discussed, disputed. (p. 41)

This went hand-in-hand with a sometimes over-intellectual approach to worship and preaching. Where not simply the *message* of the Bible but its *text* had pride of place, there was always the danger that preaching would become over-cerebral. The overarching narrative of Scripture risked getting hidden behind the minute discussion of texts or doctrinal points arising therefrom. (The Roman Catholic tradition maintained a far more embodied 'telling of the story' in their worship, but often at the cost [at least until Vatican II] of an appropriate place for preaching.)

Walker's argument suggests that a recovery of the idea that the Gospel 'story' is more fundamental than the scriptural 'text' is vital to the remedying of this situation. He calls not just for the continued telling of 'the story' but also its indwelling, and identifies liturgical renewal as one of the 'missionary imperatives' towards this goal (pp. 194–9). Here image comes into the play too. Walker encourages the churches to recover a sense of sacramentality in their worship, a use of all the senses so that we look through God's creation 'as through a window, to the world to come' (p. 196). Liturgy is, in fact, 'the regular, unceasing dramaturgical re-enactment of the story' (p. 194).

Theologically, this trend is linked to the work of Lesslie Newbigin (1986 and 1989) and the 'post-liberal' school associated with Hans Frei and George Lindbeck, emphasizing that the Church's call is not so much one of rational persuasion but of inhabiting, and inviting others to inhabit, the cultural-linguistic world of the biblical story. In literary theory, the distinction between story and text corresponds more or less to the distinction between 'story' and 'discourse'. 'The story corresponds to the "events narrated, taken from their setting in the story and reconstructed in their chronological order" (S. Chatman) . . . The discourse is the *form* given to the story by the narrator . . . ' (Marguerat and Bourquin, 1999, p. 18). 'Story' is recognized as a reality which may or may not be embodied in a text, a drama, or a ritual, but which shapes the life and thinking of cultures and keeps coming to expression in one form or another. To shift the focus in our thinking about the Bible from text to story is thus to identify an invisible reality 'behind' the text which nevertheless becomes visible in many ways both within the text and, especially, in the community which continues to seek to be formed by the text. (This point is missed in some post-liberal discourse, which eschews talk of anything 'behind' the text, as if the story were somehow identical to the text.)

With regard to image, Shane Hipps points to an interesting paradox. On the one hand, he argues, the prevalence of image culture over text in contemporary society 'is eroding and undermining imaginative creativity' (Hipps, 2009, p. 80). Applying this to the use of the Bible, we might say that to use multimedia to 'bring the Bible to life' may – unless used sparingly – cause the hearer's own faculty of engaging with Scripture imaginatively to atrophy. In addition, pictures inevitably steer the interpretation of words in particular directions. An important argument for the preservation of biblical *text* as central is that this actually *preserves* the reader's freedom of interpretation. On the other hand, Hipps identifies 'one unexpected gift of image culture . . . the resuscitation of the person of Jesus as central to our faith' (p. 81). Pointing out that much Protestant culture is heir to the tradition of Luther, who explicitly exalted doctrine over story in Scripture, Hipps claims that '[i]n an image-saturated culture, the concrete life-stories of Jesus gain traction once again' (p. 82). In evangelical circles, he says, this has been accompanied by a shift of emphasis from beliefs and doctrine to discipleship and ethics (p. 82). The readmission of image into *Church* culture may thus, positively, express and encourage a more embodied and less purely intellectual faith.

As we have seen, Walker regards *liturgy* as a key component of mission. A liturgical setting provides excellent opportunities for the recovery of the Bible as story, as well as the experiencing of the Bible as image. This is not the task of the preacher alone, but of the whole Church. One practical way in which we may see 'story' recovering its proper place is through the use of a lectionary in a wider range of churches, as the basic guide for the rehearsing of our narrative in a regular rhythm of Bible readings. Naturally, no lectionary represents a 'perfect' reading of our grand narrative, but lectionaries do connect us to the way in which the Church across time has read Scripture, and across space still does. Balancing this, the Church of England, which has traditionally used a lectionary, now has more freedom to depart from it at certain seasons; this too is a welcome development, allowing (for instance) for more extended teaching on particular biblical books.[11]

Although the idea of 'telling the story' fits well into the liturgical setting of preaching, where a community is gathered and formed, rediscovering its identity and bearing witness to its origins, it is also especially suited to conceiving the task of Christian proclamation of all kinds outside the walls of the Church. Here surely our *first* aim is not that people should understand a text but that they should start to believe that the Christian story is both true and potentially transformative of their lives.

The Bible Society has surely been right to take the idea of 'telling the story' seriously. In a western world increasingly ignorant of the gospel, it is not the details of the scriptural text which matter, as much as the grand narrative it tells. Knowledge of the Bible in its details is no doubt a desirable ideal, yet the evangelistic task is too urgent to get no further than the potentially logic-chopping business of textual exegesis. Hence the Society's recent emphasis on making the story truly 'visible' again in the 'public' spheres of politics, journalism and the arts. Walter Brueggemann, in his retrospect on the first consultation of the Scripture and Hermeneutics Seminar in 1999 (of which the Bible Society were co-sponsors), commented on the way that 'street preaching' forces us to confront the issue of what is most important in our use of the Bible. In that setting, our story is (as it were) seen in its nakedness; it is open to being contested in a way that it never is within a church building. Further, on the street 'there is very little patience with intellectual, idealistic rhetoric' (Brueggeman, 2000, p. 346). In other words (though Brueggemann does not use 'story' language here), it is 'on the streets' that we are acutely reminded that the hearing of the story, its implications and its challenges, must take priority over the understanding of the text. It is also in the open air that we may see most clearly the power of images to draw and provoke people.

Preachers must reckon with the potential and pitfalls of reconceiving Scripture as story and as image. Homiletics has taken up the theme of 'story' in two contrasting ways. A 'new homiletic' view, represented by Eugene Lowry, has recognized the enormous potential of story for engaging hearers, and explored in detail how the dynamics of narrative preaching might work (see Lowry, 2001; Graves and Schlafer, 2008). Many biblical stories have found new life through such approaches, and scriptural themes are made more gripping by being cast in a narrative form which connects the overall story of the Bible with the stories of our own lives. The effect of such preaching may well be to captivate hearers on a deeper level with the underlying dynamics of biblical narrative. On the other hand, a 'post-liberal' view, represented by Charles Campbell, argues that the 'new homiletic' has been too concerned with the creation of a particular kind of individual experience in the hearer, at the expense of simply telling the grand story of God and allowing it to shape hearers into true Christian community.[12]

We may note how in each of these approaches the text itself may recede from view. In the 'new homiletic', the preacher has considerable freedom to create narratives that represent or dramatize the connection of a biblical story with today's world, but which do not necessarily bring the text itself into the foreground of the sermon. In postliberalism, there is the possibility that the preacher's own construal of the Christian 'grand narrative' will eclipse the actual words of Scripture. Hence Walter Brueggemann's preference for a continued retelling of the Bible's 'small stories', including especially those we find uncongenial and uncomfortable (1989, pp. 69–70). Thus we may guard against imposing our own grand schemes on Scripture. Note that this may enable Brueggemann (and us) to have the best of both worlds – story *and* text in the foreground together.

What of the preacher's appropriation of the idea of the Bible as 'image'? While not neglecting the potential of actual images as an adjunct to preaching, not least in a digital age, homiletics has concentrated on the preacher's call to use *words* in an evocative way (see Day, 2005, pp. 129–57; Stevenson and Wright, 2008, pp. 41–55, 94–115). The skill here is to enable the hearer to engage their own imagination with the text, without over-imposing the preacher's own imaginative construal. This fits well with Hipps's analysis of the dangers of the image culture. At the same time, there has been recognition that the preacher's words can and must be embodied, rather than detached, affirming Hipps's insight about the image culture's 'resuscitation of Jesus' (Hipps, 2009, p. 81). This points to a necessary integration between spoken word, the imagery and symbolism of worship, and the life of preacher and congregation (Day, 2005).

Brueggemann again offers a helpful way of thinking about our use of image in communicating the Bible's message. He articulates the power of the prophetic and poetic speech of the Bible to enable hearers to 'reimagine' their world (see Brueggemann 1989 and 1993). Thus he encourages us to use and echo the Bible's actual speech-forms to allow the hearers to see the world in the light of God's great story. This guards against the danger of 'imposing' extraneous images on Scripture which might over-control hearers' imaginations, yet also strongly encourages the 'embodiment' of the word, for the preacher who does this must also have some of the instincts of the dramatist (Stevenson and Wright, 2008, pp. 82–4). Once again, perhaps this allows us to have image *and* text in the foreground, as the text itself is allowed to shape our image of the world. Brueggemann's way of thinking about preaching and Scripture holds huge promise, and perhaps has scarcely yet been sufficiently dared (at least in the UK) to make meaningful evaluation possible.

The posture of 'textual exposition' may easily become one of detachment towards the text, whereas the storyteller or picture-painter can never be detached from the story or image. The mood of storytelling and imaging is a mood of recollection, engagement and evocation, whereas the mood of exposition can be limited to one of argument and disputation. In such ways, these trends in reconceiving the nature of Scripture hold enormous potential for the preacher.

Yet there is a danger that if text gives way too much to story and image, knowledge of the actual contents of Scripture, already diminishing according to many analysts, will recede further. We run the risk of leaving the text unexplained and unexplored, and therefore of perpetuating misunderstandings or hindering appropriation of its riches. There is certainly a continuing need both for the individual parts of Scripture to be understood as literature against their historical background and for the parts to be related to the whole in a manner that has theological integrity.

Thus James W. Thompson's call for a resumption of the preacher's teaching role, using a range of methods including rational argumentation, is to be welcomed (Thompson, 2001). Whether this teaching role is carried out in the traditionally formal way from a pulpit in the course of worship, or extended to other venues and spheres, is a secondary matter compared to the basic need. Only so, as Michael Pasquarello III also argues (2005), will we fulfil our pastoral task as successors to the great apostles and teachers of the Church.

In years to come the preacher will continue to need to combine this role as teacher – especially teacher of the Bible – with other roles as proclaimer, storyteller, imagist and wise guide. In practical terms, this means that while we should certainly not lose the balanced stimulation offered by Brueggemann to lively, performative forms of speech, narrative and otherwise, we should not neglect the essential tasks of explanation. For example, in a sermon on Daniel 12.3, 'Those who are wise will be like the shining of the sky, and those who lead many to righteousness like the stars for ever and ever', I sought to help the congregation both *feel* the beauty and majesty of its imagery and *understand* the Hebrew notions of 'wisdom' and 'righteousness'. There is no reason why the emphasis has to be *either* on evocation *or* on explanation: it can be on both.

From pastoral distance to pastoral realism

A teacher who prepares a class thinking that the students have done much less, or much more, prior study of the subject than they actually have is in for a shock – and so, also, are the students!

Preachers have often operated from a rather ideal and naive view of their congregation's engagement with Scripture. On the one hand they have underestimated it, in that many may well have been nourished on Scripture devotionally for many years, and thought long and hard over its difficult passages. This can lead to patronizing or trivializing in the pulpit. On the other hand they have also overestimated it, and betrayed this by language which assumes a greater theological grasp, or historical interest, than most members have had the opportunity to acquire. In Harry Emerson Fosdick's famous jibe, most people do not come to church 'desperately anxious to discover what happened to the Jebusites' (1957, p. 92).

An important recent development in practical theology is the study of 'ordinary hermeneutics', that is, the processes and principles by which the Bible is *actually* interpreted in the Church – as opposed to the 'ideal' ways by which we sometimes tell ourselves it is or should be interpreted.[13] This study exposes the contradictions and tensions that often exist between the way the Bible is interpreted by preachers, and the way it is interpreted through the words of songs and hymns, in study groups, and by individuals. For instance, a home group may be led by someone whose theology is in marked distinction from that of the pastor. This will inevitably affect the members' understanding of the Bible, and lead to confusion. In some churches, many members are regular attenders at Christian festivals and conferences. There they learn new songs and, sometimes, ways of thinking and speaking which may be imported to the local church and exercise a considerable influence. This may act as a filter to the preacher's words, so that anything the preacher says which does not accord with the perspective gained at the festival or conference will be filtered out.

Writers such as Leonora Tubbs Tisdale (1997) have rightly emphasized the importance for preaching of the preacher's in-depth knowledge of the congregation's culture, circumstances and history. The study of 'ordinary hermeneutics' suggests that one vital aspect of this is knowledge of how the congregation, and various groups and individuals within it, *actually* understand the Bible. The preacher will then be able to address questions that are really being asked, and lead the congregation on to new encounters with Scripture on the basis of those they have already had.

In achieving this goal, it is hard to see any substitute for the slow, patient process of getting to know individuals and sharing in group studies. Such a process will not only enable the preacher to focus their use of the Bible more carefully but also remind him or her of the different frameworks that everyone (the preacher included) brings to the text – theological, cultural and personal.[14] A 'reformed' preacher should be sensitized to the way a 'catholic' or a 'charismatic' reads the text, and vice versa. A white British preacher should be sensitized to the way an Afro-Carribean British person reads the text, and vice versa. A male preacher should be sensitized to the way women may read a text, and vice versa. A preacher with a 'sensing' psychological preference should be sensitized to the way a hearer with an 'intuitive' preference may read the text, and vice versa. This need entail no loss of fundamental conviction on anyone's part – though no conviction should be beyond adjustment on the basis of shared listening to God. It is a matter of better understanding of others' perspectives and thus better ability to communicate from one's own to theirs. Empirical-theological studies such as those of Andrew Rogers, Andrew Village and Leslie Francis give us plenty of resources for doing this. It is to be hoped that such studies will continue and that preachers will take full advantage of them.[15]

Naturally, the diversity of perspectives and theologies in a single congregation can be bewildering to a preacher, and one might well despair of ever communicating with it as a whole entity. However, careful listening and preparation can enable preachers to extend themselves and their own engagement with Scripture such that 'one gospel' can by received by 'many ears' (Jeter et al., 2002).

In all this, the trustworthiness of the preacher is crucial. It is now widely recognized that we cannot draw a neat distinction between 'interpreting' Scripture in the abstract and 'interpreting' it for others. Every act of rhetoric concerning Scripture is in itself an act of interpretation. Every interpretation is expressed in the rhetorical form of words, whether unspoken or spoken. We are seeking to persuade ourselves and each other all the time. Whether our mode of presenting Scripture is 'explaining', 'echoing' or 'enacting' (Wright, 2004, pp. 84–9), it is still an act of interpretation.

The fact that the preacher's own rhetorical agenda is inextricably bound up in the act of interpretation should not be cause for alarm. As I have argued elsewhere, it simply highlights the necessity of trusting relationships between preacher and hearers.[16] Hearers look for preachers in whom rhetoric is used transparently and honestly.[17] They do not expect omniscience or objectivity, but faithfulness to the message entrusted to them. The impossibility of completely objective knowledge, the reality that understanding is fundamentally a relational not an intellectual affair: these should not threaten preachers or the Church in the slightest. The more relational an event preaching is, the more it may reflect the wonder of the Word made flesh (Stevenson and Wright, 2008, pp. 123–4).

What does this mean in practice? It will mean, surely, that while sermons should never be lectures on hermeneutical theory(!), the preacher of the future will be more conscious of his or her aims and strategies in interpreting the text, and subject them to divine ethical scrutiny. It will mean sensing the right balance between seeking various kinds of textual significance – historical, literary, sociological and ideological – while holding them all within a theological framework that does not deny but somehow encompasses them. Here there is an increasing body of scholarly material to draw upon.[18] It will mean acknowledging the limitations of one's own perspective, and the previous experience with the text that one brings to sermon preparation; and though one should neither seek to escape this perspective nor be ashamed of it, it can at least be opened up to other perspectives (Stevenson and Wright, 2008, pp. 66–7). It will mean a willingness to be an interpreter of the world around as well as, and in the light of, the text itself (pp. 64–5). It will mean a readiness to be challenged about any particular interpretation one has offered, without being defensive. It will mean acknowledging that God's truth is not vested in the preacher, but in Christ alone, and is constantly to be sought and discovered by his people as a whole. That in turn should lead to initiation of groups to share in the study of the Scriptures both in preparation for and in response to the sermon.

Conclusion

Exciting times surely lie ahead for the use of the Bible in preaching. While there is no sign that the Bible will lose its traditional place at the heart of the Church, there is every sign that we are poised to be able to communicate its message in freshly creative ways. This will entail the judicious use of the new technology which already forms a significant medium for the ancient texts. It will entail the recovery of the story and stories which lie behind and within the texts, and using them to enable people to re-imagine the world in the light of God's grand narrative. It will entail continued explanation of that which is obscure. It will entail a frank recognition of the diverse ways in which people in churches experience and understand the Bible, and a mutually trusting, relational way of working with them so as together to hear more accurately, through the Bible's words, the living word of God.

Notes

1. Augustine, *Confessions* viii.12.
2. http://www.codexsinaiticus.org/en/codex/default.aspx
3. http://www.bibleresources.org.uk/pages/data.asp?layout=book.htm&id=929
4. For interesting reflections on the truth of Marshall McLuhan's maxim 'the medium is the message' as it relates to contemporary technology and the Church, see Hipps, 2005.
5. Julia McGuinness reported that Wesley Owen, the former chain of Christian bookshops, sold one million Bibles each year: 'The Great Bible Dilemma', *Church Times*, 23 October 2009, pp. 20–1.
6. See for instance the blog of Professor Michael Quicke, formerly Principal of Spurgeon's College, London, who teaches preaching at Northern Baptist Seminary, Chicago: http://michaelquicke.blogspot.com/; and, in the UK, the blog of Richard Littledale, Minister of Teddington Baptist Church and a contributor to this volume: http://richardlittledale.wordpress.com/
7. For Lyotard, the means to prevent a new reign of terror and control in the computer age was simple: 'give the public free access to the memory and data banks' (1984, p. 67): In retrospect, Lyotard's words sound naive: we know that free access to data online by no means entails our liberation from the power of big corporations, advertising and intrusion into our private lives.
8. http://en.wikipedia.org/wiki/Main_Page
9. See, for example, the description of some of the Society's multimedia resources currently available: 'star casts and narrators kindle the imagination with stunning new and classic stories . . . experience the

passion and power of God's story through superb Bible-related films and programmes . . . enjoy grippingly told, award-winning and great animation stories': http://www.bibleresources.org.uk/pages/10.htm, accessed 16 November 2009.

10. See, for example, David Schlafer's discussion of image, narrative and argument as three possible structuring principles of preaching (1992); also Troeger, 1990.

11. 'During Ordinary Time (that is between the Presentation and Ash Wednesday and between Trinity Sunday and Advent Sunday), authorized lectionary provision remains the norm but, after due consultation with the Parochial Church Council, the minister may, from time to time, depart from the lectionary provision for pastoral reasons or preaching or teaching purposes': from 'Rules to Order How the Psalter and the Rest of Holy Scripture are Appointed to Be Read', in *Common Worship*: http://www.cofe.anglican.org/worship/liturgy/commonworship/texts/lect/lectrules.html

12. For this approach see Campbell, 1997. For reflections on the debate see Peter K. Stevenson, 'Preaching and Narrative', in Day, Astley and Francis, 2005, pp. 101–6.

13. See Andrew Rogers, 'Ordinary hermeneutics and the local church', *The Bible in Transmission* (Summer 2007), pp. 18–21; and Village, 2007. A colloquium on Ordinary Hermeneutics was arranged by the Bible Society and the Evangelical Alliance in April 2009.

14. On the psychological dimensions of preaching and hermeneutics see Francis and Village, 2008.

15. In addition to the items mentioned above, see Leslie J. Francis's books on the way that people of different personalities may interact with the Gospels: 2000, 2001, 2002. The literature on gender and preaching also has direct relevance to the handling of the Bible: see Durber, 2007; Mathews, 2003; Rogers, 2007; Walton and Durber, 1994.

16. See my 'Exegesis and the Preacher', *Evangel* 17.2 (Summer 1999), pp. 62–7, especially 67.

17. This is true not just for preachers but for anyone employing persuasive speech. See Booth, 2004. pp. 39–54.

18. See, for example: the Scripture and Hermeneutics Series, 8 vols (Carlisle / Milton Keynes / Grand Rapids: Paternoster / Zondervan, 2000–7); the *Journal of Theological Interpretation*, founded in 2007; Adam et al., 2006; Treier, 2008; Vanhoozer, 2005; Wright, 2002.

References

Adam, A. K. M. et al., 2006, *Reading Scripture with the Church: Toward a Hermeneutic for Theological Interpretation*, Grand Rapids: Baker Academic.

Booth, Wayne C., 2004, *The Rhetoric of Rhetoric: The Quest for Effective Communication*, Oxford: Blackwell.

Brueggemann, Walter, 1989, *Finally Comes the Poet: Daring Speech for Proclamation*, Minneapolis: Fortress.

_____, 1993, *Texts under Negotiation: The Bible and Postmodern Imagination*, Minneapolis: Fortress.

_____, 2000, 'A First Retrospect on the Consultation', in Craig Bartholomew, Colin Greene and Karl Möller (eds), *Renewing Biblical Interpretation*, Scripture and Hermeneutics Series vol. 1, Carlisle/Grand Rapids: Paternoster/Zondervan, pp. 342–7.

Campbell, Charles L., 1997, *Preaching Jesus: New Directions for Homiletics in Hans Frei's Postliberal Theology*, Grand Rapids: Eerdmans.

Day, David, 2005, *Embodying the Word: A Preacher's Guide*, London: SPCK.

Day, David, Jeff Astley and Leslie J. Francis (eds), 2005, *Making Connections: A Reader on Preaching*, Aldershot: Ashgate.

Durber, Susan, 2007, *Preaching like a Woman*, London: SPCK.

Fosdick, Harry Emerson, 1957, *The Living of These Days: An Autobiography*, London: SCM Press.

Francis, Leslie J., 2000, *Exploring Luke's Gospel: A Guide to the Gospel Readings in the Revised Common Lectionary*, London: Mowbray.

_____, 2001, *Exploring Matthew's Gospel: A Guide to the Gospel Readings in the Revised Common Lectionary*, London: Mowbray.

_____, 2002, *Exploring Mark's Gospel: An Aid for Readers and Preachers Using Year B of the Revised Common Lectionary*, London: Continuum.

Francis, Leslie J., and Andrew Village, 2008, *Preaching with All our Souls: A Study in Hermeneutics and Psychological Type*, London: Continuum.

Graves, Mike, and David Schlafer (eds), 2008, *What's the Shape of Narrative Preaching? Essays in Honour of Eugene L. Lowry*, St Louis: Chalice.

Hipps, Shane, 2005, *The Hidden Power of Electronic Culture: How Media Shapes Faith, the Gospel and Church*, Grand Rapids: Zondervan.

_____, 2009, *Flickering Pixels: How Technology Shapes Your Faith*, Grand Rapids: Zondervan.

Howe, Mark, 2007, *Online Church? First Steps towards Virtual Incarnation*, Cambridge: Grove.

Jeter, Joseph R., Ronald J. Allen and A. Wineman, 2002, *One Gospel, Many Ears: Preaching for Different Listeners in the Congregation*, St Louis: Chalice.

Lowry, Eugene L., 2001, *The Homiletical Plot: The Sermon as Narrative Art Form*, expanded edn, Louisville: Westminster John Knox.

Lyotard, Jean-François, 1984, *The Postmodern Condition: A Report on Knowledge*, trans. Geoff Bennington and Brian Massumi, Manchester: Manchester University Press.

Marguerat, Daniel, and Yvan Bourquin, 1999, *How to Read Bible Stories: An Introduction to Narrative Criticism*, trans. John Bowden, London: SCM Press.

Mathews, Alice P., 2003, *Preaching That Speaks to Women*, Leicester: InterVarsity Press.

Newbigin, Lesslie, 1986, *Foolishness to the Greeks: The Gospel and Western Culture*, London: SPCK.

_____, 1989, *The Gospel in a Pluralist Society*, London: SPCK.

Pasquarello, Michael, III, 2005, *Sacred Rhetoric: Preaching as a Theological and Pastoral Practice of the Church*, Grand Rapids: Eerdmans.

Rogers, Andrew, 2007, 'Reading Scripture in congregations: towards an ordinary hermeneutics', in Andrew Walker and Luke Bretherton (eds), *Remembering Our Future: Explorations in Deep Church*, Milton Keynes: Paternoster, pp. 81–107.

Schlafer, David J., 1992, *Surviving the Sermon: A Guide to Preaching for Those Who Have to Listen*, Cambridge, MA: Cowley.

Stevenson, Geoffrey, and Stephen Wright, 2008, *Preaching with Humanity: A Practical Guide for Today's Church*, London: Church House Publishing.

Thompson, James W., 2001, *Preaching like Paul: Homiletical Wisdom for Today*, Louisville: Westminster John Knox.

Tisdale, Leonora Tubbs, 1997, *Preaching as Local Theology and Folk Art*, Minneapolis: Fortress.

Treier, Daniel J., 2008, *Introducing Theological Interpretation of Scripture: Recovering a Christian Practice*, Nottingham: Apollos.

Troeger, Thomas H., 1990, *Imagining a Sermon*, Nashville: Abingdon.

Vanhoozer, Kevin J. (ed.), 2005, *Dictionary for Theological Interpretation of the Bible*, Grand Rapids: Baker.

Village, Andrew, 2007, *The Bible and Lay People: An Empirical Approach to Ordinary Hermeneutics*, Aldershot: Ashgate.

Walker, Andrew, 1996, *Telling the Story: Gospel, Mission and Culture*, London: SPCK.

Walton, Heather, and Susan Durber, 1994, *Silence in Heaven: A Book of Women's Preaching*, London: SCM Press.

Wright, Stephen, 2002, 'The Bible as sacrament', *Anvil* 19.2 (May 2002), pp. 81–7.

_____, 2004, 'The use of the Bible', in Geoffrey Hunter, Gethin Thomas and Stephen Wright (eds), *A Preacher's Companion: Essays from the College of Preachers*, Oxford: Bible Reading Fellowship, pp. 84–9.

8

Preaching on the News

PAUL JOHNS

Every week preachers preach good sermons that make no reference whatsoever to the news. Every week equally good preachers do refer in some way to news stories. You may say that we get enough news outside church without bringing it inside. So why, if we look to the future of preaching, should we make more of a point of preaching on the news?

Recent research suggests that people frequently find that sermons help them to understand God, Jesus and the Bible better; less frequently do they challenge them to think seriously about the news and controversial public issues (CODEC, 2010). Does that matter? Is there something missing from preaching that nourishes the interior life of the Christian but shies away from tackling the news of the world? Are there cultural changes afoot, especially to do with the way the world comes at us through the news, which challenge us to rebalance the content of our preaching? I suggest the answer to both questions is 'yes'.

Typically, in my experience of listening to sermons, preachers who do bring the news into their sermons do so for one of two reasons. Either a suitable news story helps to illustrate a point in the Bible text or else it provides evidence of the need for some kind of Christian ethical action to which the Bible text points. There's nothing wrong with weaving news into the sermon for these purposes; there's much to commend it. However, I want to argue that preaching on the news means going beyond treating the news as a databank of illustrations and evidence. It includes that; but it goes further in claiming that, to put it simply, God speaks through the news. So, news is more than illustration, more than context. It is something through which God's word is heard. Therefore we preachers should listen out for God in the texts of the news as we listen out for God in the texts of the Bible. The 'Godword' which we preachers humbly struggle to discern and then share with a particular congregation on a particular Sunday emerges and takes shape out of a dialogue between two texts, biblical and news. And that has implications for the way we read the Bible and the news for preaching, and implications for the way we preach.

I am not suggesting that we should drop all preaching that does not refer to the news, and go all out for holding the Bible in one hand while the other zaps at a TV news clip displayed with impressive technique on a screen behind the pulpit. I do, however, want to argue that there are reasons to do with our news culture and reasons to do with the wellbeing of the Church – its pastoral life, its mission and its theological grasp – all of which point to the conclusion that preaching on the news is important, and there ought to be more of it in future.

Why does much of our preaching keep the news at arm's length rather than wrestling with it? I can think of three reasons. First, if you scan some of the most popular books on preaching, you find that, while they rightly have much to say about how to interpret biblical texts, they have comparatively little to say about how preachers should interpret contemporary experience, public events in particular. Second, there is the dominant modern intellectual tradition, through which, since the Enlightenment, revelation has given ground to reason as the source of truth. Knowledge is objective, belief subjective. Events are a matter of fact, God is a matter of belief. God and events occupy different worlds. This discourages preachers from bringing news into the pulpit (or from taking the Bible into the pub). Third, on top of that, the legacy of the Protestant Reformation has not helped the cause of news preaching. Elevating the Bible as the word of God has had the effect of diminishing the world, in Christian minds, as the place of God.[1]

For these reasons we end up with lots of preaching on lectionary readings to sustain congregational interest in the scriptural word of God, and not much considered preaching about current events except as insofar as they serve to illustrate biblical truth, or to demonstrate the need for Christians to go out and live better lives in the world.

Christians watch, hear or read the same news as everybody else. However, our first reaction isn't normally to ask, 'What is God saying . . . ?' through this or that event; nor for us preachers to add, 'So what should I be saying?' Yet there are a number of reasons why, I suggest, future preaching needs to dig more into the news.

There are pastoral reasons. People are often troubled by the news, especially by events that seem to defy the biblical view of God's world. Graffiti scratched on the outside wall of my local Methodist church says: 'If God is good, why does He let bad things happen?' It is a question often asked inside as well as outside the Church. There's a continuing troubling dissonance between what is and what we are taught to believe should be ('Why have you brought us into the wilderness?'); and an anxiety about knowing what to do about it ('How shall we sing the Lord's song in a strange land?'). So there is a need for pastoral preaching on news events which reframes present troubles as echoes of a biblical past, and which proposes a Christian response to present troubles as a realization here and now of the future to which the Bible points.

Then there are mission reasons. For many the Christian revelation appears implausible, and therefore irrelevant to public experience. If the Church is to fulfil its mission, we have to be able to subvert the perceived implausibility by proclaiming that Jesus is Lord in terms that make coherent sense of issues and events in the world that Christians inhabit along with everyone else. Our mission requires that we are not dumb in the face of the news, but ready always 'to give account of the hope that is in us', an account that makes sense in the context of current events. Preaching on the news is one important way of equipping the Church for mission.

There are reasons to do with the news media itself. We are not engaged with an inert world waiting passively for the gospel to imprint itself. There are powerful institutional forces at large, shaping our values, making our news. Collectively, 'the media' are among the most powerful.[2] This brings us up against the cultural changes that are, I suggest, pressing the Church, and preachers in particular, to be more articulate in the face of the news. Part of what we call experience is direct and personal, but only part. For the rest, our only way of accessing it is through the news. The news media do not simply report what is. That's well understood. They have the power to select, to interpret, and thus to shape our consciousness of the world, and our understanding of the world, which is God's world. They have the power and they use it. And most of us spend more time exposed to the news than we do listening to sermons.

There is more news now than ever before. It's more immediate. We are served with breaking news day and night. It comes from more sources, not only professional journalists but also ordinary folk with mobile phones and webcams. It is accessible in more ways, press, radio stations, TV channels and websites. Technology makes it easy to convey visual images instantly across the world, and the news that makes most impact is visual news. The gathering and presentation of news is subject to many pressures – of time, of staff shortages, of commercial and political interest. The border between news and entertainment is blurred. Observers of the world of news media paint a picture of a world in which some media work with courage and integrity in pursuit of the truth, while others are accused of 'churnalism', cutting editorial corners to be first with an audience-grabbing headline or dramatic footage.[3] Media technology brings the world Jesus came to save closer to us. Yet in doing so it is constantly editing our perception of it and our attitude to it.

Given the mixed quality of news coverage, we're bound to ask the awkward question: how can reportage so variable, so open to human manipulation be media through which God speaks. Is it really worth preaching on the news if you can't believe what you read in the papers? One answer is to say that God speaks through events, not the reporting of them. That isn't a very satisfactory reply, since, for most of us most of the time, we have access to the event only through the reporting of it. A better answer could be that God speaks both in the event and in the reporting of it; and that since God is God of a fallen world we must listen out for his word in both good and bad events (in the Bible as well as in the news) and good and bad journalism.

News reporting, like any other human activity, is inherently ambiguous, both in need of redemption and potentially a means of redemption; but we should never, I suggest, think of it as something about which and through which an omnipresent God has nothing to say. 'The news', and the reporting of it, is a matter for serious theological interest. The news therefore should be of concern to a preacher who, on a Sunday, has the opportunity to reframe biblically the congregation's consciousness of the world, saturated by the news media from Monday to Saturday.

This brings us to the Bible itself as a strong reason for more preaching on the news. More preaching on the news definitely does not mean less preaching on the Bible. Theologically it takes its stand on the Bible, on a Christian understanding of the Bible both as a record of God's revelation of himself and as an account of events through which God has revealed himself.

The Bible is revelation and history combined. It is revelation on its own terms, not accountable to any definition of revelation outside itself. It is history on its own terms, not accountable to any definition of history outside itself. It tells us that God makes himself known in what he says and what he does in the realm of human experience; that he entrusts his self-revelation to fallible people – prophets in the Old Testament, apostles in the New. It's characteristic of God, and important for news preaching, that God reveals himself in the particular, to particular people through particular events at particular times and places. Revelation and history come together uniquely, definitively and decisively in the particular person of Jesus and the events of his life.

In one sense the Bible is complete. There are no more books to be added to it; no more texts bearing revelation or history. Yet the Bible is not a closed book. It points us forward to a final consummation of God's purpose, beyond the biblical record, still in the future. The Bible itself leads us to expect that, as long as there is more history, more events, we may expect more revelation. Therefore we should be looking for more 'Godwords', in history in the making, that is, in the news. We live in the same aeon of resurrection, hope and expectation as the first Christians. We should expect to discern God at work in our current events as they did in theirs.

Bible writers created narrative about events. The events may not all be history as the modern world would define history. However, it is important that they are reported as taking place in this world, not the world of the gods, and they concerned the life of God's people, and not any other people. The purpose of the narratives was not just to entertain (though no doubt they did that, and we tend to ignore their entertainment value). They were told and written to sustain communal consciousness and identity in a world often uncertain and hostile.

Today, in our postmodern thought-world, interest in communal narrative, in overarching stories, has declined. Narrative is a matter of personal choice. You can buy into this one or that. The media offer a variety of choice on a variety of platforms. Mum and Dad watch *News at Ten* downstairs; the kids surf the net upstairs, or create their own newsworld on Facebook.

A crucial function of news preaching is to recreate communal narrative in a culture of fragmented individualistic identities; to take news stories in which Godwords are embedded and recast them in the context of the biblical narratives, and so, as it were, to create extensions of the biblical news stories by grafting new contemporary news stories onto them.

Secular media report events in a secular way. There is no room to squeeze Godwords into their news gathering, editing, reporting. What preaching on the news needs is its own theological space, its own editorial desk, from which to scan, select and interpret the news, to enable people to hear the voice of God in the corridors of power.

We have to become more skilful at bringing the texts of the Bible into play with the texts of the news. It isn't just a matter of using biblical text to interpret news text. If God's word is somewhere embedded, like a war correspondent, in the news and the events it reports, news text becomes the interpreter of biblical text. Each text becomes a picture frame for the other.

And that, I suggest, requires a change of emphasis in the way we go about exegesis for preaching. Most text books on preaching set things out in a line. You take your Bible text, you study it, you discern its meaning and then you think about how to apply it to the congregation you have in mind. At this point, the applying point, you may bring in a news story, to illustrate the text or to demonstrate the need for action called for by the text. Preaching on the news suggests a different approach. We bring the news text on stage at the start. We have the two actors – biblical text and news text – before us at the same time; we watch the interplay, follow carefully the dialogue. And out of that dialogue we discern the Godword to be preached.

To help us interpret this dialogue, we need a range of theological perspectives. First we need a balanced perspective which affirms both the Bible and experience as sources of Godwords; not subordinating one to the other. This does not of course mean that Bible and experience are equivalent. It means that they lead us to God in different and complementary ways; and that each is necessary to the other. There are two pitfalls to avoid. The first is to think that the world of experience makes sense only if fitted into the world of the Bible. This devalues all non-scriptural interpretations of the news, and reduces events to the status of illustrations of biblical truth. The second is to think that the world of experience can be fully affirmed only by translating the gospel without significant remainder into the language of common human experience. This reduces the Bible by making it a signpost to reality rather than a description of reality, and risks turning Jesus into a symbol of all good things. To preach the gospel and to preach on the news at the same time requires a theological middle ground, territory where the preacher can name grace in events as well as in Scripture, and can name 'disgrace' in Scripture (tales of idolatry and violence and texts of terror) as well as in events.

Then we need other books on the shelf offering different theological perspectives for interpreting different kinds of news events. Like the early Christians, we need to discover theology by wrestling with different questions in different contexts – how to relate to pagan government (obedience or resistance) and pagan culture (whether or not to eat food devoted to idols). Here are three different theological mirrors that I find useful.

The first is a theology of institutional power (see Wink, 1992, and Campbell, 2002). The activities of big institutions – governments and corporations – provide much of our news. A theology of 'the powers' understands them to be both spiritual and material. The ambiguity of kingship in the Old Testament witnesses to the powers as both good and evil (1 Samuel 8). Jesus offered a critique of the exercise of institutional power (Mark 10.41–5). The powers are part of God's creation (Col. 1.16). But they are fallen; Jesus was crucified by the powers personified in Caiaphas and Pilate (Mark 15.15; John 11.50). Now, through the cross, the powers have been taken captive by Christ (Col. 2.15), and his resurrection paves the way for their redemption (Col. 1.20).

A different kind of theological perspective is needed for engaging biblically with the world of popular culture (see Lynch, 2005). Popular culture features substantially in the news. It feeds the media with a stream
of stories. Very often these are human interest stories, about the doings
of personalities associated with a TV show, a music group, a sport. The
news stories about them place them in the ongoing discourse of popular
culture, often in ways intended to make for controversy in the discourse.
One only has to name John Terry, for example.[4] The discourse of popular culture revolves round themes like youth, beauty, health, wealth, sex,
domestic life, lifestyle, image and identity. However, this discourse is not
monochrome gossip. Popular is not the same as trivial. Popular culture
has its own internal critics; the voices of stand-up satire on TV and in
clubs, for example, and many films exploring serious issues through entertaining narrative.

Popular culture is therefore a varied and open discourse carried on in
the media. It's an open discourse that cries out for theological reflection.
The need is not for a theology that stuffily dismisses popular culture as
inherently opposed to Christ, nor for one that trendily embraces it, deter-
mined to find something of Christ in everything. The need is for a theology
of critical engagement. Critical engagement requires a listening theology,
one which allows the events that make up popular culture to speak before they are spoken to. This is one that acknowledges in cultural life a
deep ambiguity. Much like household life in New Testament Ephesus,
it can be an opportunity for either exploitation or sacramental living
(Eph. 6.5–9). It is a theology which acknowledges that the narratives of
an alien culture surrounding the Church can be adapted to be powerful
narrative for the Church; much as Jewish exiles first listened to and then
adopted the Babylonian flood myth and turned it into one of their own
most popular stories (Genesis 6–8). It is also a theology prepared to
challenge the dominant myths of popular culture; to reframe for example
the pervasive myth of redemptive violence (only violent goodies can purge
the world of violent baddies) in terms of the violence of the crucifixion
seen through the lens of resurrection.[5] It is a theology prepared to step
outside its own comfort zone, tease out of the everyday a discussion of the
big issues of life, as did Jesus at the well with the Samaritan woman (John
4). This is a perspective that recognizes in culture both the means of redemption and the need for redemption, and reminds us that the Church,
the body of Christ, can neither wholly live within nor wholly achieve its
mission without engagement with popular culture.

Many news stories deal with dislocation. Dislocation happens when
the reality we thought we knew and within which we felt secure changes

and seems to leave us stranded. The change may be sudden, like a natural disaster, or the crash of a bank, or the announcement of massive redundancy. It may be gradual like the process of global warming, or the slow but nonetheless troubling transformation of a monocultural neighbourhood into a multicultural one. It is the experience of familiar landmarks disappearing, reality as I have known it changing and pitching me into uncertainty. Dislocating experience is heavily reported in the media, often in contradictory and alarmist ways.

Thus there is a need for a contextual theology of dislocation (see Brueggemann, 1997), to redescribe specific experiences of dislocation in terms of experience recorded in biblical texts; a theology that helps to answer the question, 'How can we look at this experience differently and therefore live through it differently?' The Bible has much to say about dislocation and with it relocation. In the Old Testament, God's people were dislocated from the security of slavery and relocated in the wholly different reality of the wilderness (Exod. 17.3, 4). Later came the fundamental and formative dislocation: from homeland to exile (for example, Lam. 1.10, 15). In the New Testament comes the dislocation of the crucifixion followed by a relocation in the new world of the resurrection (for example, Luke 24.13–35; 2 Cor. 5.17; Eph. 2.11–13).

The need is for a theological perspective that enables the building of hermeneutical bridges between biblical and present experience of dislocation. This could be a perspective that utilizes the metaphor of 'exile'. The function of the metaphor is to enable dislocated people to reconstrue reality as they see it, to learn to live with uncertainty and to find a new 'home' and purpose in a world looked at differently in the light of the gospel (Jer. 29.4–7; Eph. 4.17–24).

As long as there are news stories that revolve around dislocation the news preacher needs to be able to answer the question, 'So how are we to live in Babylon?' The answer is twofold. The first part is practical, almost comically obvious: 'build houses and live in them' (Jer. 29.5). The second is theological: 'seek the welfare of the city; in it you will find yours' (v. 7). The question is about a particular place and time. The answer both responds to the question on its own terms and goes beyond it.

You can see the same pattern at work in 2 Corinthians 1.15–20: the implicit 'news story' is discontent in the Corinthian church with Paul's leadership style, in particular his apparently vacillating travel plans. The response is the text of Paul's letter. In this he seeks first to justify himself, directly answering the complaint, then goes beyond self-justification to make a distinctive and profound theological affirmation about Christ (v. 20), an affirmation that emerges directly out of the context of acrimony over the event.

Again, the same pattern is at work in Mark 10.41–5. The event is the disciples jockeying for position, like politicians bidding for cabinet posts after their leader has won the election. Jesus deals directly with the bid for power. Then he reframes the whole business of power in the context of his own forthcoming death, powerlessness as service.

This is the pattern for news preaching. The crucial word to be spoken, the punchline, comes from outside the event as experienced by those to whom the word is addressed. At the same time, however, it is the event as they experience it that shapes and contextualizes the word to be spoken. The primary intention in news preaching generally is not to explain either the Gospel text or the news text but to affirm the gospel in the context of the news text, as a transformation, which enables hearers to look at experienced events differently, and therefore be empowered to live differently in the world of events.

How then can we bring two different types of text, biblical and news, together, get them to 'talk' to each other, and discern in the dialogue the Godword to be preached? Consider the word dialogue. It's a dialogue between two different kinds of texts. For Christians the biblical text has special status. If the gospel is to be preached, the biblical text must always have the last theological word. Nonetheless, if we accept that God speaks through events, then the news that reports those events must be treated with respect on its own terms. Dialogue also implies a certain openness in the interchange, a willingness in both parties to allow new meaning and insight to emerge from the encounter. The truth, that is the Godword to be preached, lies not in the news story alone, not in the biblical text alone, but in the conversation between them. Since news is by definition new, and a particular news text and a particular biblical text will not have met before, it follows that the process of dialogue is not a matter of discovering meaning that was there already, but a matter of creating new meaning.

Thus, for example, in Acts 17, Paul preaching to or conversing with the Athenians is interpreting the Christian God in terms of Athenian experience of idols and vice versa. Paul confers new meaning on the altar 'to the unknown god' and new meaning on the Judaeo-Christian concept of God by restating it in terms relevant to the practice of pagan worship in Athens.

Conferring new meaning is surely the business of the Holy Spirit. The preacher needs to allow the Spirit workspace; to keep hobbyhorses reined in, so that his or her own interests and opinions don't intrude too much into the dialogue. The Spirit cannot be contained by mechanistic explanation (John 3.8). Nonetheless, experience suggest that certain forms of language are useful ways of channelling the Spirit and of enabling her to help us make connections between Bible and news, and thence to shape a sermon on the news.

These are forms of language commonplace in the Bible as well as in other literature and, for that matter, in everyday speech. Essentially they are forms that generate meaning by comparing one thing with another, or talking of one thing in terms of another; in other words, analogy, typology and metaphor. The choice of analogy and the creation of metaphor is an act of imagination. And imagination is God's gift. Imagination let loose can lead to fantasy; but news preaching requires imagination tethered at one end to the Bible and at the other to current events. The biblical text does not have a fixed meaning. It invites interpretation. The news text is by definition new. The biblical text has not met it before. Thus any insight that comes out of comparing the two will be new. It will also be particular, the word to be spoken, to shape understanding, arising from the bringing together of these two texts and no others.

The comparing of the two will not exhaust the meaning of either the biblical or the news text. Jesus said: 'The kingdom of heaven is like a grain of mustard seed' (Mark 4.31). The latter doesn't say all that Jesus had to say about the former; but it does shine light on it. At the time of September 11, 2001, more than one observer drew a parallel between the attack on the World Trade Center and the story of the tower of Babel (Genesis 11). September 11th had not happened before, so the comparison was a new one, and therefore the meaning to be drawn from it is also new. The comparison is thought provoking, but it doesn't say all that is to be said about either the Bible story or September 11th.

When comparing biblical and news text, the differences that an analogy throws up are as important as, often more important than, the similarities: 'You have heard it said . . . but I say . . . ' (for example, Matt. 5.33, 34). It is often in the differences that the transcendent gospel breaks into the dialogue between the two texts. Compare, for example, Mark 8.31–3 with reports of the death of Jade Goody (in March 2009). There are similarities. Both Jesus and Jade Goody spoke in advance about their dying, publicly and controversially. But there is a very obvious difference. Reports of Jade Goody's death were for many sad and moving; but her death was not 'for us'.

Typology is useful as a kind of one-way analogy. A biblical event or person confers meaning on a contemporary one while retaining the meaning given it by its place in the Bible. Thus the suffering servant of Isaiah 53 confers the meaning of atonement on the death of Jesus. The Exodus narrative has conferred meaning on twentieth-century liberation movements. A political leader who proposes an immigration policy to help rather than exclude economic migrants could be a lesser Joseph (Gen. 45.4–8). A modern prescient observer of our investment banking system before the crash of 2008/9 could be called a second Jeremiah.

Metaphor is an intense form of comparison to generate new meaning. It goes beyond 'that is like or not like that' comparison, by talking about one thing in terms of another. The Bible is highly metaphoric throughout: God is Father, Jesus is Word, the Church is the body of Christ. Some metaphors are so familiar that we forget they are metaphors. However, metaphor that is freshly coined when a particular news story opens up can have particular power to disclose meaning. Thus we have 'casino capitalism' to describe the behaviour of some investment bankers, or, more strikingly, they are 'Arthur Scargills in pinstripes'.[6]

Consider periodic news stories about controversy over the headdress of Muslim women, especially the burka, once described as 'a mark of separation'.[7] Set these alongside 2 Corinthians 4.3–6. You could then say, 'God chooses not to wear a burka.' The burka is thus a metaphor for self-concealment. To say that a burka conceals the wearer's face is not the only thing to be said about the burka. To say that we see God in the face of Jesus is not the only thing to be said about God. However, the burka as a metaphor is, it can be argued, fresh, relevant and revealing when this particular issue in the news encounters this particular text in a sermon.

Imagine a sermon preached in the context of a local event, the first night of the village pantomime. 'In the death and resurrection of Jesus God has already turned the pumpkin into a coach so that we, our grandchildren and great-grandchildren can all board the coach and go to the ball. And the days of the ugly sisters are numbered.' You could say that this is no more than an amusing metaphor, even a trivial one. It may throw little light on the atonement. Alternatively, you could say that to use a pantomime storyline as a metaphor for salvation is to make the point that the appeal of the panto story is in the way it articulates deep-seated human longing for transformation and fulfilment to which the act of God in Christ is the ultimate answer.

Both burka and Cinderella are metaphors provided by the world outside the Bible. Alternatively, biblical text can provide a metaphor for the news. One example could be the Temple in need of cleansing by Jesus as a metaphor for the need to expunge the abuse of MPs' expenses.

If the future preaching repertoire needs to include more sermons on the news, there are implications first for the preacher, then for the congregation and then for the sermon in which both preacher and congregation engage.

The obvious implication for preachers is the need to follow the news carefully as an integral part of sermon preparation. This means cultivating the skill to 'read' the news, to understand the nature of news journalism, the conventions and pressures associated with news-gathering and presentation. All of this points to the need to give all of us preachers more opportunities in future for training in media literacy.

Concerning the congregation, the first point is that research mentioned at the beginning of this chapter suggests the congregations are likely to welcome more preaching on issues in the news, preaching which helps them to look at them differently. The second is to do with the place of the news in worship. News preaching deals with two kinds of text, biblical and news, sacred and secular. The congregation will probably look at the different kinds of text from different points of view. The biblical reading is customary, part of the ministry of the word. It is accepted as in some sense authoritative and true. The news text is not customary, not part of the ministry of the word, nor can it be accepted as true or authoritative. It may be controversial, the subject of differing and strongly held opinions within the congregation. There are implications for the preacher in these differences. He or she needs to make the congregation aware of the news text, either during the sermon or elsewhere in the worship; to show a pulpit awareness of differing levels of interest in any news story and of contrasting views about it. In doing so he or she is, as it were, articulating the voice of the congregation before the biblical text as well as the voice of the biblical text before the congregation.

Then there are issues to do with the sermon. One of these is the use of the visual. News reports that make most impact on consciousness are highly visual, on TV and the internet, and they are particular stories, with images of particular people and places. This visual particularity invites questions about the use of the visual – news photos or video clips – in sermons. This is debatable. Technical questions apart, the visual image can be seen as a powerful aid or as an over-powerful illustration. It may add impact to the sermon or spoil a speech act which should, it can be argued, be above all a conversation between preacher and congregation.

Finally, there is the question as to whether news preaching lends itself to any particular form of sermon. Because it deals so much in dialogue between sacred and secular texts, news preaching is perhaps more peculiarly bi-vocal than customary preaching. It follows, I suggest, that the notion of dialogue which should, I have argued, govern the preparation to preach should also shape the sermon; so that the congregation are led move by move toward the local Godword arising from the texts in conversation. This suggests inductive sermon, construction that has the effect of creating new narrative out of an interweaving of news and biblical text. A suitable metaphor for the shape of the sermon might be a vertical spiral. The preacher seeks to lift the congregation by moving between biblical and news text and back again, each move taking the congregation towards the apex of the spiral. The apex of the spiral and the end-point of the sermon is the concluding affirmation, in the context of the news, of the gospel of cross and resurrection, the gospel of Jesus as Lord of, among all else, the news headlines.

Notes

1. This is a line of thought set out in Alistair McGrath, 2004, *The Twilight of Atheism*, London: Random House.
2. National TV news is in the hands of just three big companies – BBC, ITN and BSkyB; just four publishers control 70 per cent of UK local and regional press. Source: Commission of Inquiry into the Future of Civil Society, reported in *The Guardian*, 13 March 2010.
3. See for example Borschel, 2001, and Davies, 2009. See also the report of the Commission of Inquiry into the Future of Civil Society, 17 March 2010.
4. John Terry, the footballer, was much in the news during February 2010.
5. This is a theme of Jolyon Mitchell, 2007, *Media Violence and Christian Ethics*, Cambridge: Cambridge University Press.
6. Nick Clegg, speaking at a LibDem party conference, 13 March 2010, reported in *The Guardian*.
7. Thus Tony Blair in November 2006.

References

Borschel, Audrey, 2001, *Preaching Prophetically When the News Disturbs*, Atlanta: Chalice Press.

Brueggemann, Walter, 1997, *Cadences of Home*, Louisville: Westminster John Knox Press.

Campbell, Charles, 2002, *The Word before the Powers*, Louisville: Westminster John Knox.

CODEC, 2010, *The View from the Pew*, Durham: St John's College, Durham University.

Paul Johns

Davies, Nick, 2009, *Flat Earth News*, London: Vintage.
Lynch, Gordon, 2005, *Understanding Theology and Popular Culture*, Oxford: Blackwell.
Wink, Walter, 1992, *Engaging the Powers*, Minneapolis: Augsburg Fortress.

9

Preaching for All

Inclusivity and the Future of Preaching in All-Age Worship

MARGARET WITHERS

Travelling along a busy motorway one winter evening in 1992 I confided to a friend that I planned to write a book on all-age worship. 'You mean some talks for children?' she responded. Well, the car remained on the road, and the book was eventually written but, nearly twenty years later, a common perception still lingers that an all-age service is either geared towards children with the adults being little more than an audience or that it is the usual service with a few tweaks and a 'stunt from the front' in place of the sermon.

It is vital, therefore, to review what is meant by all-age worship before exploring the challenges and opportunities of preaching at such services in the future.

Basic principles of all-age worship

In one sense, almost every congregation is all-age because 'age' is not just about years, but about spiritual experience and individual faith journeys as well as familiarity with the Bible, Christian doctrine and being part of a worshipping community.

Even in a tiny community, the main Sunday service will have a congregation with a wide mixture of beliefs and experiences of life. Children should take part for at least part of it, and sometimes there will be visitors, uniformed organizations, civic dignitaries, couples planning to marry at the church, and families attending a child's baptism. Some of the adults and children will be committed Christians. Others will have some knowledge of the Christian faith, while a few may be members of other faiths or none. Several will be 'enquirers': people who are asking questions or who have come to turning-points in their lives, and are interested in exploring them from a Christian perspective.

After half a century of 'unchurching' the nation, it cannot be guaranteed that anyone of less than about 60 will know anything about Christianity. A child of 5 from a Christian family, who has been in church or Sunday school each week and prays at home, will be more familiar with well-known Bible stories and church services than an occasional attendee aged 50. An elderly man, who has been on numerous study days, may sit next to a young woman with learning difficulties but a deep personal faith. A large percentage of the adult population knows nothing beyond a few stories connected with Christmas but over a million children attend church schools, some of which are consciously Christian and rooted in worship.

Assuming that children in any church service are a separate group is a simplification of the real situation. As numerous studies have shown, people learn in a variety of ways and adults as well as children will benefit from hands-on activities, movement and group discussion as effective ways of learning and worshipping God. Many of the things that are perceived as being child-friendly in worship are helpful to some adults as well. Adults who are frail or in wheelchairs can have the same difficulty as small people in seeing what is going on. Visually impaired adults and young children like to read from large-print service sheets and so on.

Rather than working to the lowest common denominator, all-age worship aims to engage and challenge each person so that they can give and receive in their own way. Music, actions, pictures and light often speak more strongly than words, so form an integral part of the teaching in any service and, at times, may be vehicles for teaching in themselves.

Having taken those principles on board, the fact remains that any service in which children are genuinely involved will be different from one where only adults are present. Children add a freshness and vitality to a service that spreads right through church life. Their questions and perceptions often make adults pause for thought. Churches that have admitted children to Holy Communion have found their congregations have been transformed by the commitment and reverence shown by their youngest members.[1]

Worshipping and learning through all the senses

It is widely accepted that people learn and retain information for a longer time through sight than hearing, and even more through doing. Recent research indicates that 'kinaesthetic' methods of learning, through discussion, movement and practical activities in groups, are the most effective way of learning for a significant majority of the population, especially men and boys. This needs to become a major factor in our thinking on how we lead and preach at any service, but especially one that aims to include people of all ages and backgrounds.

Together for a Season, a series of all-age services, suggests ways of creative worship while using the Church of England's *Common Worship*. The layout of each service is tabulated with four headings:

Structure and movement   Text/words   Multi-sensory   Participation

How often do preachers and worship leaders look beyond the first two headings? This is not about looking for gimmicks to make a dull service more entertaining. Very little worship is boring in itself; it is the way that it is led. If we add elaborate visual aids or witty jokes simply in order to make a service exciting and appealing, we will find that they have under-mined the worship so that its shape and message are lost. Multi-sensory worship is about deepening the experience of God by helping us to wor-ship him with our whole selves. Joy and laughter are part of enjoying his presence but they are not ends in themselves.

Most worship takes place in a wonderful teaching aid – the church building. Many services are held in ancient buildings with music, stained glass and furnishings designed to give a sense of God's presence and the beauty of holiness. They are wonderful preaching aids if used imagina-tively. Others are held in modern churches, multi-purpose buildings or school halls. They are more flexible so give different opportunities for creative teaching through layout, drama, movement and visual effects.

Every church furnishing – the cross, lectern, pulpit, altar or communion table, baptistery or font – has a symbolic meaning. A font placed near the entrance gives a different message from one moved into the centre of the building for a baptism. A communion service held with the chairs in a circle gives a different message from one with seats in rows some distance away. An open Bible displayed on a large lectern or read from the pulpit teaches us about its importance, and so on.

Posture and movement make us part of the worship. Standing for prayers feels different from sitting or kneeling. Actions like bowing the head, gestures with hands, or sharing the Peace with a stranger often teach better than long explanations or effusive welcomes.

Murals and stained glass taught the faith to generations of people who could not read. The Northern European Protestant tradition – and we are all affected by it to a certain extent – saw these images as distractions and put a stress on the written word, but much is being rediscovered across all traditions. Colour, light, music, silence, movement, drama and visual effects are being used in churches and chapels that would not have considered such things twenty years ago.

At the same time, there is a shift away from the book culture to visual effects through television, DVDs, the internet and small bites of information rather than lengthy descriptions. We need to engage with today's culture in the same way, by using the signs and symbols around us when we preach: stained glass, pictures, icons, liturgical colours, light, pictures, icons, banners and displays as well as film and computer-generated materials.

We often burden our preaching with lengthy explanations when a simple image will convey the message more effectively. Children forming a tableau for a nativity play, the sun shining through a stained-glass window, a stark cross in a silent church on Good Friday will stay in the mind long after the words are forgotten.

Preparing to preach at all-age services

Preaching at this kind of worship is about getting ideas. Treat Scripture, the story of God's relationship with his people, as a springboard for your thoughts. This involves using your imagination, and then thinking creatively. Communicate with the people in charge of the music, with readers, with prayers and with the young people. Be prepared to use other people's skills and talents to help you to choose music, rehearse drama or create visual effects.

Bible readings in an all-age service may follow a lectionary or be chosen to fit a theme. Either method has its advantages and pitfalls.

If you are following a lectionary, ask yourself:

1 What are these readings saying?
2 How can they be presented to a congregation of different ages and levels of understanding?
3 Are any adaptations necessary?

The Christian year is a wonderful gift. It covers the story of our faith, every emotion and every aspect of our lives. Using the lectionary gives continuity with other weeks for the regular congregation and children's groups and ensures that a wide range of Scripture is used. Be prepared to set aside some of the more gruesome parts of the Old Testament or Paul's most pensive arguments when appropriate. Always be on the lookout for ideas, quotations, stories and resources and record them so that you have them to hand to support your teaching when needed.

The questions are similar but in a different order for a **thematic** service:

1 What is the intended focus of this service?
2 How can it be presented to a congregation of different ages and levels of understanding?
3 Which Scripture readings will help to develop this theme?

Thematic services give opportunities to focus on a particular situation in the news or a special occasion for the church or wider community. They are most appropriate for services geared towards children: the end of the school year or after a holiday club. Several Christian charities provide materials that can be adapted to local needs.[2] There is, however, a real danger of reusing a few Bible readings so that the overall Christian message is distorted or becomes superficial. Some people will just attend family services so this may be the only Christian teaching they ever receive.

Having studied and prayed about the readings, think through what resources, including those in the church building, will be helpful, and ask three further questions:

4 Will music, drama or visual aids help to put the message across?
5 How will we involve people of all ages to worship with their whole selves?
6 What will give a sense of the presence of God with time and space for prayer?

Best practice

Jesus often sat to teach his friends. This was the rabbinic tradition, and put him on the same level as his hearers, so that they could make eye contact and even touch each other. We recall how he drew in the dust and cuddled a child that was standing by him. Try to create similar intimacy by being either seated or standing near the front rows. You could invite anyone who cannot see clearly to move to the front and for the children to sit around you on hassocks or the carpet.

Memorize what you have to say, or put a few keywords on a card. That will allow you to gesture with your hands and handle visual aids or computer-generated materials easily. It will also give you freedom to move around. If you are telling a story, see that you make eye contact and tell it directly to the congregation. Your tone of voice, timing and pace can take adults as well as children on a voyage in their own imagination. Let your posture and actions illustrate your story. Walk when a person goes on a journey. Sit or stand when he does. Speak slowly and lower your head when the situation is sad. Pause to create suspense. Lift your head, smile and lighten your tone when the story is happy or joyful.

Relate the theme of the service to today's culture and current interests or use them to open your teaching and get attention. People of all ages will know about the latest popular television programmes or cult stars. If you are using these topics, research your subject carefully, usually with the help of a youngster, and always be honest about your interests and preferences.

Use your church building or, if you are leading worship in a school, use the displays or the topics being studied as part of your teaching. Other visual aids must be large and clear. If you decide to use children to help you, rehearse them before the service or assembly. Always tell them when they can put down the particular items and thank them before they return to their seats.

Some family services are a non-stop hour of activity and noise. While any service needs to move at a steady pace, it is important to allow time for silent reflection during the prayers and after the readings and preaching. Children are used to being silent at school and will respond well. Their minds are less cluttered than ours so they often find praying easy while adults are dealing with distractions. Many adults lead frenetic lives in a noisy world and a time of silence to think about a Scripture reading or to make a prayer one's own may be the only quiet space in the week.

Common preaching methods and examples

We have already seen how and when aspects of the worship or surroundings can be vehicles for teaching. The following suggestions are some of the most common ways of preaching at all-age services. The examples are not perfect models, but a few simple ideas to show how a congregation can participate creatively within the teaching.

Interactive commentary on Bible readings

One of the most popular ways of preaching is a commentary on the Bible reading with interaction or visual aids. This can vary from inviting discussion to using visual aids, including puppets, PowerPoint or clips from DVDs. Occasionally it can involve the whole congregation in reflecting on the reading through responses and even actions. This can form a sermon or be an extended introduction or follow-up to the reading or readings.

Inviting the congregation to handle visual aids or create something as part of the teaching adds the sense of touch to the worship. Simple acts like making palm crosses or modelling with clay can be a response to the teaching. In a small congregation, or a class at school, various visual aids and artefacts can be passed around during the teaching or after the service. This need not be complicated: the simplest ideas are usually the most effective.

Example: The Three Gifts

The gifts that the Magi offered to Jesus are full of symbolism. They lose much of their mystique when they are only talked about or illustrated with a paper crown and a joss stick. For the preaching at an Epiphany service, pass around a gold-plated chalice (if you can borrow one) or other golden item and leave incense to smoulder while the congregation smells it and watches the smoke rise up like a prayer to God. Oil of myrrh can be bought from most alternative medicine shops and reminds us of Jesus as a healer as well as dying for us. Invite the congregation to put a dab of myrrh on their fingers or to anoint each other while learning about the meaning of the Magi's gifts and what they teach about the person of Jesus as King, God and Saviour.

A related story

Reinforcing a reading or the theme with a related story is a common form of preaching at any service. Well-known characters like Dr Who, Homer Simpson, or a particular football player will immediately get the young people's attention and can then be used as a bridge or an example of the message of your teaching. If you do this, see that you really know your subject. Children cannot be conned! If you give the wrong actor's name to a particular Time Lord or make a football player score too few goals in a special match, your message will be lost along with your credibility.

Using the Bible with young people can be difficult. Don't start by saying where the story has come from but tell it in your own words or write your own version, and then put it in context. The parables were stories about everyday people and situations that Jesus' listeners would have recognized. Keep them alive in a similar way.

One of the effects of 'Godly Play' is that it encourages people to respond through a more open-ended meditative approach to a Bible passage. Rather than tying it up with neat answers, consider ending your preaching with an open-ended question, such as, 'I wonder which part of this story was the most important, for you', or, 'I wonder what you would have said or done if you were that person'. Then leave a short silence for reflection before continuing the service.

Drama

Using drama adds visual effect, movement, colour and variety of voices to our preaching. Many Gospel and some Old Testament passages are stories that can be read dramatically, keywords on cards can be held up or a small group can mime a Bible reading while it is read.

Acting a short play based on a Bible reading or following a reading with a short drama to reflect on it will be teaching in themselves and may not need a sermon as well. There are a number of biblically based short plays published for church use, and the Iona series of dialogues, *Eh Jesus . . . Yes, Peter?* are still available (see, for example, Hopwood, 2001, and Bell and Maule, 2004). If you plan to teach through drama, see that you use both adults and children and have strong speakers. Keep it short and simple with clear movements and a sense of pace. Most church dramas are too long and complicated.

Example: A mime based on Luke 10.1–12

This is based on the story of Jesus sending out the 72 evangelists to proclaim the kingdom of God. It needs a narrator and 5 groups of people: evangelists, waylayers, people in the welcoming town, sick people and unwelcoming people, but each group needs only one or two people. Each evangelist needs to wear a rucksack and flip-flops to be discarded when instructed. A basket of bread can be used for offering hospitality and a walking stick is a good symbol for illness.

When rehearsing, give clear instructions about moving on a particular word or sentence so that the action synchronizes with the text. If the reader cannot see the players have a prompter hidden behind a pillar to indicate any pauses or reminders of movements. Simple movements like smiling and beckoning for friendship, standing and walking when healed, and turning away for unfriendliness are all that is required.

A *taught service or a running sermon*

A 'taught service' is often appreciated by people who are unfamiliar with church worship and wonder why, for example, a service starts with a confession of sins, what is meant by 'the word of the Lord' and the significance of sharing the Peace or ending with a dismissal. It is especially appropriate in eucharistic worship, which is full of symbolism that is often taken for granted. When a service is conducted with brief explanations during it, the preaching could simply draw together points already explained or discussed. This could involve the whole congregation through inviting comments or asking questions. It is useful to anticipate some of the possible problem answers and be prepared to take them on board as part of the teaching.

A 'running sermon' is exactly what it says – the teaching runs through the whole service, either by being an almost continuous commentary or through linking the parts of the worship with the Bible readings. It is especially appropriate in an informal service where there is no strong structure. The teaching may speak for itself or could be drawn together at some point before the final prayers and hymn.

Example: A Palm Sunday Passion reading

This interactive version of a shortened Passion story (from Pilate's judgement to Jesus' burial) with teaching, visual aids and a prayer takes the form of a journey around the church with a verse of a hymn sung in between each section.

Visual aids – a bowl of water, a large cross, nails and so on – are placed around the church, and the congregation can be invited either to follow the preacher to each one or to stay in their places. Each reading is followed with a brief reflection on it while the congregation are invited to act – washing their hands, hammering nails, stretching their arms out and so on – then has a prayer for those in similar situations: judges, prisoners of conscience, the dying and the bereaved. The whole service could end by lighting a candle as a sign of hope of the resurrection and the congregation leaving quietly.

Dialogue

A question-and-answer session or some sort of quiz can be effective but should not be the only way of preaching at a family service. An opening question or two is very effective in engaging the congregation, but if you use it too frequently or ask too many questions, it can focus on one or two children rather than being a learning time for everyone. Always include the adults as much as the children. Do not assume that they know all the answers; indeed, a family service or worship at a toddler group may provide some of your most effective teaching to adults as they can learn in a safe environment. The minister of a large Methodist church once commented that he always prayed that there would be a family service on Trinity Sunday, because it allowed him to put a tricycle in the pulpit without the adults feeling patronized!

Always seek to affirm people, especially children. A bald 'Wrong' or a put-down teaches nothing. Teaching something about the answer that has been offered and then explaining why another one is more accurate, for example, asking what we celebrate on Ascension day, is often answered with, 'the Resurrection'. Explaining that this is also an important event, but we celebrate it at Easter, then prompting the correct answer – 'What does "ascend" mean?' 'Where is Jesus now?' – teaches two things rather than one. A youngster with learning difficulties or who is unhappy at school needs to know the love of God and acceptance of the church family more than most other people. There will be no SATs or GCSEs in the kingdom of God.

Frequency and type of services

Having explored the reasons for having inclusive worship and the styles and methods of preaching within or as an integral part of the liturgy, we come to pattern and type of all-age services. Each presents different challenges and opportunities.

Everyone together

Some churches have decided that every service should be all-age worship with children and adults together. In some cases, notably new congregations, 'Fresh Expressions' and some independent churches, the congregation is genuinely inclusive. In most Roman Catholic, Orthodox and a few Anglican churches the practice is for the whole worshipping community to meet for the Eucharist every Sunday, and the children will be expected to learn through the colour, movement and symbolism of the liturgy as well as direct teaching.

Other churches of all traditions have tiny congregations or few facilities, so everyone worships together for practical reasons. The congregation may feel that it has failed because the numbers are small or that everything would be better if the children were not there. The challenge is to stress the positive aspects of a congregation where everyone is known and valued, and to give the highest standard of teaching possible that includes everyone. A family service is often a special occasion in a rural area when the local church is only used occasionally. Whatever the reason, the preacher has to remember that this may be the only time that the particular congregation will attend church and it is important to feed and challenge the regular and informed worshippers as well as the least formed.

A more common practice is to have an all-age service once a month. This will take one of four forms:

1 Informal service
2 Based on a teaching course, for example, *SALT* or *Roots*[3]
3 Service of the Word
4 Eucharist or Holy Communion

A DIY Family Service

An informal service is the most difficult to prepare and deliver because it means starting, maybe literally, with a blank sheet of paper. A tendency is to design it linearly so that it becomes a hotchpotch of items strung together with no identifiable focus. It needs a clear theme that carries through the readings, prayers and music, with the teaching being a vital strand that may run through the service and be summed up in the 'sermon'. Preachers need a clear objective – what do we want to impart and by what means do we do it – and to be able to ask afterwards whether they have achieved it.

Service of the Word and Holy Communion

Both of these services have strong structures that can act as a skeleton to hang the teaching on. A Eucharist is the more straightforward service because it has a clear focus and rich symbolism. At the heart of it is a meal. It can be a simple or elaborate celebration but it is still a shared meal.

Some churches have been celebrating the Eucharist imaginatively for a quarter of a century with special music, simplified texts and all-age groups fully involved. Admitting children to Holy Communion in churches of most denominations has encouraged many churches to try to see their worship through the eyes of a child with the stress on the experience of the presence of God in his word and sacrament as much as direct teaching about him. In others it is still regarded as a service for committed adults with children and enquirers fitting around the edge.

Ideally a Eucharist will be a truly all-age service in which everyone is equally involved. Some children will receive Holy Communion while adults are blessed. Members of a uniformed organization may lead the prayers, a family present the elements, and a group of youngsters act out the Gospel reading. The richness of the service gives huge opportunities for teaching about it and throughout it, thus drawing in people who attend it only occasionally.

Occasional services

Nearly every church has occasional services that are geared towards families and occasional attendees: Christingle, Crib service, Mothering Sunday, Harvest Thanksgiving and a memorial service for All Souls. Uniformed organizations may attend church on Remembrance Sunday and St George's Tide. They are easily dismissed as 'fringe activities' and given to lay preachers or Readers rather than clergy. If you are in that situation, rejoice that you have been handed such a gift! They are usually the best-attended services of the year and present enormous opportunities for reaching people who rarely darken the doors of any church. That presents challenges in itself. They will be one of the most difficult services you will ever lead, so take time to prepare them carefully.

Preaching in school

Most clergy and preachers would be thrilled to find a congregation of several hundred people of all ages and backgrounds on a Sunday morning. That is exactly what they have when they lead collective worship in the local school or at a special service in church. Although children will be in the majority, teachers and other staff, and, in many instances, parents and governors, will also be present, making an all-age community.

Even experienced teachers can find leading worship with the whole school daunting. The age range can span from literally 5 to 65, and it is expected to be a memorable experience for everyone. Some teachers feel ill at ease with the whole idea of worshipping God, so visitors from a local church are usually welcomed to lead worship or give a talk. Worship in any school should be 'broadly Christian' but in a church school it will follow the doctrine of the particular denomination. Always seek advice from the school about what sort of teaching is appropriate.

Preaching with under-fives, their parents and carers

A similar situation exists at a buggy service or worship in a toddler group. The children, their parents and the leaders, who may be older or retired, make an instant congregation of three generations. Some of the parents will want to bring their children up as Christians. Others may have had negative experiences or stereotyped views about the way that Christians behave. They may feel that the Christian story is, if not untrue, irrelevant in today's world.

The teaching in a buggy service will not just be a short story or talk for the children, but will allow time for questions and discussion, while they are playing. Some parents may start to enquire about the Christian faith because the atmosphere is informal and relaxed. Others may not own to any belief but want their children to know something of the Christian story. Time will come when it is appropriate to enter into dialogue.

Christian festivals, baptisms or dedication of babies, support for a troubled parent with an offer of prayer are great teaching opportunities and may be the preparation for the first steps of a journey of faith.

Looking forward

In 1991 a report, *All God's Children?*, stated that only 11 per cent of children were in contact with a church and the number was falling.[4] Other statistics presented similar falls and predicted that the Church would be collapsing by about 2016. They did not take account of human beings' infinite ability to adapt, or the power of the Holy Spirit!

After years of falling numbers, the tide is beginning to turn. Two centuries of learned segregation, with children being nurtured in Sunday schools while the adults worshipped separately, presents challenges for the Church to address as it struggles to re-engage with children and adults who have little, if any, experience of the Christian faith.

Many churches have responded by having regular all-age services. Occasional services with a strong theme are well attended, and numbers of people in contact with a church are rising as more churches find imaginative and varied ways of engaging with them. Most initiatives like 'Fresh Expressions' and cell groups are genuinely inclusive, and mid-week clubs, toddler groups and family activities like 'Messy Church'[5] are now valued as worship in their own right.

We are living in a visual age. People rely increasingly on film, DVDs, texting and soundbites for information. They learn in a variety of ways with a stress on working in groups, discussion and practical activities. The answer to the question whether formal preaching from a static pulpit is the most effective way of teaching congregations of mixed ages with a wide breadth of spiritual experience is, clearly, 'no'. On the other hand, the opportunities for imaginative teaching that uses all the senses and allows everyone to enjoy a sense of the presence of God is enormous.

This leads to a second question, which is asked by Lucy Moore, founder of Messy Church. She writes,

> Is the church service the occasion for the main learning of church members to take place, or should it happen elsewhere? And if it is done sensitively and imaginatively can an all-age service open up possibilities for worship, learning, wonder, fellowship and meeting God during the rest of the week, rather than being the only time we expect any of this to happen? Again this is so much easier to manage if expectations have not already been set by generations of learned segregation.

> It is also worth considering that if all-age worship means 'dumbing-down', is that OK, even once a month? Surely it is possible to have a regular service which challenges and feeds everybody together? (Moore, 2010, p. 30.)

How will this affect the ministry of preaching? Rather than just preparing one large sermon, preachers will find that they are regularly teaching several groups, sometimes in informal settings that lend themselves to discussion and creative activities. They will increasingly use music, drama and visual effects in a main Sunday service to teach a gathered community of all ages and backgrounds. This will lead to demands for training in different styles and methods of teaching. It may also affirm ways of teaching that have hitherto been thought of as inappropriate for church.

What will such a church be like?

- It will speak in each person's own language
- It will engage, in that it will be geared towards people's needs or cultures
- It will be inclusive – genuinely all-age
- It will nurture – telling the story so that everyone can understand it

- It will transform – giving each person an opportunity to have an encounter with the living God.

That changes lives.

Notes

1. Debate of the Church of England's General Synod on *Children and Holy Communion: A Review* (GS 1576), 5 July 2005.
2. Christian Aid, www.christianaid.org.uk; Church Mission Society, www.cms-uk.org; Mission to Seafarers (Sea Sunday), www.mission toseafarers.org.
3. www.rootsontheweb.com.
4. General Synod of the Church of England, GS 988.
5. www.messychurch.org.uk.

References

Ambrose, Gill (ed.), 2006–9, *Together for a Season*, vols 1–3, London: Church House Publishing.

Bell, John L., and Graham Maule, 2004, *Jesus and Peter: Off-the-Record Conversations*, Glasgow: Wild Goose.

Hopwood, Dave, 2001, *A Fistful of Sketches*, London: Church House Publishing.

Moore, Lucy, 2010, *All Age Worship*, London: Bible Reading Fellowship.

10

The Future of Language in Preaching

IAN PAUL

The past is a foreign country; they do things differently there.

So runs the famous opening line of L. P. Hartley's *The Go Between*, introducing a story told largely in flashback, suggesting that past and present have an unbridgeable discontinuity. But given that today is the tomorrow that we worried about yesterday, the same could be suggested of the future – it, too, is a foreign country, and woe betide anyone who dares to predict the lie of the land in that country. Many have foundered on the rock of certainty regarding what tomorrow's world will be.[1] But the reassuring thing is to note that, however different a country the past is, it seemed to be populated by people with very similar concerns to our own, albeit expressed in different terms – concerns about meaning, personal significance, security and destiny, and above all (within the Christian tradition) a concern to make sense of what God has done for us in Christ, and how that is to be made known in the world around them. We can be confident that the strange land of the future will similarly be populated with people whose concerns we understand and can identify with.

To explore the future of language in preaching, we need to have a working assumption about what 'preaching' is. In teaching homiletics, I work with the understanding that preaching is expressing the answer to the question: 'What is God saying through this text to these people in this place at this time?' This working definition has important connections with Karl Barth's explanation of preaching in *Homiletics*:

Preaching is the attempt enjoined upon the church to serve God's own Word, through one who is called hereto, by expounding a biblical text in human words and making it relevant to contemporaries in intimation of what they have to hear from God himself. (Barth, 1991, p. 44)

My definition of it assumes two key poles of preaching – the world of Scripture and the world of those listening to the preaching – and that there is a need to close some sort of gap between these two worlds. My own definition makes more explicit two important assumptions. The first is that there is a hermeneutical dimension to preaching, in fact, a doubly hermeneutical dimension to preaching, in that the preacher is seeking to interpret both the text in question and the situation ('these people in this place at this time') in question. Confidence in preaching therefore has to be subject to a double humility in the face of the provisional nature of all interpretation. The second assumption my definition makes is that there is a necessary prophetic element in preaching, in that the discernment of what God is saying in a particular situation is, in biblical terms, the ministry of the prophet.[2]

This still leaves the question of the context of preaching we are considering. Darrell Johnson helpfully categorizes the contexts of preaching under four broad headings, formed from considering the audience and the place of preaching – to believers or unbelievers, in either a sacred or a secular place (Johnson, 2009, p. 32). For the purposes of this discussion, I will primarily have in mind one of these situations, the addressing of believers within a sacred space, though the observations could equally apply to the other three.[3]

If the task of preaching, then, relates to these two poles of Scripture and the context of listeners, what are the trends that will endure which might affect this task? I believe that they fall into two main areas.

The accelerating decline in biblical literacy and growing hostility to Christian faith

Every Christmas time there appears to be the mandatory story about how few people – especially young people – know the basic facts of the Christmas story. But research demonstrates that this is a long-term issue, and not just a source of seasonal entertainment. The National Biblical Literacy Survey found that:

> 62% of respondents did not know the parable of the Prodigal Son and 60% could not name anything about the story of the Good Samaritan. One respondent said David and Goliath was the name of a ship, while another thought Daniel – who survived being thrown into the lions' den – was the Lion King.[4]

Interestingly, the survey (funded by a consortium of national churches, charitable trusts and Bible agencies) also found that people turned to the Bible in times of emotional need, but how can they use the Bible if they know so little about it?[5]

This decline in biblical literacy is also found within the churches. As I have attended different churches as a visiting preacher, I have often been struck by how little time and attention is given to the reading of Scripture together. Ironically, it is often in those churches that declare themselves to be particularly 'Bible based', and which have little formal liturgy, that there is commonly only one Bible reading, where Anglican liturgy would have had them read from the Old Testament, the New Testament letters, the Gospels, the psalms and possibly a biblical 'canticle'.[6] But reading the Scriptures alone is not enough; the work of Jeff Astley and Ann Christie on 'ordinary theology' highlights how a large proportion of Anglicans do not hold core biblical doctrines about Christology and the atonement (Astley and Christie, 2007).[7] So at St John's, part of preparation for all forms of lay and ordained ministry is to take a basic course giving an overview of the Bible's contents, and this is something we find all students benefit from.

Levels of hostility to Christian faith in Britain are harder to measure, and there is always a tendency to see 'persecution' whenever there is opposition to some Christian agency or another. But several high-profile cases of Christians being seen to be under pressure for their beliefs in the workplace have contributed to a sense of hostility, along with an increasingly vocal atheist lobby led by figures like Richard Dawkins. A church minister, who had spent the last 30 years in mission work abroad and just returned to the UK, commented to me recently how much harder it was to talk about faith in the UK now than when he first left.

The recognition of the importance and power of language

This second area is demonstrated in some truly surprising trends in education, the media and popular culture, including:

- The increase in *radio listening*, this year believed to be up by 9 per cent.
- The effect of the *Labour government's initiatives* in numeracy and literacy. I was amused by a conversation with the headteacher of my children's school last year, when I asked about my children's awareness of different genres of writing. 'It is all about meta-cognition!' he replied; in their literacy strategy (developed in conjunction with Nottingham Trent University), they are developing skills in genre recognition by focusing on reading and writing a different genre of literature each half term. Thus at age nine the pupils are overtaking

most graduates in their understanding of what Douglas Stuart and Gordon Fee identify as a key element of biblical literacy.[8]

- Actual *use of the internet* as an interactive medium, which, despite the importance of picture and video material, is very often text-based. Children asked to 'research' a subject on the internet are very often engaged in activities that in practice look very similar to reading an article in an encyclopaedia, and adult usage often makes high demands of literacy. The growth of blogs, in particular, has led to a veritable explosion of verbiage; from an academic and a ministry perspective, I simply find I cannot keep up with all that is being written.

- The extraordinary rise of *stand-up comedy* in the last few years, a form of entertainment entirely dependent on the crafting and use of words. To those objecting to the form of the monologue sermon as unsustainable in the contemporary context, I point out that people will pay very good money to listen to 90 minutes of monologue at the Apollo Theatre in London! There might be problems with many monologue sermons, but stand-up comedy says that the problem does not simply lie in the monologue *form* itself!

- The return of *rhetoric within political speech*, the prime example here being that of Barack Obama. Writing on the day Obama was due to give his Inaugural Presidential Speech, Razia Iqbal quotes Tony Blair's former speech-writer Philip Collins: Obama at his absolute best 'combines a poetic form of expression with a poetic compression of meaning, while rarely straying from ordinary language. His speeches do take wing, but the flight comes from the rhythm of the sentences as much as the elevation of the language.'[9] Obama's speech on that day is replete with classical techniques and strategies of rhetoric.[10]

What is needed in preaching that will effectively connect the world of Scripture with the world of contemporary listeners, in the face of declining familiarity with and welcome of the Bible and its message, and this awareness of the power of language? I believe there are two main requirements, each with an important qualification.

A rediscovery of rhetoric . . .

Paul Scott Wilson, in his masterly introduction to *The Practice of Preaching*, argues that preaching must be engaging and persuasive, but not in the first instance for practical reasons. Rather, he argues that theology itself is rhetorical because it is relational, in that it seeks to be a place of encounter between God and his people (1994, Ch. 3). Anthony Thiselton says something similar in the opening of his recent *The Hermeneutics of Doctrine*. The early creeds were never mere statements of propositions to which the Church gave intellectual assent; they were always expressions of 'dispositions', fundamental orientations that affected the whole of life (2007, Ch. 1).

If theology is rhetorical, in the sense that its goal is 'faithful persuasion', Wilson argues that homiletics must also be rhetorical, since it is the 'completion' of theology:

> I believe that the sermon is not the dilution of theology; it is rather the completion of theology, made complete through Christ speaking it and constituting the church through it. We might even say that the church is most truly the church when it is preaching in worship, for it is through the Word and sacrament that salvation comes to the world, and it is through our lives being transformed in the cruciform image that our acts of justice, mercy, peace, and love are begun once more in power. (Wilson, 1994, p. 70)

Against an 'old homiletic', propositional approach to preaching, Wilson believes that preaching is 'never simply the exchange of information from preacher to congregation' (p. 77), but must involve persuasive engagement. In doing this, preaching must rediscover Aristotle's ancient rhetorical categories of *logos*, the appeal to rational argument and facts, *ethos*, the integrity and character, even plausibility, of the speaker, and *pathos*, or emotional appeal.

> Our preaching must be experienced as integrating head, heart and soul (or loosely: logos, ethos and pathos). Homiletical theology is not an intellectual exercise that results in the cool dispensing of knowledge over a prescription counter; it involves our entire lives in devotional purpose. (pp. 79–80)

Interestingly, some of the examples of the recovery of the importance of language in culture appear to have discovered this very thing. In 'observational' comedy, one of the most prominent forms of contemporary stand-up, the rational facts of a situation (*logos*) are extrapolated into a *reductio ad absurdum*; as a result, the comic is left in an absurd situation, with which we sympathize (*pathos*); and all the while the comic uses various devices to establish rapport with the audience (*ethos*) – the comic is very much 'one of us' and even (in a sense) goes through these experiences on our behalf.

Proponents of the 'new homiletic' have argued for a more radical rethinking of the sermon as a performative engagement. But the need to rediscover rhetoric is more fundamental and all-encompassing; contemporary preachers need to develop basic skills of communication, 'asking alliteration's artful aid' (as I was once taught),[11] structuring in threes,[12] creating narrative tension by delayed resolution – and so on. I found the experience of giving 2-minute *Pause for Thought* talks on Radio 2 transformative of my preaching, since it demanded a scripting and crafting of language that a 30-minute sermon never asked for. So I require all those studying homiletics at St John's to preach a two-minute sermon to their peers. Discovering how much you can say in such a short time when you take care, they then sometimes wonder why they ever needed 20 minutes or more!

Given the sense of growing hostility to Christian faith, the importance of good, persuasive, engaging preaching is not just about satisfying religious consumers in the supermarket of faith. Increasingly, Christians in the West need to have good reasons for what they believe, and encouraging faith involves continually making a persuasive case for trusting in God.

. . . rooted in a rediscovery of the rhetoric of Scripture

If Wilson is correct in claiming that theology is inherently rhetorical, it comes as no surprise to find a whole range of rhetorical strategies in Scripture itself. This has become particularly evident since the rise of literary and rhetorical criticism within biblical studies since the 1960s and 1970s. Alan Culpepper's *Anatomy of the Fourth Gospel: A Study in Literary Design* in the early 1980s has shaped study of John's Gospel ever since. Ben Witherington's influential commentaries on the New Testament are usually styled 'socio-rhetorical' studies, and while they might not necessarily be particularly radical in their critical outlook,[13] the terminology is highly significant. 'Socio-rhetorical' criticism claims to combine the 'objective', 'behind-the-text'[14] dimensions of historical criticism with the 'subjective', 'within-the-text' dimensions of literary and rhetorical criticism, asking the historical 'in front of the text' question: 'What was the rhetorical impact of this text in that historical context?' The preacher, if using the working definition I began with, will in the light of this then want to ask the next question: 'What might the rhetorical impact of this text be in the contemporary context?'

Ron Boyd-Macmillan, in his exploration of rhetoric in preaching, delightfully draws out the threefold nature of Paul's argument about the resurrection in 1 Corinthians 15:

- Verses 1 to 11: the facts of the gospel that Paul 'received' and 'passed on' (*logos*)
- Verses 12 to 49: answering possible questions and objections, establishing the plausibility of Paul's argument and his credibility (*ethos*)
- Verses 50 to 58: Paul's emotional and evocative climax, leading him to clinch the argument with a final exhortation (*pathos*).

Boyd-Macmillan links this to the ability of the great preachers of the patristic era and later to 'effortlessly change gear' in their speaking and preaching (2006, pp. 103–5 and 142–4).

There is, of course, a wonderful irony here, in that at the beginning of the letter Paul has protested in the strongest terms that he has set aside this world's wisdom or 'superior eloquence' (1 Cor. 1.20; 2.1, NET), and perhaps Paul has in mind here the need to distance himself from professional rhetoricians who sought merely to entertain or make money. (There might well be the same danger today – though I cannot myself recall anyone saying, 'I'm not going to that church anymore; it is just too entertaining'!)

Similar examples of biblical rhetoric abound, if only we will see them.

- In a class on the letter of James, one of the students studying the Greek text pointed out that the seemingly (in English) unordered description of 'the wisdom from above' in James 3.17 in fact consists of a pair of triples, the first group all beginning with the letter epsilon and the second group all beginning with the letter alpha.
- A sermon class was discussing a sermon on Ephesians 4.20–24 (admittedly an unusually short text to preach on), but we discovered a natural threefold structure to Paul's comments in verses 22 to 24: 'You were taught . . . to lay aside the old humanity . . . to be renewed . . . to put on the new humanity . . . ' [15]
- For some time I had thought of the notion of chiastic structure in biblical texts (the form A–B–C–D–C′–B′–A′) to be a somewhat artificial and arbitrary assumption, until I discovered as a preacher that it is a natural way to speak, and one that creates and sustains interest in the listener. In fact, it can bear a striking resemblance to

Eugene Lowry's proposal to develop a 'homiletical plot' in preaching (Lowry, 2001).[16]

If the preacher is charged with closing the gap between the world of Scripture and the world of the contemporary listener, it could be imagined that paying more attention to the one pulls you away from the other. But in fact moving further into Scripture does not take you away from your listeners, since Scripture is a rhetorically shaped act of communication, and so offers natural strategies for rhetorical engagement with the contemporary world.

A rediscovery of metaphor and the poetic . . .

Of all aspects of rhetoric, the use of metaphor is the most powerful, but the most misunderstood. And yet, said Aristotle, whoever wants to master speech must master metaphor.

Far and away my favourite film is the epic trilogy that is Peter Jackson's rendering of J. R. R. Tolkien's *Lord of the Rings*. One of the most moving moments in the trilogy comes in the third film. All seems lost. Minas Tirith is under siege; the walls have been breached; orcs are running amok killing all in their path. The world of men is about to fall. In a brief pause in the fighting, Pippin the hobbit and Gandalf the wizard find themselves on a terrace of the city with a few moments to reflect.

> Pippin: I didn't think it would end this way.
> Gandalf: End? No, the journey does not end here. Death is just another path, one that we all must take. The grey rain curtain of this world rolls back, and all turns to silver glass. And then you see it.
> Pippin: What, Gandalf? See what?
> Gandalf: White shores . . . and beyond, a far green country under a swift sunrise.
> Pippin: Well, that isn't so bad.
> Gandalf: No. No it isn't.

With hope renewed and vision rekindled, they plunge once again into the fray of battle – and very soon the tide has turned.

What is so striking is how such a powerful and poignant description of life beyond death is offered in so few words. They were words written by Tolkien himself (as is almost all the dialogue in the films) but in the book come at the very end, as Frodo sails with Gandalf and the elves from the Grey Havens in the last boat to the Undying Lands. This short dialogue demonstrates the power of poetic metaphor to move and to inspire.

Tom Wright, current bishop of Durham, was speaking in London recently at a Fulcrum conference.[17] Talking of the current context of British culture, he commented on attitudes to faith and atheism:

> There is all the difference in the world between waking up in a single bed and waking up in a double bed with nobody the other side. Many in our western culture may be atheists or agnostics, but they still find themselves wondering why the other side of the bed still feels warm, and the sheets a little rumpled. And I think this is true in ways that were not the case even ten, let alone thirty years ago.

Again – powerful, transforming and remarkably concise.

Why does poetic speech have such an effect? Our words 'poetic', 'poetry' and 'poem' are all derived from the Greek word *poeio* meaning 'to make'. When we write something poetic we are making something new – and new connection between words which sheds new light. The way poetry does this is through metaphor; the meaning of a word is carried ('-phor') beyond ('meta-') its original meaning to something new.

Metaphor has made a comeback in recent years, along with other aspects of rhetoric, in academic reflection on issues of knowledge in relation to religion, and one of its champions has been the French philosopher Paul Ricœur.[18] Ricœur built on the analysis of previous commentators (particularly I. A. Richards [1936] and Monroe Beardsley [1958, 1962, 1967]) to notice that metaphor involves three elements – the subject of the metaphor (the thing the metaphor is about, implicitly or explicitly), the vehicle (the word you are using to describe the subject) and the tenor (what it is you are communicating in the metaphor). In simple metaphors it is easy to identify the different elements. In the saying 'This is a pig of a problem' the subject is the problem, and vehicle is 'pig' and the tenor has to do with difficulty. But in most use, things get a little more complicated. In my first example, the subject is death, the vehicle is a sea journey (actually from Middle Earth to the Undying Lands in the book) and the tenor is . . . well, something hope-filled to do with perfection and peace, drawing on archetypal imagery with perhaps echoes of childhood idyll.

. . . rooted in a rediscovery of the metaphors of Scripture

But Ricœur went much further in describing the importance of metaphor. For one thing, metaphor is the key way in which language develops to describe new realities. If you have 'surfed' the internet today, worried about 'inflation' (a metaphor coined in the eighteenth century) or reflected on how much your behaviour was shaped by your genes, those little 'packets' of information affecting your make-up, then you can see how dependent we are on metaphors for giving us a grasp of the complicated world we live in. Once a metaphor has been coined, as it becomes part of common usage then the tenor of the metaphor actually becomes part of the (lexical) meaning of the word – but not before another aspect of reality has been conquered.

This relates to Ricœur's other key claim. Metaphor does not simply embellish language; it is also an important part of the way we construct our perception of the world. Metaphor has cognitive content; it tells us what reality is like, as much as (so-called) scientific language.[19] This is a big challenge to our Enlightenment heritage in the West, but it is good for Christian belief, since so much biblical language about God is metaphorical. God is a creator, he is father, he is commander of the heavenly army (the meaning behind the Hebrew translated 'almighty') and so on. Jesus is rescuer, shepherd, gate, light, bread and path. These metaphors are not simply figures that can be explained better in a rational, propositional way; they are claims about spiritual reality which cannot be substituted. Even secular counsellors are recognizing the importance of metaphor in the way we perceive our worlds. I recently came across a website of someone offering to transform my outlook on life by offering new metaphors through which to see myself. Metaphors give us a powerful handle on reality. This is why the book of Revelation is at once the most mysterious but also most powerful book of the Bible, because it is so highly metaphorical.

In making claims about reality, metaphors don't simply describe one thing as another, but bring two aspects of our perceptual world into contact with one another. I remember as a fairly new father the first time I read Psalm 103.13 at a funeral service: 'As a father has compassion on his children, so the LORD has compassion on his faithful followers.' Not only was God father-like in his dealings with people; I was to be compassionate-God-like in my dealings with my children! This makes metaphor crucial for preaching, since we are always trying to make these connections between the two worlds of the text and of our hearers. I realized this when I reflected on sermons I had heard on David and Goliath. They almost always ended up with some form of the question: 'What are the giants you are facing in your life?'

We can not only see the possibilities of this kind of metaphorical bridging or extension within preaching; very often they are given for us in the text of Scripture, since (as Paul reminds us in 1 Corinthians 15) this good news has already been preached once, to the first generation of believers. So, while Mark recounts the crisis of the disciples in the boat during 'a great storm of wind' (4.37), and Luke 'a storm of wind' (8.23), for Matthew it is a *seismos*, a great 'shaking' (8.24). For Matthew, then, the voice of Jesus, which rebukes the wind and brings a calm, is a voice that can bring calm to any of life's storms, any 'shaking' of faith; this metaphorical 'surplus of meaning' is already evident in the text.

So, what is the future of language in preaching? In this strange new world, preachers will need to deploy persuasive speech, rooted in the rhetoric of biblical theology, that makes real, relevant and attractive the biblical metaphors describing what God has done for us in Christ and how this transforms and refigures our world.[20]

Notes

1. My favourite is the (possibly apocryphal) prediction of the former President of the Olivetti Corporation, who confidently asserted that in future the world would be in need of at most four computers.
2. Anthony Thiselton, in both his longer NIGTC commentary on 1 Corinthians (2000), and his shorter commentary (2006), connects the spiritual gift of prophecy in 1 Corinthians 12 with contemporary preaching, but (to my mind) collapses prophecy too much *into* preaching. Preaching is irreducibly prophetic if it is anything, but there is a prophetic ministry that happens in places other than the pulpit, exercised by people other than 'the preacher'.
3. Although this is very often the implicit assumption of context behind many discussions of preaching, both the vocabulary of preaching/ proclamation in the New Testament and the social settings in which it took place won't allow for such a limitation. See Jeremy Thomson's (1996) excellent study on this, especially ch. 2.
4. http://news.bbc.co.uk/1/hi/england/wear/8146460.stm accessed March 2010.
5. Lack of Bible knowledge is also becoming a serious issue in the academic study of literature and the arts. The former Poet Laureate Andrew Motion said that lack of the Bible and classical mythology made it 'difficult to even get beyond go', when teaching some of his recent students. John Mullan, professor of English at University College London, comments: 'I recently have interviewed quite a lot of candidates who have done Measure for Measure, Shakespeare's play, for "A" level. Not a single one of them seemed to have known the title comes from Christ's Sermon on the Mount and that might

make a difference to what the play's about.' See http://news.bbc. co.uk/1/hi/entertainment/7894563.stm accessed March 2010. American teachers and academics are also trying to get around the division between religion and state to teach the Bible as a cultural artefact. See http://blogs.usatoday.com/oped/2009/08/column-teach-the-bible-of-course-.html accessed March 2010.

6. It is worth noting that often in these churches the Bible is explored in other contexts, such as small groups. But it seems to me that there is a great danger in letting go of this corporate engagement in the context of public worship.

7. See their excellent summary. Interestingly, those identifying as 'evangelical' did hold to biblical doctrines, and Astley and Christie note that 'They appear to have been explicitly taught christological orthodoxy as part of what they call "*classic evangelical thinking*"' (2007, p. 11; italics theirs). Their recommendation is that we ought to broaden our idea of what constitutes 'orthodoxy', though perhaps a more obvious conclusion is that Anglicans should be better taught about their faith.

8. In Fee and Stuart 1983 and later editions, the entire framework of which is genre recognition. I am aware that this growth in literacy is very uneven, given the continuing poor levels of attainment particularly in areas of social deprivation. Rather than uniformly increasing literacy, government education policy could be seen to have both increased but also polarized literacy, with certain social groups becoming more literate but a continuing underclass remaining functionally illiterate.

9. Quoted in Razia Iqbals's BBC blog from Tuesday 20 January 2009, http://www.bbc.co.uk/blogs/thereporters/raziaiqbal/2009/01/the_power_of_language.html accessed in March 2010.

10. Both transcripts of the speech itself and analyses of its features are plentiful on the internet.

11. See the section 'How to give a talk', in Watson, 1985.

12. From Barack Obama's Inaugural Presidential Address: 'Homes have been lost; jobs shed; businesses shuttered . . . all are equal, all are free, and all deserve a chance . . . the risk-takers, the doers, the makers of things . . . For us, they packed up . . . /For us, they toiled . . . /For us, they fought and died . . . we have duties to ourselves, our nation, and the world . . . This is the price . . . /This is the source . . . /This is the meaning . . . ' and so on!

13. This is certainly the case for his 2003 New Cambridge Bible Commentary on Revelation, the one I am most familiar with.

14. The terms 'behind the text', 'within the text' and 'in front of the text' arise from the work of Paul Ricœur.

15. Assuming, for the moment, Pauline authorship.
16. To see the connection with chiasmus, take Lowry's 'loop' picture and turn it on its side.
17. Fulcrum is a network of 'open' evangelicalism in the Church of England; see www.fulcrum-anglican.org.uk.
18. On this, see particularly Ricœur, 1970, 1976 and 1977, the last most notable by the abysmal translation of its French title, *Le Metaphor Vive*. For an excellent introduction to Ricœur's work, see Stiver, 2001.
19. And there is a whole fruitful area of apologetic discussion to be had in exploring the relation between metaphors in religious language and models in science.
20. Some of the material here first appeared in an article on 'Poetry as Preaching' in *The Preacher* magazine. I am grateful to Dr Mark Bonnington for kick-starting some ideas on this subject, to Andrew Talbert for some very helpful research that supported the writing of this chapter, and to Geoffrey Stevenson for his extraordinary editorial patience.

References

Astley, Jeff, and Ann Christie, 2007, *Taking Ordinary Theology Seriously*, Cambridge: Grove Books.

Barth, Karl, 1991, *Homiletics*, trans. Geoffrey W. Bromiley and Donald E. Daniels, Louisville, KY: Westminster John Knox Press.

Beardsley, Monroe, 1958, *Aesthetics: Problems in the Philosophy of Criticism*, New York: Harcourt, Brace & World.

_____, 1962, 'The metaphorical twist', *Philosophy and Phenomenological Research* 22, pp. 293–307.

_____, 1967, 'Metaphor', in *Encyclopedia of Philosophy*, ed. Paul Edwards, New York: Macmillan, pp. 284–9.

Boyd-Macmillan, Ron, 2006, *Explosive Preaching: Letters on Detonating the Gospel in the 21st Century*, Milton Keynes: Paternoster.

Culpepper, Alan, 1983, *Anatomy of the Fourth Gospel: A Study in Literary Design*, Philadelphia: Fortress Press.

Fee, Gordon, and Douglas Stuart, 1983, *How to Read the Bible for All Its Worth*, London: Scripture Union.

Johnson, Darrell, 2009, *The Glory of Preaching: Participating in God's Transformation of the World*, Downers Grove, IL: IVP Academic.

Lowry, Eugene, 2001, *The Homiletical Plot: The Sermon as Narrative Art Form*, expanded edn, Louisville: Westminster John Knox Press.

Paul, Ian, 2008, 'Poetry as Preaching', *The Preacher* 130, July, pp. 5–6.

Richards, I. A., 1936, *The Philosophy of Rhetoric*, Oxford: Oxford University Press.

Ricœur, Paul, 1970, *Freud and Philosophy: An Essay on Interpretation*, New Haven: Yale University Press.

_____, 1976, *Interpretation Theory: Discourse and the Surplus of Meaning*, Fort Worth: Texas Christian University Press.

_____, 1977, *The Rule of Metaphor: Multi-Disciplinary Studies of the Creation of Meaning in Language*, London: Routledge.

Stiver, Dan, 2001, *Theology after Ricœur: New Directions in Hermeneutical Theology*, Louisville: Westminister John Knox Press.

Thiselton, Anthony C., 2000, *The First Epistle to the Corinthians: A Commentary on the Greek Text*, The New International Greek Testament Commentary, Carlisle: Pasternoster.

_____, 2006, *First Corinthians: A Shorter Exegetical and Pastoral Commentary*, Grand Rapids, Mich.: William B. Eerdmans.

_____, 2007, *The Hermeneutics of Doctrine*, Grand Rapids, MI: Eerdmans.

Thomson, Jeremy, 1996, *Preaching as Dialogue*, Cambridge: Grove Books.

Watson, David, 1985, *Discipleship*, London: Hodder and Stoughton.

Wilson, Paul Scott, 1994, *The Practice of Preaching*, rev. edn, Nashville: Abingdon.

Witherington, Ben, III, 2003, *Revelation*, New Cambridge Bible Commentary, Cambridge: Cambridge University Press.

I I

Sermon Form in a Digital Future

RICHARD LITTLEDALE

Introduction

In years gone by vending machines only ever seemed to sell quite ordinary things, like cigarettes or chocolate bars. Since then, however, they have really taken off, and you can buy all kinds of weird and wonderful things from them. I have seen machines selling everything from live fishing bait to piping hot baguettes in an old Norman town.

So how about a sermon-vending machine? With a simple coin inserted in the slot, a sermon could be delivered to the customer on the forecourt, or in the library, or even in the shopping centre. For wider appeal, they could be colour-coded to suit your mood, or labelled with an appropriate 'emoticon' to ease selection. A smiley face could indicate an upbeat, affirming sermon, while a sad one could warn of a challenging one and so on. In no time at all, sermons could be delivered to the masses, available on demand at any time of day or night.

Some might argue that this has already happened, with the increasing popularity of the podcast. Thousands of churches now offer 'banks' of recorded sermons via the worldwide web to a global audience. The cost is minimal to the church and non-existent to the customer. The sermons can be selected on the basis of preacher, subject, biblical material, or date preached. Once downloaded, they can be transferred to portable media and listened to in the car, on the beach, or even in the gym. The potential audience is in the millions, and the need for attendance at church is non-existent.

Without too much effort we could gaze into the future to a point where attendance at church to listen to a sermon would seem as strange as writing this book in a flowing hand with a fountain pen, or as self-indulgent as smoking on a crowded bus. We could all leave our cars at home, give the planet a breather by not driving to church, and tune in at home to a live-streaming webcast of this week's sermon instead. Of course, if we didn't fancy it, we could always tune in to last week's instead, or hop channels to another church for a change of theology. Those with bigger budgets may be able to use holographic technology – permitting them the dubious privilege of hosting a three-dimensional broadcast preacher in their living room! Is this the future of preaching?

The threat of technology

A future where preaching is altogether divorced from a face-to-face encounter between a real preacher, warts and all, and a real congregation with all their faults, is a bleak one indeed. Hard-wired into the human psyche is our need to hear the most important and profound messages in person. Anyone who has ever sought to find out information about a relative in hospital and has been confronted instead with an automated phone menu will know what this is all about. Preaching, surely, reflects our need for human encounter and arises out of a relationship between preacher and people? This is why the most fruitful preaching is often that which arises out of an established, local, ministry, rather than the hit-and-run of the itinerant preacher. In a local setting, there is a sense in which preaching is 'organic'. It grows out of the soil of shared experience, and is watered by the sweat and tears of preacher and people alike. It both arises from, and comments upon, their lives together. When a pastor preaches on long-suffering on a Sunday, after burying a beloved servant of the church on the previous Friday, there is something to be read in his eyes by those who were there at both. This will not be possible for the person who simply 'tunes in' to the sermon from a distance podcast or streaming audio.

From the first oracles delivered by the prophets of old, on through Jesus on the Mount, to Paul in the Areopagus and Desmond Tutu on the streets of Cape Town – preaching has been incarnational. Preachers have paved the way for their message with their lives and sometimes paid its price with their deaths. Preaching is not truth delivered in a pre-packaged way, as one might receive notes of a lecture which you were unable to attend. Richard Lischer asks, in *The End of Words*, 'how does one reduce to a series of bullet points Abraham's journey of faith or the Lord's agony in Gethsemane?' (2005, p. 26). He goes on to ask what Martin Luther King's 'I have a dream' speech might have looked like in PowerPoint. Preaching is truth dwelling in flesh and blood, which has not only a voice, but arms and legs too. For every preacher this is a mixed blessing – for the truth preached on Sunday will be judged by the life lived on Monday. It is a mixed blessing for the congregation too – for the hands they raised in blessing on the Sunday must be used to serve their fellow man on a Monday. Incarnated preaching is a mixed blessing, but it *is* a blessing –

and it will not be available to a congregation who are linked only by technology.

There is a sense, too, in which sermons should not live forever. Although as Christians we may baulk at the description, to an extent every sermon is existential – making the most of the unrepeatable moment in which it is preached and useless thereafter. Like the manna of old, descending as God's bountiful provision for his people fresh each day, it goes off if kept too long. Of course there are some sermons of such staggering beauty and immense depth that they will be studied and appreciated long after their language seems antiquated and their points of cultural reference have disappeared into obscurity. However, they are few and far between. The technology that delivers a back catalogue of sermons to your desktop may be delivering a stale diet to your faith.

The promise of technology

It is all too easy to demonize technology, and to set about it with a Luddite hammer, which we mistakenly label as 'faith'. Christianity, which harnessed the printing press to bring the Bible to the masses and uses helicopters to rescue the remotest victims of natural disaster, should not fight shy of technology that could benefit the preacher. For all the concerns about the use of technology in preaching, the worldwide web nonetheless opens up an audience for our preaching of which our forebears could not have dreamt. With the use of simple, affordable, technology, your sermon preached today could be heard tomorrow by millions, even in places where the gospel is forbidden. Not only that, but the hours you spent in preparing and writing it will not be over and done with in the twenty minutes or so it takes to preach it. A person who was there on Sunday and missed a particular nuance can listen to it again and again to clarify it in their mind. A person who is too hesitant to ever come on Sunday can nonetheless hear an authentic word.

Technology can enhance the live delivery of that word too. Presentation software, such as PowerPoint, can be a tremendous asset to the preacher if used carefully. On the 25th anniversary of its launch Microsoft claimed that the average PowerPoint presentation lasted 250 minutes.[1] Thankfully few sermons last quite so long, but preachers can use this technology to enhance their 20 or 25 minutes. For visual learners in the congregation, the use of one or two carefully selected images can really enhance the verbal message. Two or three phrases can provide a helpful 'map' of where the sermon is heading, too, and can help with retention of the points made. Not only this, but the fact that they can be revealed gradually as the sermon progresses can ensure that everybody clearly understands where the sermon has been and where it is heading. Of course, it must be used with restraint. All too often the ease of using this technology leads to us being cavalier in its application. A set of slides with moving graphics, animated texts and zany colour schemes can be so 'busy' that they distract the congregation from what is being said, rather than underpinning it. Clicking the mouse button in haste may lead to both preacher and people repenting at leisure.

There are a number of simple rules that should be observed when using this software. First, it should only enhance the verbal material delivered by the preacher, rather than the sermon relying upon it. This is a lesson I was taught very powerfully when preaching with an old-fashioned overhead projector in India. When the electricity supply cannot be relied upon, it is unwise to depend too much on your visual aids. Furthermore, a sermon that makes no sense without the visual material excludes those who cannot see. Second, an overall colour scheme of words and background should be chosen for ease of viewing. Contrast is important – either dark on light or light on dark. A softer colour palate, however, will be better for those with any mild visual impairment. Third, the few words of each bullet point should be in the biggest and simplest font that the slide will accommodate, and any pictures should be inserted with a border. A white border is best on a dark background and a black border on a white one. This will ensure that the image stands out on the slide. Finally, slide transitions and custom animations of text and graphics should be kept as simple as possible. A slide that is too busy or zany will simply distract the congregation.

Affordable technology can also allow the congregation to span the miles in ways hitherto impossible. At a youth service on the theme of trust and courage, our sermon was preached by a missionary live from his home in Ethiopia. Sitting there in his distant home, to which faith and trust had taken him, he addressed the issues over the phone to the waiting congregation in London, while his picture was projected onto a screen behind the pulpit. Although this was done via an ordinary phone line, it could also have been done for nothing over broadband-based phone via two computers. It gave an edge to the theme, and also allowed the congregation to stay 'as one', even when separated by distance. In years gone by this kind of thing would have been beyond the budget and know-how of many congregations. Thankfully this is no longer the case, and we can explore creative ways of engaging the more distant members of the congregation in the ministry of the Word.

Technology can also help to extend the life of the sermon beyond the time when it was preached. This is the case not only with podcasts, as discussed above, but also with the interactive applications that typify Web2.0. Live 'chatter' sites such as Twitter mean that the content of a sermon can be discussed by preacher, congregation and anyone else who wants to join in within minutes of the close of the service at which it is preached. A person too shy to tackle the preacher directly about a point that was obscure or provocative in the sermon might be very happy to do so online. Blogging provides a facility for a reasoned and protracted debate on issues raised by the sermon in the week after it is preached. People whose lifestyle would not permit them to attend a church Bible study or discussion group can participate in such a debate even on their way to work.

Another development of Web 2.0 is the creation of virtual congregations that exist only in cyberspace. One such is Second Life, founded by Linden Lab in 1999.[2] In this virtual world there are shops, entertainment venues, academic centres and even sacred spaces. Some of these venues are owned by private individuals, some by commercial organizations, and some by colleges and universities. At any one time in this virtual space there may be live music performances, business seminars, academic tutorials and marketing promotions taking place. Everyone who participates in this virtual world creates a visual representation or 'avatar' of themselves that can travel from (virtual) place to place and converse with the avatars of others. In 2007 the Anglican Cathedral of Second Life was opened. In this virtual worship space people can meet, pray, worship and discuss much as they could in its real equivalent. It now has over 400 members, holds services twice each Sunday, and hosts midweek prayer and Bible study meetings. During a service, the 'avatars' of people attending sit in the pews, participate in the liturgy and listen to a recorded sermon. One of the more bizarre aspects of this is that the congregation may consist of everything from pink-haired punk rockers and fantasy creatures with wings to suited businessmen. However, it also means that people who would otherwise be kept from Christian worship are able to attend. A paraplegic person, with no hope of moving beyond the walls of her home, can worship alongside people from other towns, countries and even continents.

This, surely, is a brave new world of technology? Like any other brave new world, its rules are as yet unwritten, and its territory uncharted. Mistakes will be made. Some old traditions will be thoughtlessly discarded and some new trends carelessly embraced. However, if the word is to be preached to 'every creature' then some of them may have to be found in the virtual world. We can either dismiss environments such as Second Life as the vacuous preserve of the technological geek, or we can look to see what opportunities it might present for the furtherance of the gospel.

A new context

Changes in the future will be brought about not just by the way that sermons are delivered but also by the context into which they are delivered. Following the discovery that many young British Muslims were being radicalized by preaching in their mosques, and in the wake of Imam Abu Hamza's arrest and deportation, the Religious and Racial Hatred Act was enacted in 2006. This Act forbade the use of preaching to incite religious and racial hatred. Reactions were mixed among the Christian community, with some perceiving it as a curtailment of religious liberty and others as a sensible move. What is clear, however, was that for the first time in several generations the British government was taking preaching so seriously that it had to be policed. Instead of seeing it as the province of the harmless cleric, it was seen as a powerful tool to motivate and inspire – either for good or for ill. Preaching in such a context is a different animal from the one with which many preachers have grown up. Training for preaching and the delivery of sermons will have to be treated with the utmost seriousness within the Church when those outside the Church are acknowledging its importance in this way.

Another change in the context has been brought about by political upheaval on the other side of the Atlantic. In President Barack Obama the United States of America has elected a president who often sounds more like a preacher. The content and tone of his addresses often carry the cadences of the pulpit more than those of the debating chamber. The structure of his speeches and the poetry of his language have given public speaking a good name once again. Many hardened pundits and political commentators have found themselves, almost reluctantly, acknowledging the power of rhetoric. In such a context, preachers should find themselves with a new liberty to express the Bible's timeless truths with a poetic and prophetic intensity too long neglected. We cannot, surely, allow the politicians to tug the heartstrings harder than the preachers?

The battle, however, is not over. Many will still point to the fact that outside the Church (and now the Senate House) there are few places where one talks and many listen. School classrooms, where pupils once sat in serried ranks to listen in silence to the wisdom of their teacher, are now very different places. Today they are noisy places, with all kinds of student–teacher interaction and group learning. The same could be said for higher education, where only a small proportion of learning is delivered in the lecture format. In the workplace, too, continuing professional development is more often delivered through interaction and group work than by one speaking and all listening. Set against such a backdrop, preaching can seem old-fashioned. The preacher delivering received wisdom to a silent group where there is no interaction or challenge can seem autocratic and out of place. We should not, though, be thoughtlessly swept along by this view.

We can point to the biblical story and show that on many occasions God has used the mode of preaching to address the needs of many through the inspired individual. We see this when Ezra addressed the crowds of the faithful in the rebuilt city of Jerusalem. Builders who had just downed tools from their construction work picked them up one last time to construct a wooden pulpit so that a preacher could stand upon it, read from God's words and make God-sense of all the changes they had been through. In this particular instance there was not only a preacher but also a group of his assistants who passed through the crowd explaining the word preached to the crowd. There is some uncertainty about the translation of Nehemiah 8.8, since the preacher's assistants may have been 'translating' the preached word, 'explaining' the preached word or, literally, 'chopping it up'. What is clear is that they were performing a vital task in making the word of God clear in a situation of uncertainty and confusion.

Similarly in the heady chaos of Jerusalem on Pentecost day, Peter took to the stage, raising his voice above the hubbub of the crowd and articulating these perplexing events in the light of ancient promises. From his words 'let me explain this to you' in Acts 2.14 flowed the first recorded sermon of the Christian Church. As the tapestry of church history unfurled, the preachers were there at many of its key stages, in order to make sense of what was happening both inside and outside the churches. Reformation inside the Church and warfare outside of it brought preachers to the fore in order to speak a holy word to a waiting crowd. That this is still the case is evidenced by the upsurge of church attendance at times of crisis. It was seen in the wake of the Twin Towers attack in New York in 2001 and also in the first few months of global recession. Despite the accusations of preaching seeming outmoded or autocratic, people still need preachers, it would seem. Rumours of the death of preaching have been greatly exaggerated.

A new language

The fact that preaching still has a place, however, should not make the preachers complacent. Indeed, the fact that they are needed should make them all the more resolved to hone their skills. In order to do so in such a way as to maintain and improve their role in public life, they may need to look beyond the theological seminaries to sharpen their preaching reflexes. Many global corporations spend huge amounts of money on their internal and external communication. A whole industry has sprung up around motivational communication and change empowerment. Since both are in the Church's remit, albeit for different reasons, they should be studied by preachers too.

One element of this 'secular' communication industry is the power of story to motivate and inspire on the grand scale. Top-flight managers are taught to listen to the story of their employees, and then to reflect it back with the story of their organization's goals and aspirations. Many of the world's most successful companies have built a narrative around their particular product and the contribution it makes to human life. That narrative is presented to the consumer, discussed in the boardroom and fed back to the staff at every level. Since churches are communities of faith built around the great narrative of salvation there is scope for them to perform a similar operation. It would be a sad thing if a Christian finds more motivational rhetoric in the workplace than in the Church. This means that preachers need to be good not only at articulating the great story in the pulpit but also at hearing it in the little stories of faith and triumph in the congregation. These should then be reflected back in such a way as to preserve the anonymity of their source but to encourage the wider body of believers. Clearly this takes a great deal of skill, but it can pay enormous dividends in motivating the faith community to achieve great things together as they hear that it is working.

In order to harness this great power of story, as Jesus and the prophets have done before them, the preacher must be prepared to work hard. He or she must be prepared to invest more time in the simple reading of Scripture, unfettered by commentaries or reference works, than they have ever done before. Through this 'deep' reading of Scripture not only the words but also the rhythms, the timbre, the very essence of this living word will permeate them. A great storyteller must really hear the story before ever it is told. The same goes for hearing the little stories of faith in the congregation too. Hours spent listening to seemingly inconsequential chatter are not an alternative to the serious work of sermon preparation, but part of it. To feel the heartbeat of the people in the street, or in their homes, or at the hospital bed, means that the story of faith can be told in a way that resonates. When it is told, the preacher must be prepared to invest extra time in choosing the words for the telling. Like a cabinetmaker poring over a selection of veneers to choose one with just the right pattern in the grain, so the preacher must linger long over his or her vocabulary in order to achieve the right effect. It is worth taking twice as long to choose half as many words if the story is to be told with power and conviction.

Outside the Church, communicators are not only unleashing the power of story to motivate but also looking to the unspoken elements of verbal communication, such as stance, posture, gesture and even facial expression. People training to communicate outside the Church will be taught not only to read body and facial language but also to write it. Thus, for instance, a speaker who wants to reflect on what has been will step back from the podium. A speaker who wants to put forward a brave new concept will step forward towards his audience, and one who wants to exude calm and competence will work on minimizing his movement in order to project stability and trustworthiness. A great example of this can be seen in Barack Obama's acceptance speech at the Democrat Convention on 28 August 2008. His stable posture and restrained gestures were designed to draw attention away from his youth and towards his qualities as a statesman.

Neurolinguistic programming, first introduced in the 1970s, teaches communicators to read the micro-gestures of the faces on those with whom they communicate. This is not just the obvious ones like the eyes drifting to the watch or falling shut which mean that the attention is waning. Instead they are much more subtle, such as the eyes drifting up and to the left when a person reflects on a past action or up and to the right when contemplating a new project. Skilled communicators are able not just to read these but also to use them to underpin their words in many subtle ways. Even an experienced preacher may have to return to practising a sermon or two in front of the mirror if he wants to harness all these insights.

Such things may seem a long way from the homiletics classroom. Indeed, to some they may seem like some form of witch-doctoring. However, if preaching is to retain a hearing in the noisy marketplace of ideas, then it must keep up. Preachers must develop great skills in reading their congregations, and capitalize on the full panoply of communicators' skills. There was a time when preachers were the only educated and skilful orators out there. This is no longer so, and they must hone their skills wherever they can, or be silenced.

Plus ça change

It is important, however, to retain a sense of perspective. Technological changes may mean that preaching is delivered in different formats.

A congregation may no longer gather at the same place and time to hear a sermon any more than they all gather at the same place and time to watch television. Not only that, but developments in the field of human communication may mean that verbal and non-verbal communication are constantly changing. Preachers must be aware of these things if they want to be heard. There are some things, though, that will always remain the same for preaching. These things are unchanged whether the sermon is delivered by streaming video or on a street corner. They will abide whether the sermon is delivered in a palace of glass and steel or in a musty church hall.

Relationship

Successful communication is born of integral relationships. Regardless of the technology through which they deliver their sermons, preachers will find in the future that the quality of the congregation's listening on a Sunday will depend upon the quality of their own listening Monday to Friday. They may have to work harder on this, as economic constraints mean that more adult members of the congregation will be working long hours and will not be seen in church from one week's end to the other. Indeed for some, the financial constraints may be so severe that attending church at all will be impossible, because working on numerous Sundays is a financial necessity. In such circumstances a preacher may find himself in the role of workplace chaplain if he wants to develop more than a passing acquaintance with his congregation.

Creative space

I am not referring to the space in which the sermon is delivered, nor even to the one in which it is crafted, but rather, the space between pulpit and pew (or lectern and chair) and the energy that infuses it. The very air between the two needs to be charged with energy and expectancy if a genuinely divine encounter is to happen in the space of the sermon. The preacher needs to bring all their prayerful endeavour and linguistic dexterity into that space. Phrases that 'will do' should be consciously exchanged for those that will excel. Words that will pass should be swapped for those that will tingle with energy. Equally, the listeners should not feel that their job is done simply by presenting themselves before the preacher and placing bottoms on seats. There is a work to be done in the days leading up to the sermon as urgent prayers are offered for the preacher's anointing and insight. Even as the sermon is delivered the praying should not stop, for the preacher's reticence or ineptitude may at times only be rectified by the prayers of others.

Discipline

Discipline is a terribly old-fashioned word, and one that is not popular with either preachers or listeners. However, no amount of resources or equipment will lift from the preacher the need for the disciplines associated with mining spiritual gold from the deep seams of Scripture. Time must be given to reading the text as it stands. Time must be given to reading what others have to say about it. Time, above all, must be spent in prayer in order to see what God has to say about it. In all our discussions about the form and delivery of sermons in the future, we must not forget that unless they are prepared they cannot be delivered. This preparation consists in preparing not just the words themselves but also the heart and mouth of the one who will deliver them. Time spent by preachers on their knees will repay dividends when they stand up to speak on God's behalf.

Diet

In any discussion of contemporary or future preaching, it is tempting to rush into a redefinition of those subjects upon which the preacher should touch. A world with instant communication, seismic economic shifts and global meltdown cries out for a different preaching diet, we are told. The preacher must be relevant in such a world as this. Indeed, he or she must – but relevant about what, and to whom? If relevant means preaching about today's news topic, then it may well be out of date by the time we preach it tomorrow. And anyway, isn't preaching more about tomorrow, or even the day after tomorrow, than it is about today? The preacher's skill has always been twofold. In the first place he must exercise sufficient discernment to make God-sense of the things that go on around about him or her. In the second place he must learn to articulate that spiritual understanding in such a way that people are transformed. In the future the diet of preaching should be no more dominated by contemporary issues than it is today.

Coupled with this increasing global awareness is decreasing biblical awareness. In 2009 the National Biblical Literacy survey revealed that though 75 per cent of those asked owned a Bible few ever read it; 57 per cent of respondents, for instance, knew nothing about the story of

Joseph and his brothers and 60 per cent appeared never to have heard of the Good Samaritan. In such a context the preacher must increasingly act as the bridge between the puzzling events of today and the timeless truths of Scripture. Like the Men of Issachar in 1 Chronicles 12, he needs to 'understand the times and know what Israel should do'. This skill will also involve identifying the underlying issues in the topic of the day. Thus a story on sub-prime mortgages might be a story of greed, while a story about licensing life-saving drugs abroad might be all about neighbour love. These particular skills are discussed elsewhere in the chapter on preaching the news.

Conclusion

Until the sound of every human voice falls silent, there will be a place for the voice of the preacher. It may be heard directly from pulpit to pew, or indirectly via webcam and broadband. Since we are the children of a speaking God, we are speaking creatures, and will remain so. The form of the sermon is less important than its formulation out of the soil of Scripture and the cultural air we breathe. The key element of its delivery is not the technology or the technique but the devotion involved. The preachers of the future, if they exist, are people who devote every fibre and sinew of their being to the task, and trust to God to make use of their efforts.

Notes

1. http://news.bbc.co.uk/1/hi/magazine/8207849.stm
2. http://secondlife.com.

Reference

Lischer, Richard, 2005, *The End of Words*, Grand Rapids: Eerdmans.

PART THREE

People

12

Preaching and Personality

The SIFT Approach

LESLIE J. FRANCIS

Introduction

The SIFT (sensing, intuition, feeling and thinking) method of biblical hermeneutics and liturgical preaching was first introduced and tested in my book *Personality Type and Scripture* (Francis, 1997) after ten years or so of routinely using the method in my own preaching and of exploring the wider relevance and application through workshops and training events for clergy and lay ministers. I have been particularly grateful to two colleagues for working with me on refining, applying and testing the underlying theory and the practical applications of the method. First, Bishop Peter Atkins collaborated with me in applying the method systematically to the Gospel readings set by the *Revised Common Lectionary* for the principal Sunday services. Together, we tested the method on 152 Gospel lections. At least as far as the four canonical Gospels are concerned, the method was shown to be robust and generally applicable (see Francis and Atkins, 2000, 2001, 2002). Second, Professor Andrew Village collaborated with me in examining the theoretical bases of the method within the broader context of contemporary hermeneutical approaches. The method was shown to be coherent and connected with the wider literature (see Francis and Village, 2008).

The claim to have established a fresh approach to biblical hermeneutics and liturgical preaching is a bold claim. Some indeed might consider such an innovation is both unnecessary and unwise given the long-established history both of biblical interpretation and of biblical preaching (in both liturgical and non-liturgical contexts). Defence of the SIFT method rests on three fields of debate: contemporary developments in hermeneutics; a theology of individual differences grounded in a strong doctrine of creation; and an appreciation of psychological type theory. My aim in this chapter is to discuss these three issues, to explore the connection between psychological type and preaching and to define the SIFT approach. Then I will display the method in practice.

Leslie J. Francis

Contemporary hermeneutics

A major development in the theory and practice of biblical criticism in recent years has concerned the emergence of the crucial issue of perspective or standpoint in the reading and interpretation of biblical texts. The issue of perspective or standpoint takes seriously the role of the reader in interpretation. Within this tradition of biblical hermeneutics particular attention has been given to the formative influence of the social location of the reader, as so well illustrated by the title of the volumes edited by Segovia and Tolbert (1995), *Reading from This Place*. In their preface to this collection of essays, Segovia and Tolbert (1995, vol. 1, p. ix) draw attention to the way in which the foundation was set by such movements as feminist criticism, literacy criticism, sociological analysis, and liberation and contextual theologies, all of which questioned the implied claims of the older and established exegetical and theological methods to promote universal and objective interpretation under the construct of an objective and scientific reader. Thus, according to Segovia and Tolbert (1995, vol. 1, p. ix),

> factors traditionally left out of consideration were now becoming areas of exploration – for example, gender, race, ethnic origins, class, sexual orientation, religious affiliation, and socio-political contexts – with a focus on real, flesh-and-blood readers . . . whose reading and interpretation of the texts were seen as affected by their social location.

In other words, concepts, theories and heuristic tools of modern sociology were becoming powerful instruments in the discipline of biblical hermeneutics.

The key perspective of sociology within the process of biblical hermeneutics is made explicit in an essay by Segovia:

> I believe that the time has come to introduce the real reader, the flesh-and-blood reader, fully and explicitly, into the theory and practice of biblical criticism; to acknowledge that no reading, informed or uninformed, takes place in a social vacuum or desert . . . with a view of all readings as constructs proceeding from, dependent upon, and addressing a particular social location . . . I should like to propose, therefore, the beginning of a hermeneutical framework for taking the flesh-and-blood reader seriously in biblical criticism, not so much as a unique and independent individual but rather as a member of distinct and identifiable social configurations. (1995, vol. 1, pp. 57–8)

The SIFT method of biblical hermeneutics and liturgical preaching takes very seriously two themes proposed by this stream within contemporary hermeneutical theory. The first theme concerns the active role of the reader in the interpretative process. The second theme concerns the constructive role of the social sciences (specifically sociology) in sharpening understanding and appreciation of the distinctive contexts within which interpretation takes place. The bold contribution of the SIFT method is to suggest that psychology should be invited to offer a perspective on biblical hermeneutics alongside the perspective offered by sociology. The rationale for such a contribution is supported by the growing appreciation of the perspective offered by the theology of individual differences.

Theology of individual differences

The theology of individual differences, grounded in a strong doctrine of creation, argues that a certain deep level of human difference (in which psychology takes a proper interest) reflects the intentionality of the divine creator. If such a view can be maintained, it has significant implications for understanding and interpreting the role of the reader in biblical hermeneutics.

A primary task of the Christian theologian is to test the logic and internal coherence of claims made within Christian teaching. The use of psychological insights into the interpretation and proclamation of Scripture needs to be rigorously tested against (and integrated within) a coherent understanding of the major themes of Christian teaching as encapsulated, for example, by the key doctrines of creation, fall, salvation through the person of Christ, and sanctification through the work of the Holy Spirit.

The psychological insight on which we are drawing concerns the identification of the deep-seated components of human personality and belongs to the tradition known as the 'psychology of individual differences'. According to our understanding, the psychology of individual differences can be grounded within a 'theology of individual differences'. This notion of the theology of individual differences is first and foremost grounded in a Christian doctrine of creation. The biblical basis for this doctrine of creation is informed by Genesis 1.27:

God created humankind in the image of God, in the image of God, God created them, male and female God created them. (Author's translation.)

The key insight provided by this biblical basis for a doctrine of creation is that God embraces diversity and that such diversity is reflected in those created in the image of God. The notion that God embraces diversity is clearly consistent with the Christian doctrine of Trinity and was also clearly anticipated within that strand in the opening books of the Old Testament that use a plural noun for God, as in Genesis 1.27.

In contrast with the narrative concerning Adam and Eve, a doctrine of creation grounded in Genesis 1.27 is committed theologically to recognizing both men and women to be created equally in the image of God, and to arguing that individual differences that are created equal (male and female) need to be accorded equal value and equal status. If such a theology of individual differences holds good for sex differences then, by extension, such a theology should hold good also for other differences equally grounded in creation, that is to say in the intentionality of the divine creator. Such differences may well include those of ethnicity and those of personality. Before examining the implications of such a view, the Christian doctrine of creation needs to be set alongside the Christian doctrine of the fall.

The key point made by the Christian doctrine of the fall is that the image of the creator seen in the human creature is no longer unsullied. The image has been corrupted. The task to be undertaken by a sound theology of individual differences is to attempt to untangle those differences that can reasonably be posited to reflect the fall and those that persist as proper indicators of the image and of the intention of the divine creator. Those individual differences that reflect the corruption brought about by the fall must rightly be subject to the saving and transforming power of Christ (the doctrine of redemption) and the perfecting power of the Holy Spirit (the doctrine of sanctification). Those individual differences that reflect the divine image of the creator may need to be given proper respect and value in the hermeneutical dialogue between text and interpretation.

In the light of a doctrine of creation grounded in Genesis 1.27, the individual difference of sex (male and female) may be properly seen as reflecting creation rather than fall. As a consequence it becomes theologically inappropriate to call, say, on men to repent and to become women, or on women to repent and to become men. The argument seems equally strong to propose that the individual difference of ethnicity may be properly seen as reflecting creation rather than fall. Again, as a consequence, it becomes theologically inappropriate to call, say, on white people to repent and to become people of colour, or on people of colour to repent and to become white. There are, of course, enormous political implications that emerge from such a simple (and profound) theology of individual differences.

While the case may seem relatively clear-cut in respect of sex and ethnicity, the argument regarding individual differences in personality may prove to be somewhat more controversial. The problem arises, at least in part, from a real lack of clarity regarding ways in which the term personality itself can be used, especially in colloquial usage. The professional debate needs to be sharpened, therefore, by distinguishing between two related, but potentially very distinct, terms (personality and character) and further by distinguishing between two related, but potentially very distinct, branches of psychology in which the term personality is used (normal psychology and abnormal psychology).

Normal psychology is concerned with describing, understanding and interpreting variations within the normal population. In this context 'personality' is employed to define some of those normal variations. Abnormal psychology is concerned with describing, understanding and responding to psychological abnormalities and mental disorders of varying degrees of severity. In this context 'personality disorder' is employed to characterize dysfunctional behaviour. The ensuing discussion is rooted in the analysis of normal personality as distinct from a concern with personality disorders.

As generally employed within the normal psychology of individual differences, the term personality is reserved for those deep-seated individual differences that reflect something of the individual's genetic roots, while character reflects individual qualities that are nearer the surface. Qualities that define personality are largely immutable (like sex and ethnicity), while qualities that define character are open to change and to development. Qualities that define personality should be morally neutral and value-free (like sex and ethnicity), while qualities that define character should be highly significant in terms of morality and personal values.

An example of individual differences in personality is provided by the well-understood distinction between introversion and extraversion. Personality theory does not claim that extraverts are (in any sense) better or worse than introverts. Introverts and extraverts are just different and, as a consequence, introverts can do some things better than extraverts and extraverts can do some things better than introverts. In other words, introverts do not need to become extraverts in order to become better people, nor do extraverts need to become introverts in order to become better people.

An example of individual differences in character is provided by the equally well-understood distinction between pride and humility. Moral theology is clear that one of these qualities is far superior to the other. Pride is looked upon as a consequence of the fall. This is not how in the beginning God intended people to be. Humility is looked upon as a sign of God's grace and redemption. This is how God intends redeemed people to become.

Thus, while normal personality is value neutral, character is heavily value-laden. An extravert can develop a good character, sharing the fruits of the Spirit as described in Galatians 5 (love, joy, peace, patience, kindness, generosity, faithfulness, gentleness and self-control), or an extravert can develop a bad character, sharing the works of the flesh as also described in Galatians 5 (licentiousness, strife, jealousy, anger, quarrels, envy and drunkenness). An introvert also has equal opportunities to develop a good character or to develop a bad character.

Psychological type theory

Psychological type theory proposes a model of normal personality, which has proved itself to be accessible and attractive to several branches of practical theology (Osborn and Osborn, 1991; Michael and Norrisey, 1984; Duncan, 1993; Goldsmith and Wharton, 1993; Baab, 1998), even though the application of this theory remains controversial among some religious and theological commentators (Leech, 1996; Lloyd, 2007). Psychological type theory has its origins in pioneering and creative work by Carl Jung (see, for example, Jung, 1971), but has been developed, clarified and popularized through a range of psychological assessment devices that have been applied within religious and theological contexts, most notably the Myers-Briggs Type Indicator (Myers and McCaulley, 1985), the Keirsey Temperament Sorter (Keirsey and Bates, 1978) and the Francis Psychological Type Scales (Francis, 2005).

The two orientations are concerned with where psychological energy is drawn from and focused. On the one hand, extraverts are orientated toward the outer world; they are energized by the events and people around them. They enjoy communicating and thrive in stimulating and exciting environments. They tend to focus their attention on what is happening outside themselves. They are usually open people, easy to get to know, and enjoy having many friends. On the other hand, introverts are orientated toward their inner world; they are energized by their inner ideas and concepts. They enjoy solitude, silence and contemplation, as they tend to focus their attention on what is happening in their inner life. They may prefer to have a small circle of intimate friends rather than many acquaintances.

The two perceiving functions are concerned with the way in which people perceive information. On the one hand, sensing types focus on the realities of a situation as perceived by the senses. They tend to focus on specific details, rather than on the overall picture. They are concerned with the actual, the real and the practical, and they tend to be down-to-earth and matter-of-fact. On the other hand, intuitive types focus on the possibilities of a situation, perceiving meanings and relationships. They may feel that perception by the senses is not as valuable as information gained when indirect associations and concepts impact on their perception. They focus on the overall picture, rather than on specific facts and data.

The two judging functions are concerned with the processes by which people make decisions and judgements. On the one hand, thinking types make judgements based on objective, impersonal logic. They value integrity and justice. They are known for their truthfulness and for their desire for fairness. They consider conforming to principles to be of more importance than cultivating harmony. On the other hand, feeling types make judgements based on subjective, personal values. They value compassion and mercy. They are known for their tactfulness, for their desire for peace and for their empathic capacity. They are more concerned to promote harmony than to adhere to abstract principles.

The two attitudes toward the outer world are concerned with which of the two sets of functions (that is, perceiving or judging) is preferred in dealings with the outer world. On the one hand, judging types seek to order, rationalize and structure their outer world, as they actively judge external stimuli. They enjoy routine and established patterns. They prefer to follow schedules in order to reach an established goal and may make use of lists, timetables or diaries. They tend to be punctual, organized and tidy. They prefer to make decisions quickly and to stick to their conclusions once made. On the other hand, perceiving types do not seek to impose order on the outer world, but are more reflective, perceptive and open, as they passively perceive external stimuli. They have a flexible, open-ended approach to life. They enjoy change and spontaneity. They prefer to leave projects open in order to adapt and improve them. Their behaviour may often seem impulsive and unplanned.

Jung's view is that each individual develops one of the perceiving functions (sensing or intuition) at the expense of the other and one of the judging functions (feeling or thinking) at the expense of the other. Moreover, for each individual either the preferred perceiving function or the preferred judging function takes preference over the other, leading to the emergence of one dominant function that shapes the individual's dominant approach to life. Dominant sensing shapes the practical person. Dominant intuition shapes the imaginative person. Dominant feeling shapes the humane person. Dominant thinking shapes the analytic person. According to Jungian type theory, the function paired with the dominant function is known as the 'inferior function'. It is here that individuals experience most difficulty. Thus dominant sensers may struggle with intuition; dominant intuitives may struggle with sensing; dominant feelers may struggle with thinking; and dominant thinkers may struggle with feeling.

The bold contribution of the SIFT method of biblical hermeneutics and liturgical preaching is to suggest that psychological type theory provides a coherent framework within which to locate both the role of the reader in biblical interpretation and the experience of the preacher in communication within the liturgical community.

Psychological type and preaching

Although it is the two core processes of perceiving (sensing and intuition) and judging (feeling and thinking) that are key to the SIFT method of biblical hermeneutics and liturgical preaching, the orientations (extraversion and introversion) and the attitudes toward the outer world (judging and perceiving) also are of considerable relevance to the ways in which preachers set about their task.

Introversion and extraversion

On the one hand, introverts like quiet for concentration. They want to be able to shut off the distractions of the outer world and turn inwards. Introverts work best alone and may dislike distractions and interruptions from other people. Introverts prefer to learn by reading rather than by discussing with others. They are reflective people who probe inwardly for stimulation.

In order to engage fully and effectively with their ministry of preaching, introverted preachers need to be able to step back from the business of daily life and to create enough space and solitude to reflect on the text of Scripture and on the context of the community among whom they will be preaching. For some, this may mean going into their own room and closing the door. For some, this may mean creating their own internal island of quiet on a busy train, in a busy street or in a crowded room. To be really creative introverts need to feel that they can be immune from interruption and distraction. The thought of the telephone sitting on the desk ready to ring at any moment may distract the introvert from settling to the task. For the introverted preacher the stimulation for reflection comes from the books on the shelf and the ideas stored in the mind.

On the other hand, extraverts like variety and action. They like to have other people around them, and enjoy the stimulation of interruptions. Extraverts prefer to learn by talking things through with other people. They often find that their own ideas become clarified through communicating them with others. They are active people who scan the outer environment for stimulation.

In order to engage fully and effectively with this ministry of preaching, extraverted preachers need to be able to engage with others in order to talk about and to discuss the text of Scripture and the context of the community among whom they will be preaching. For the extravert, sitting in a quiet room may be disabling. For the extravert, being left alone with the pile of commentaries may be quite unproductive. To be really creative, extraverts need to feel that they can discuss their developing ideas with others and seek clarification though dialogue and conversation. Extraverts would rather address their questions by asking others than by searching through reference books. A proper understanding of their own psychological type preferences may encourage a group of extraverted preachers to meet in order to discuss their sermon preparation. Or they may agree to speak by telephone as they recognize the need to draw on each other's support.

Psychological insight into the differences between introverts and extraverts makes it clear that there may be no one right way in which to prepare for preaching, but that there are different ways in which extraverts and introverts may do so more effectively. The difficulty, however, arises when introverted preachers try to teach extraverts to do things the introverted way, or vice versa.

Judging and perceiving

On the one hand, individuals who prefer to relate to the outer world with a judging process present a planned and orderly approach to life. They prefer to have a settled system in place and display a preference for closure. Judging types schedule projects so that each step gets done on time. They work best when they can plan their work in advance and then follow that plan. Judging types tend to be satisfied when they have finished what they set out to achieve. They dislike having to revise their decisions and having to take fresh information into account.

In order to engage fully and effectively with their ministry of preaching, judging preachers need to be able to plan and to structure their preparation and then to be able to implement that framework. For some this may mean structuring sermon preparation into the plan for the whole week.

There are some judging preachers who may follow the discipline of studying the text on Monday, relating the text to the local context on Tuesday, and writing out the whole sermon on Wednesday. That task completed, it is now possible to choose the hymns, to design the posters and to organize participation well in advance. There are other judging preachers who may plan a whole course of sermons weeks in advance and have everything ready and planned in the file for a whole sequence of Sundays well ahead of schedule.

On the other hand, individuals who prefer to relate to the outer world with a perceiving process present a flexible and spontaneous approach to life. They prefer to keep plans and organization to a minimum and display a preference for openness. Perceiving types adapt well to changing situations. They make allowances for new information and for changes in the situations in which they are living or acting. Perceiving types do not mind leaving things open for last-minute changes. They work best under pressure and get a lot accomplished at the last minute under the constraints of a deadline.

In order to engage fully and effectively with their ministry of preaching, perceiving preachers need to be able to keep their options open for as long as possible. For some this may mean reflecting on many different passages of Scripture during the course of the week, collecting and reflecting on apparently unrelated experiences and ideas, and resisting choosing the hymns and selecting the music until as late as possible. Perceiving preachers need the pressures that build up late on Saturday evening or early on Sunday morning before everything really begins to fall into place.

Psychological insight into the differences between judgers and perceivers makes it clear that there may be no one right way in which to prepare for preaching, but that there are different ways in which judgers and perceivers may do so more effectively. The difficulty, however, arises when preachers who prefer judging try to teach perceivers to do things the judging way, or vice versa.

Psychological type and the SIFT Method

In essence, the SIFT method of biblical hermeneutics and liturgical preaching systematically addresses to each passage of Scripture the four sets of questions posed by the four psychological functions of sensing (S), intuition (I), feeling (F) and thinking (T). The two perceiving functions (sensing and intuition) are applied first, since the perceiving process is concerned with gathering information and ideas. This is what Jung referred to as the irrational process, because it is unconcerned with making judgements or with formulating evaluations. The two judging functions (feeling and thinking) are applied second, since the judging process is concerned with evaluating information and ideas. Both feeling and thinking are described by Jung as rational functions, since they are concerned with making judgements and with formulating evaluations.

The first step in the SIFT method is to address the sensing perspective. It is the sensing perspective that gets to grips with the text itself and that gives proper attention to the details of the passage and may wish to draw on insights of historical methods of biblical scholarship in order to draw in 'facts' from other parts of the Bible. The first set of questions asks, 'How does this passage speak to the sensing function? What are the facts and details? What is there to see, to hear, to touch, to smell and to taste?'

When sensing types hear a passage of Scripture, they want to savour all the detail of the text and may become fascinated by descriptions that appeal to their senses. They tend to start from a fairly literal interest in what is being said. Sensing types may want to find out all they can about the passage and about the facts that stand behind the passage. They welcome preachers who lead them into the passage by repeating the story and by giving them time to observe and to appreciate the details. Sensing types quickly lose the thread if they are bombarded with too many possibilities too quickly.

The second step in the SIFT method is to address the intuitive perspective. It is the intuitive perspective that relates the biblical text to wider issues and concerns. The second set of questions asks, 'How does this passage speak to the intuitive function? What is there to speak to the imagination, to forge links with current situations, to illuminate issues in our lives?'

When intuitive types hear a passage of Scripture, they want to know how that passage will fire their imagination and stimulate their ideas. They tend to focus not on the literal meaning of what is being said but on the possibilities and challenges implied. Intuitive types may want to explore all of the possible directions in which the passage could lead. They welcome preachers who throw out suggestions and brainstorm possibilities, whether or not these are obviously linked to the passage, whether or not these ideas are followed through. Intuitive types quickly become bored with too much detail, too many facts and too much repetition.

The third step in the SIFT method is to address the feeling perspective. It is the feeling perspective that examines the human interest in the biblical text and learns the lessons of God for harmonious and compassionate living. The third set of questions asks, 'How does this passage speak to the feeling function? What is there to speak about fundamental human values, about the relationships between people, and about what it is to be truly human?'

When feeling types hear a passage of Scripture they want to know what the passage has to say about personal values and about human relationships. They empathize deeply with people in the story and with the human drama in the narrative. Feeling types are keen to get inside the lives of people about whom they hear in Scripture. They want to explore what it felt like to be there at the time and how those feelings help to illuminate their Christian journey today. They welcome preachers who take time to develop the human dimension of the passage and who apply the passage to issues of compassion, harmony and trust. Feeling types quickly lose interest in theological debates that explore abstract issues without clear application to personal relationships.

The fourth step in the SIFT method is to address the thinking perspective. It is the thinking perspective that examines the theological interest in the biblical text and that reflects rationally and critically on issues of principle. The fourth set of questions asks, 'How does this passage speak to the thinking function? What is there to speak to the mind, to challenge us on issues of truth and justice, and to provoke profound theological thinking?'

When thinking types hear a passage of Scripture, they want to know what the passage has to say about principles of truth and justice. They get caught up with the principles involved in the story and with the various kinds of truth-claims being made. Thinking types are often keen to do theology and to follow through the implications and the logic of the positions they adopt. Some thinkers apply this perspective to a literal interpretation of Scripture, while other thinkers are more at home with the liberal interpretation of Scripture. They welcome preachers who are fully alert to the logical and to the theological implications of their themes. They value sermons that debate fundamental issues of integrity and righteousness. Thinking types quickly lose interest in sermons that concentrate on applications to personal relationships but fail to debate critically issues of theology and morality.

Applying the SIFT Method

On the Third Sunday in Advent (the day when I settled down to write this chapter) the *Book of Common Prayer* (Church of England, 1662) offered as its Gospel reading Matthew 11.2–10. In some ways, the choice of a passage that profiles John the Baptist sets an appropriate note for the Advent theme. In other ways, the choice is odd because it assumes knowledge of so many scriptural passages before its message and relevance to Advent become clear. So here is one example of the SIFT method that seemed pertinent on the day of writing.

Sensing

For the sensing perspective, I took my 'text' from the very end of the passage: 'Behold, I send my messenger before thy face.' Here is the story of the messenger.

Become sensing people and recall the details of the story. See the old man Zechariah as he entered the sanctuary of the Lord to offer the incense. Hear the angelic salutation as the angel foretells the birth of John the Baptist. Share the old man's disbelief as he laughs in scorn at the absurdity of becoming a father so late in life.

Become sensing people and recall the details of the story. See the old woman Elizabeth (Zechariah's wife) as her cousin Mary (Jesus' mother) visited her home. Hear Mary's famous song as she proclaims the future of Elizabeth's unborn son: 'My soul doth magnify the Lord, and my spirit hath rejoiced in God my saviour.' Share the old woman's joy as she embraces the future of her son.

Become sensing people and recall the details of the story. See the old man Zechariah, struck dumb because of his disbelief, as he comes to the circumcision of his son and writes on the tablet 'His name is John.' Hear Zechariah's famous song as he, too, proclaims the future of his son: 'Blessed be the Lord God of Israel, for he hath visited and redeemed his people.' Share the celebration as the aged parents rejoice.

Become sensing people and recall the details of the story. See the young man John go off to test his vocation by the edge of the River Jordan, as he turns his back on the city to explore the spirituality of the wilderness. Hear the young man John proclaim baptism for repentance. Hear the young man John chastise the indigenous people ('You vipers' brood!') and exhort the foreign soldiers ('No bullying, no blackmail.'). Share the amazement of the crowd as they wonder at his authority and courage.

Become sensing people and recall the details of the story. See the young man John led away to be incarcerated in Herod's prison. Hear the growing exasperation, sense the growing uncertainty as John begins to question everything going on around hm. Hear the charge that John gives to his disciples: 'Go and ask Jesus: are you the one who is come or are we to expect another?' Share John's profound Advent quest as he seeks to test the truth of the revelation.

Intuition

For the intuitive perspective, I took my 'text' from Jesus' question to the crowd: 'What went ye out in the wilderness to see?' Here is the question to stimulate the imagination.

Become intuitive people and interrogate the deep purpose of your Advent quest. Perhaps you went out into the wilderness of Advent to link with history. Perhaps you were attracted to John because he evoked the good old days when God was thought to be highly visible and very active in day-to-day events of the world. So is your quest for a nostalgic religion that celebrates the past but leaves the present largely untouched?

Become intuitive people and interrogate the deep purpose of your Advent quest. Perhaps you went out into the wilderness of Advent to hear a comforting story about the future. Perhaps you were attracted to John because he pointed to a coming saviour. Perhaps you were attracted to John, because he foretold the good days to come, when God would be back in charge of the heavens and the kingdom of God would be established on earth. So is your quest for a futuristic religion that puts its hope in the future but leaves the present largely untouched?

Become intuitive people and interrogate the deep purpose of your Advent quest. Perhaps you went out into the wilderness of Advent to hear your prejudices confirmed by John's enthusiastic teaching. Perhaps you were attracted to John because he had harsh things to say about religious leaders. Perhaps you were attracted to John because he had harsh things to say about tax collectors. Perhaps you were attracted to John because he had harsh things to say about the military. So is your quest for a judgemental religion that puts other people in their place but that leaves your life largely untouched?

Become intuitive people and interrogate the deep purpose of your Advent quest. Perhaps you went out into the wilderness of Advent to hold up a mirror to your own life. Perhaps you were attracted to John because he calls you to make a profound evaluation of your own life. Perhaps you were attracted to John because he calls you to radical personal repentance. Perhaps you were attracted to John because he calls you to deep transformation in readiness to welcome the Christmas nativity of your Lord and Saviour? So is your quest for a personal religion that transforms your life for good?

172

Each year Advent gives you the opportunity to reflect on what you went out into the wilderness to see.

Feeling

For the feeling perspective, I took my 'text' from the very heart of the passage: 'John sent two of his disciples to Jesus with this message'.

Become feeling people and put yourself in John's shoes: it could not have been an easy life being John. Right from the start there was an enormous expectation put on John. If Zechariah had told John but half of what the angel had told him, John would have had so much to live up to. If Elizabeth had told John half of Mary's song of prophecy, John would have had so much to live up to. The call of the forerunner was no easy call to carry.

Become feeling people and put yourself in John's shoes: it could not have been an easy life being John. From the day he strode into the wilderness and took up his position by the River Jordan there was an enormous expectation put on John. From the day he put on the robes of Elijah with the camel's hair and the leather girdle there was an enormous expectation put on John. From the moment that the people began to flock to hear his message and to receive his baptism there was an enormous expectation put on John. The call of the forerunner was no easy call to carry.

Become feeling people and put yourself in John's shoes: it could not have been an easy life being John. From the day he began to speak his mind and to call the indigenous people, 'You vipers' brood!', there was bound to be growing dislike. From the day he began to speak his mind and tell the tax gatherers, 'Exact no more than the assessment', there was bound to be growing dislike. From the day he began to speak his mind and to tell the occupying soldiers, 'No bullying, no blackmail', there was bound to be growing dislike. The call of the forerunner was no easy call to carry.

Become feeling people and put yourself in John's shoes: it could not have been an easy life being John. From the day he decided to make public criticism of King Herod's relationship with Herodias, his brother Philip's wife, the prison doors began to close around him. Robbed of his personal freedom, his self-confidence was soon to follow. No wonder John began to doubt the very heart of his mission. No wonder John sent out envoys to ask Jesus the very question that authenticated the forerunner's mission. 'Are you the One who is to come, or are we to expect another?' The call of the forerunner was no easy call to carry.

Thinking

For the thinking perspective, I took my 'text' from Jesus' reply to John's enquiry: 'go and show John again those things which ye do hear and see'.

Become thinking people and consider the experiential basis of your faith. On this occasion, Jesus was asked to validate his identity. He did not appeal to his personal authority and proclaim, 'I am the Lord's anointed.' On this occasion when Jesus was asked to establish his role in the divine plan for drawing in the reign of God, he did not appeal to his personal authority and proclaim, 'I am the Bread of Life, the true Vine.'

Become thinking people and consider the experiential basis of your faith. On this occasion when Jesus was asked to validate his identity, he did not appeal to the authority of Scripture and recite his davidic lineage. On this occasion when Jesus was asked to establish his role in the divine plan for drawing in the reign of God, he did not appeal to the authority of Scripture and recite the texts that referred to himself.

Become thinking people and consider the experiential basis of your faith. On this occasion when Jesus was asked to authenticate his identity, he invited John to reflect on his personal experience, to reflect on the things he saw and heard. When the blind recover their sight, the reign of God is visible. When the deaf hear, the reign of God is audible. When the lame recover their strength, the reign of God is tangible.

Become thinking people and consider the experiential basis of your faith. When the bread is taken, when the blessing is spoken, when the pieces are broken, when the people are given the bread of life, the reign of God is tasted on the tongue. When the wine is poured, when the cup is blessed, when the people are given the true vine, the reign of God is tasted on the lips.

Become thinking people and share the experiential basis of your faith with all who ask who it is whom you follow, who it is whom you serve. Indeed, the one for whom we have been waiting has come in the person of Jesus, the Christ.

Conclusion

The SIFT method of biblical hermeneutics and liturgical preaching emerged from theological reflection on the application of personality theory for a richer appreciation of the role of the reader in the hermeneutical process. Like so many contemporary developments in personality psychology and in empirical theology, a real strength of this approach is that it can be subjected to proper empirical investigation and testing. Support for the approach has already been provided by the empirical studies reported by Village and Francis (2005), Francis, Robbins and Village (2009) and Francis (in press). Such studies provide a real foundation for a new empirical science of preaching, embracing the fields of psychology, hermeneutics and homiletics.

References

Baab, L. M., 1998, *Personality Type in Congregations: How to Work with Others More Effectively*, Washington, DC: Alban Institute.

Church of England, 1662, *The Book of Common Prayer*, Oxford: Oxford University Press.

Duncan, B., 1993, *Pray Your Way: Your Personality and God*, London: Darton, Longman and Todd.

Francis, L. J., 1997, *Personality Type and Scripture: Exploring Mark's Gospel*, London: Mowbray.

___, 2005, 'Psychological type and biblical hermeneutics: SIFT method of preaching', in D. Day, J. Astley and L. J. Francis (eds), *Making Connections: A Reader on Preaching*, Aldershot: Ashgate, pp. 75–82.

___ (in press), 'Psychological type and biblical hermeneutics in examining the SIFT approach among Anglican preachers'.

Francis, L. J., and P. Atkins, 2000, *Exploring Luke's Gospel: A Guide to the Gospel Readings in the Revised Common Lectionary*, London: Mowbray.

___, 2001, *Exploring Matthew's Gospel: A Guide to the Gospel Readings in the Revised Common Lectionary*, London: Mowbray.

___, 2002, *Exploring Mark's Gospel: An Aid for Readers and Preachers Using Year B of the Revised Common Lectionary*, London: Continuum.

Francis, L. J., M. Robbins and A. Village, 2009, 'Psychological type and the pulpit: an empirical enquiry concerning preachers and the SIFT method of biblical hermeneutics', *HTS Theological Studies* 65.1, article 161, 7 pages.

Francis, L. J., and A. Village, 2008, *Preaching with All Our Soul*, London: Continuum.

Goldsmith, M., and M. Wharton, 1993, *Knowing Me Knowing You*, London: SPCK.

Jung, C. G., 1971, *Psychological Types: The Collected Works*, vol. 6, London: Routledge and Kegan Paul.

Keirsey, D., and M. Bates, 1978, *Please Understand Me*, Del Mar, CA: Prometheus Nemesis.

Leech, K. (ed.), 1996, *Myers-Briggs: Some Critical Reflections*, Croydon: Jubilee Group.

Lloyd, J. B., 2007, 'Opposition from Christians to Myers-Briggs personality typing: an analysis and evaluation', *Journal of Beliefs and Values* 28, pp. 111–23.

Michael, C. P., and M. C. Norrisey, 1984, *Prayer and Temperament: Different Prayer Forms for Different Personality Types*, Charlottesville, VA: Open Door.

Myers, I. B., and M. H. McCaulley, 1985, *Manual: A Guide to the Development and Use of the Myers-Briggs Type Indicator*, Palo Alto, CA: Consulting Psychologists Press.

Osborn, L., and D. Osborn, 1991, *God's Diverse People*, London: Daybreak.

Segovia, F. F., 1995, 'Toward a hermeneutic of the diaspora: a hermeneutic of otherness and engagement', in F. F. Segovia and M. A. Tolbert (eds), *Reading from This Place: Social Location and Biblical Interpretation in the United States*, 2 vols, Minneapolis, MN: Fortress Press, vol. 1, pp. 57–73.

Village, A., and L. J. Francis, 2005, 'The relationship of psychological type preferences to biblical interpretation', *Journal of Empirical Theology* 18.1, pp. 74–89.

13

The Preacher's Inner Life

SUSAN DURBER

In church communities there is always a good deal of fretting mixed up with double doses of guilt. I remember a conversation once in a church gathering about whether we were doing enough, or the right sort of, mission. A very wise retired missionary there told us that we didn't need to worry quite so much as we thought, that of course we were doing mission, whether we thought we were or not. In every encounter we have with anyone, we would be presenting in obvious and subtle ways who we are, what shapes us, the faith that makes us.

I feel rather the same about a subject like 'the inner life of the preacher'. As I set out to write this chapter I thought, at first, that what I needed to do was reflect on how to make sure that we who are preachers fill our souls up with enough good things so that we can preach the gospel faithfully to others. We've all had the experience, I expect, of feeling on a Sunday morning, or whenever it is, that we are empty, used-up, with nothing really to give. Our spirits sometimes seem to be starving, listless, nothing much doing. We feel as though the inside of us is hollow, that we are empty vessels. And so the task is to make sure that the vessels remain full, or at least full enough. So you might expect, from this chapter, the usual exhortations to pray more, to read more 'spiritual' books, to listen to Mozart or Bob Dylan regularly, to keep your relationships in good order and to take the spiritual equivalent of brisk regular walks.

However, as important as all those things are, that's not what I want to argue at all. I want to say something more like what my wise missionary friend said, and to suggest that there may be more going on in you anyway than the usual ways of thinking about all this suggest. What makes us believe and, perhaps more important, feel that we are empty, or not filled with the 'right' sort of things? I want to start by questioning the kind of metaphors we use as we speak of the challenge before us as preachers to have something to say, and something important to say, and to suggest an alternative way of looking at it. For example, I wonder whether it really helps very much to think of ourselves as having an outer and an 'inner' life, with all the possibilities that opens up for images of emptiness. Sometimes life does feel like that and the metaphor does seem to fit. But it is a metaphor and a metaphor that has, for good and ill, shaped how we understand what it means to practise faith and to speak of it. But maybe there are alternative ways of thinking that might help us or even set us free. I remember once being struck, when a theologian I much respected said that there is no such thing as 'spirituality', no such thing as an inner life. There is simply life. There is really what you do and what you are and that's in evidence in your life (just as your faith is inevitably expressed to those around you whether you are meaning to do it or not). Perhaps this talk of inner and outer life, and of fullness and emptiness in the inner life, is grounded in an unhealthy kind of dualism. Could it be possible that what we have sometimes thought of as the 'outer life', the life of the body, is as much a resource for preaching as anything we might want to call an 'inner life'? Perhaps the important thing is not to fill yourself up with a good spiritual diet, to pour better things into the outward form of your life, but instead to learn to pay more attention to the embodied life that you actually have, to the life that you have led and are leading, whether you have noticed it before or not. It may be that you have more resources in your own experience than you think. It may be that we have learned to think of some particular lives or some aspects of life as more resourceful for the preacher than others (a residual or even actual monastic model of the saintly and remarkable preacher), while ignoring the fruitful possibilities of exploring the resources of the actual lives we lead and the diverse and complex experiences we each have. It is not perhaps that a preacher needs a particular kind of 'inner' life at all, but that preachers have human lives like others, and they will find in the lives they lead the resources to discover what it might be to speak of God and to interpret the Scriptures. It is not that we should deliberately feed the inner man or woman, but recognize how the person we are is already being fed, in many ways, by God, by creation, by our ecclesial tradition or church, by experience, and by our very particular location in the world. It is puzzling, but true, that we find it possible to ignore great wells of fruitful life, knowledge and wisdom, while looking for some specific, and sometimes rather esoteric, form of spiritual knowledge and strength for which most people are easily persuaded that they are in need. This is the motes and beams story, but this time in reverse. Why are we so slow to recognize how God comes to us in the bodily lives we actually lead, and not only in the ones we imagine that properly 'spiritual' people lead? No wonder many of us feel empty, despite the fact that our lives are filled with all sorts of experiences, situations and sources of important knowledge and grace.

The lives we inhabit as human beings are a great gift and resource for preaching, but just as it is said that we use only a tiny portion of our brain when we think so I suspect is it the case that we often do not mine deeply into our experience in order to speak of God. We might feel guilty, especially as preachers, that we have not read enough of the spiritual classics, that we do not spend enough time in prayer, or that we do not feed our spirits, but we do not see that all the while we are living, learning, feeling, working, loving, suffering and rejoicing, that we are becoming human beings with rich and deep resources of situated wisdom and knowledge. We long, with some measure of guilty regret, for a rich spiritual life, but do not notice the riches that God is giving us through the life, situation and experience that we are actually having. How strange, when you reflect on it, that someone might regret not having read the writings of the desert fathers or mothers, but not see that the desert spaces in their own life may be a rich source of knowledge and insight. How sad that a woman might wish she had more academic knowledge about the Marian tradition, but not see that her own experience of motherhood might be a deep well from which to draw life-giving water. How sad that someone who labours hard with their body might believe that a proper preacher would have read more books, when we need more people to speak of the gospel from the experience of the body.

It is regrettable that many people do not think that the material of their own lives could be of real interest or significance, or that it could be a source of true wisdom. And here I do not refer to those people who repeat endlessly from the pulpit anecdotes from their own or their families' lives. We need less of that. But we need more people who will be able to seize on the real resources of their own particular and extraordinary human life, in order to preach to God's people the passion of the gospel.

If I have learned anything from being among human beings in the close ways of a minister, it is that all life stories are interesting, and indeed significant, and not just the obvious ones like Oscar Wilde or Judy Garland or C. S. Lewis. Every single human being with whom I have ever had a serious conversation has a fascinating story to tell. Iris Murdoch was once asked why she filled her novels with such extraordinary people; so many eccentrics, so many people with dark secrets and mysteries, so many people with desires of which they are ashamed, so many people with extraordinary psyches and powerful imaginations. She simply replied that she did not believe she was writing about extraordinary people at all. She was just writing about people. She knew what must be true, that all people are utterly extraordinary. We all work hard to hide it, but of course the novelist can see with the eye of God and can see what lies beneath the façade of the ordinary. It is what lies beneath that is fascinating and revealing. And it is in this extraordinariness and particularity of human life that God is made known. It is certainly the task and the privilege of a good preacher to see the extraordinary and the ordinary things in their own life and to find God there. And we are to do this in such a way that we can speak from our particular experience into the lives of others.

Of course, what I do not want to say (and I think this is a temptation of the preacher) is that we should rush to find the point at which our experience, our reading, our prayer, or indeed anything which is engaging us or shaping us, will become directly 'useful'. It is tempting to think of nothing as being of much value unless we can quote it in our sermons. A friend, who has been a preacher for several decades, recently told me about the time when *Honest to God* came out. He read it, as everyone did at the time, and was profoundly affected by it. He went to the ministers' fraternal (*sic*) meeting, eager to discuss the book and its implications. Another minister there said that he did not think Bishop Robinson's book would affect his preaching at all. My friend said immediately, 'It's transformed mine!' But in conversation afterwards they recognized that they were at cross-purposes. My friend had no intention at all of *quoting* the book in any sermon, but he knew that every time he came to look at the Scriptures and to interpret them with his congregation, he would have to bear in mind what the book was on about, and that it would shape, in future, every encounter he had with the task of interpreting and expounding the faith. The others at the fraternal had assumed that the only way a book (or anything!) could really be said to impact on preaching was by direct quotation. If we see the process like that, we shall be too eager to make 'use' of everything, too hasty to dismiss anything not directly and immediately useful, and not attentive enough to whatever God might be saying to us through any experience, whether that be from a book or, perhaps even more significantly, from an event in our lives. Being a preacher is a much more indirect task than that. It is rooted in a faithful attention to the Bible and to the human beings with whom you share community and life, and also to the lessons of your own life, the whole of that life and not just the kind of experiences that some would define as 'inner' life. I have often talked of the ways in which my experience as a woman has real implications for my preaching, that the place from which I speak is a real source of knowledge and truth. People sometimes misunderstand me and think that this means my sermons will be peppered with 'girly' stories, with stories of birth that might make people squirm or with too much raw emotion and weeping. Of course, these very objections betray much, but it is certainly not the case that drawing on your experience means telling personal stories or making yourself inappropriately vulnerable. But it does mean learning to interpret and to reflect on what God is teaching you through the days as you live and what the particular lens of your own life and experience brings to the interpretation of the Bible stories and the traditions of faith. You have the most rich and amazing resource in your very body.

I don't think preachers necessarily have to go searching for a particular kind of life, even or especially a more 'spiritual' one, but I do believe that careful attention and theological reflection on your own experience, and from that also careful attention to the experiences of others, will make you a more holy person and a good, effective preacher. I believe that God is already feeding you, in ways you may not always notice, or notice immediately. But we are all of us being fed. Our spirit has no special meal times. It is fed by the experiences that life brings us and by our ability to reflect upon them with wisdom and insight. We do not have to go to a special place to 'eat' or to feed the spirit. The spirit is fed as we raise our children, or grieve for not having them, or as we are children ourselves, as we make love or enjoy friendship or travel the world, or potter in the garden or work hard at whatever we do or enter political battles or worry about the future of the planet.

One of the contemporary preachers I most admire is Frederick Buechner, an American Presbyterian novelist and theologian. An inspired and inspiring preacher, he knows how to use the wonderful gift of his own experience and to connect his own understanding of what has happened to him with the understanding of others. He has written much autobiography, not as an exercise in personal hubris, but as a reaching for understanding of his own life and that of others. He believes that this reflection on what has happened to any of us is in itself a central task of theology and, one might say, particularly for the preacher. And, to reiterate what I said earlier, I am very chary indeed of relating direct personal experience in sermons. This will not be feeding to the lives of others. There is too much danger of embarrassing personal display and of distracting the hearer. But with that caveat, here is what Buechner has written about theology and life.

If God speaks to us at all in this world, if God speaks anywhere, it is into our personal lives that he speaks. Someone we love dies, say. Some unforeseen act of kindness or cruelty touches the heart or makes the blood run cold. We fail a friend, or a friend fails us, and we are appalled at the capacity we have for estranging the very people in our lives we need the most. Or maybe nothing extraordinary happens at all – just one day following another, helter-skelter, in the manner of days. We sleep and dream. We wake. We work. We remember and forget. We have fun and are depressed. And into the thick of it, or out of the thick of it, at moments of even the most humdrum of our days, God speaks. (1982, p. 2)

Buechner is extremely skilled at reflecting on his own experience of life and of God. He has written obviously autobiographical pieces that stand well on their own. But he has also published many, many sermons. And, though in none of his sermons do you find autobiographical reflection in quite the same way, you do find evidence of the results of his reflection on his own experience (or life) and an ability to turn to it in such a way that it can connect with the experience of others without simply drawing attention to himself. In some places today you can find a kind of obsession about ourselves and this is not something I want to encourage, particularly in the pulpit. The journalist Suzanne Moore, reviewing a clutch of autobiographies, once gave vent to near-despair at what she saw as the self-obsession and self-deception that pass for heavily marketed 'honesty' these days. She wondered whether there is today a crisis of confidence in which no one can speak for anyone outside themselves. But I think that it may be a test of a good piece of autobiography (and it is certainly a test of good preaching) that it *does* enable all of us to connect with human experience beyond our own, and that it does give us a sense of being related to human beings who, though they have very different experiences from ours, are nonetheless 'just like us'. And as we hear good storytelling and good preaching, they connect us with our *own* experience in new ways, and even with our own experience of the God who made each of us and who speaks to us within the day-to-day stuff of life, the 'once upon a time' of all our lives. So, perhaps it's not, after all, that we preachers need a particular kind of inner life, but a particular kind of relation to the lives which God has given us, not only so that we can let our life experience bear gifts of wisdom and strength to us but also so that our own lives, in all their fullness and complexity, may become a way of relating to the truths of God for others.

All good preachers will need to begin with a deep sense of gratitude for and reflection on our own lives, through which I believe God has fed us, but which we often ignore. Your life is not only your own life. It is part of what enables you to connect with others outside of yourself. You don't have to have had a particularly dramatic life to have experience that is worth reflecting on and that will serve as a good basis for preaching that connects with the lives of others. The sort of life experience I am talking about it is the kind that most of us have in one way or another: weeping, ecstasy, disappointment, boredom, desire, hope, despair, sorrow, loss, fear, shame, pain. All of these things will be experienced, though of course all embodied and situated in very different contexts, and never simply in the abstract. But in whatever ways we find ourselves experiencing what it means to be a human being, our lives give us all insight into the joy and the burden of being human. You don't have to have suffered a major bereavement to understand what it means to experience loss. But, if you know yourself well and can reflect on what happens, and if you have or develop a good imagination, you can begin to know something of what other people, the ones you are talking to, might be experiencing, rejoicing in and struggling with. And being able to connect with those to whom you are talking is a significant part of what makes preaching something life-changing and powerful, especially when you are then opening up the possibility for those listening to reflect on their own life and to understand their own story within the context of the stories of the Bible.

Having a faith means that you have to take seriously the life that God has given you so that you can enable others to hear the seriousness and significance of their lives. I think this is what many of us have failed to do well. We have, too often, ignored the food of life's experience that God has actually given us and gone in search instead for something that we imagine is more appropriate for preachers, an inner life resourced from the writings or reflections of people very different from us. And it is fine and good to look elsewhere if we have first looked also at ourselves, at the embodied and particular and situated life that God has already given us. I am talking about making good use of the experiences you have had and using them as a place of discovery that can help you to communicate more effectively to others. Your life is important, but not only your inner life, not only a specially resourced part of you, but all of the life that presses upon you and shapes you.

Let me offer an example from my own preaching. It is an excerpt from a sermon, which I can testify was fed by the events and reflections of my own life, but it is also a sermon that reflects on what it means to have an 'inner life' or a private life. So perhaps it serves a double purpose. The sermon was preached after a time when I had cared for someone who had died of cancer, a time of hugely practical tasks, a time for guarding a private space for her to say her prayers, to be ill or simply asleep. And after her death there was for me a time of lonely grieving. But all of this, in ways I could hardly appreciate at the time, fed my spirit. I was exhausted, stretched and aching with loss, but I was also growing as a human being, being re-born from a kind of death of my own. And I hope that this has somehow borne fruit in my life as a preacher. An experience like that is not one that anyone would go looking for. It's just part of life that sometimes creeps up on you whether you like it or not. But it undoubtedly fed me and changed me, and profoundly shaped my spirit. That's what I mean I think by saying that the inner life cannot be separated from just *life*. It wasn't any special spiritual kind of reading or praying that fed my spirit (I had little time, or inclination really, to read so-called 'spiritual books' during the heat of that period) but simply the raw material of life's ordinary and extraordinary happenings. And the feeding came most profoundly during and after a time when I was exhausted and drained, and one might say emptied out.

The sermon was preached on that text from Matthew's Gospel about praying in a private room rather than publicly and ostentatiously on the street.

It is tempting to picture the earliest disciples taking this teaching to heart. But it's hard to do it without thinking in all too modern terms. I can only imagine a solid kind of room – in a modern kind of house – perhaps at least a three bedroom semi – with plenty of empty rooms up and down – from the quiet bedrooms to the book-lined study – the prayer corner or the smallest room. And the disciple saying the office or having a 'quiet time' – while the life of the house murmurs in the distance as someone makes another cup of coffee, collects another email, puts another load in the washing machine or opens the door to a visitor. The disciple finds a private, quiet space and prays without benefit of trumpets. But, of course, it can't have been anything like that. The kind of privacy we have become used to and take as a right (a dubious one) was not a reality of first century life. Houses were small and crowded, and pretty much all of life was public – from washing to praying to urinating. There were not many mansions with many rooms. Our modern ideas about private 'space' are just that, modern. So perhaps this is a passage we have become used to taking literally, which we might, after all, take another way as speaking a deeper kind of truth.

In modern times we have become used to having privacy, but we are not so comfortable about being alone. And so we come, sometimes unprepared and afraid, to those experiences that we must face alone, those journeys on which no-one can come with us. A couple of years ago a young journalist called Ruth Picardie died of breast cancer. She wrote several columns about her experience of being ill and facing death, and they were published in the Observer *Life* magazine. Ruth's husband, writing about the night before the night she died, describes how Ruth struggled up the stairs with him to help put their twins (aged 2) to bed and how he suddenly realized, with such sadness, how alone she was and how, in a sense, she was already lost to him.

Our deepest joys and our deepest sorrows are most profoundly ours to have alone – in the private space that is undefined by physical walls, but is more certainly private to us than the room in which we place our pyjamas. But for us, whose private selves are made in the Christian shape, we are offered a blessing. The gospel says to us that, though alone, we need not be truly lonely, for God who sees what is in the secret places of our experience – of our praying and doing and all our living – God will have mercy on us. In the private room of our innermost selves – God is with us.

It used to frighten me a little, the thought that God could see everything in us, everything we hide from other people, every secret thought, every desire, everything in us however beautiful or loathsome, everything we would gladly shut the door on. But I think it is, after all, a blessing, to know that the God of all love and mercy is with us in the inner and private space – that we are not, finally, alone. We are not, like Euridyce, lost to the underworld, but God is wherever we go – into whatever shared heaven or private hell. God is there and is with us. We are not, after all, absolutely alone.

I had preached a sermon that spoke from the wells of my experience, a reflection on the Scriptures that came from a very bodily experience of being a carer and a mourner. But what about the life experiences you haven't had? Is it going to be enough to be at the mercy of only your *own* life's experience for spiritual food?

It is easy, of course, for us to think that we do understand all human experience, or to generalize in a crude way all human experience from our own particular and situated one. It is important to recognize that there are experiences from human life that you haven't had, but to find ways to speak to the people who sit before you waiting for a word for their lives, in their particularity. And of course, even this very openness to the lives of others will feed you.

In Walter Burghardt's wonderful book called *Preaching: The Art and the Craft* (1987) he includes an address he gave at a national symposium on preaching with a response to it given by Elisabeth Schüssler Fiorenza.

This remarkable debate illustrates powerfully the potential significance of recognizing that your own life experience is always a limited diet and of how that limitation can be addressed.

In his own lecture, Burghardt advocates 'study impregnated with experience' (1987, p. 64) as a powerful preparation for preaching. He declares that his preaching is least effective when he experiences nothing, that careful study is never enough on its own. He then describes the process he went through in preparing a particular sermon for Advent Sunday. He writes of how he read Shakespeare and Manley Hopkins, Tennessee Williams and John Henry Newman (the kinds of things any good preacher might want to read to feed the spirit) in an effort to think as broadly as possible about human experience. Then he thanks Fiorenza for her 'insightful, persuasive and moving address' (p. 68) and includes it in his book.

Fiorenza argued on the day at the symposium that the 'experience' of which Burghardt had written was actually only male experience. She said, and Burghardt then quotes her in his book, that

> For all practical purposes women of the past and of the present have not preached and are in many Christian churches still excluded from defining the role of proclamation in terms of their own experience. In such an ecclesiastical institution, the danger exists that the homily will not articulate the experience of God as the rich and pluriform experience of God's people, but that the male preacher will articulate his own experience and will declare and proclaim his own particular experience as the experience of God par excellence. What is limited and particular to his experience will be proclaimed as universal and paradigmatic for everyone. (Fiorenza in Burghardt, 1987, p. 70)

Fiorenza encourages male preachers to be attentive to a wider range of human experience and she reflects on the too many sermons she has heard against the 'male' sins of desire for power, of hubris and pride. She favours a more ecclesial and less clerical style of preaching. In turning to Burghardt's sermon for Advent, she writes:

> I was surprised that he does not think of taking into account the experiences of pregnant women and their sense of self. (Fiorenza in Burghardt, 1987, p. 76)

Interpreting Mary requires the interpretation also of women's experience today. The experience of men must no longer be allowed to be seen as the paradigm of all human experience. The experience of living in a woman's body is different and demands to be named, interpreted and remade in the pulpit.

We should not underestimate the wealth and diversity of human experience. This might be one way in which we can feed our 'inner lives' or, more properly, our 'lives' as preachers. As we become more skilled at reflecting on the significance of our own life experience, we develop a proper kind of humility before the life experiences of others. And, as we develop a keen imagination and a sympathy (in the proper sense) for other human beings, whose outward lives are different from ours in significant ways, then we find ways to let their lives speak to ours. My own spirit, my own life, will expand as I meet with or engage with people with very different lives from my own, and from such encounters I believe that God speaks. Experiences of other parts of the world, other nations, peoples, church traditions, will not only be interesting and add diversity to life, but they will also enrich our spirits in profound ways if we let them. For example, a student for ministry might well grow spiritually through engagement in Ignatian retreats or quiet days, but will also grow immeasurably (if able not only to have the experience but also not to miss the meaning) through an international placement or a community placement in an inner-city context. For every preacher the same is true. An expanded horizon of experience and understanding will feed every part of a person and give them, potentially, new knowledge of God.

I confess that I find other people fascinating, and I'm always intrigued by how people are living out the remarkable and fascinating task of being and becoming a human being. I suppose I feed my own spirit by constantly enquiring and wondering how other people tick. What makes them cry and laugh and be passionate about things? I do this of course by meeting as many people as I can, by talking with them and learning of their lives, by sharing life with them, by opening my home, by travelling when I can. And I also do it by reading novels, by looking at paintings, by reading poems, watching films, whatever it takes. Whether it's low culture or high, I soak it up. All of this can 'feed my spirit' and restore my soul, but I also believe that it can provide what a preacher needs, food for thought, reflection and theology.

When it comes to it though, I know that I can only preach with integrity from any pulpit when I preach words that have been truly forged within my own body. True learning from others cannot be the kind of learning that simply repeats their words, because from a pulpit I can only speak words that come from me. In her book *Preaching as Testimony*, Anna Carter Florence describes the fearful experience that many preachers share, of feeling that we must speak words we do not believe ourselves, or that we become a cipher for the quotations of others, 'generic talking heads' (Florence, 2007, p. 113). We leave so much of ourselves behind, but repeat the words of others, without really sharing them or owning them for ourselves. We crave the certainty that we are authoritative and effective preachers, but we, foolishly, think this can only be found through the elaborate rituals of quotation and technique that preachers play out. As she puts it, we become and we know ourselves to be 'dead preachers walking'. The answer, she suggests, is not to acquire new skills as a rhetorician, or even a new role within the Church (like ordination). She writes,

> We had to stop our endless searching for the fountain of authority. We had to give up the dream of the good preacher. Basically, we had to shut up for a while, be very still, and exercise our senses. Preaching had shown how disconnected we were, from Scripture and from ourselves; now we had to watch and wait for God to appear and show us a way of becoming whole. (p. 114)

Her response to the drama of this disconnection between what preachers are called to do and what they feel deep-down their skills and authority could ever sustain is to say that we can only ever preach with integrity if we think of preaching as testimony, as the voice that comes from the place where God has called us to be and from the encounter that we, as the people we truly are, in every aspect of ourselves, have with the texts of Scripture. She knows that many preachers feel they leave large parts of themselves behind as they preach, and yet they then feel ill-equipped. But the truth is that God has given you a life from which to speak, a community from which to speak and a tradition (which you inhabit in your body and in your location), and from this you must speak.

If you are a preacher who craves a place from which to speak with integrity, then you already have it. It is your own life and the lives of those with whom you share in community. It may not be an interior life, but it is life, in all its mess, reality and particularity. Preach your testimony from where you are. If you are hungry for food for the soul, there is so much of it waiting to be eaten. There are already, without doubt, resources within your own life's experience, even the very day-to-day happenings of an ordinary, yet extraordinary, human life. There are also plenty of ways of discovering how it is that other people are experiencing this human life, if you have eyes to see them. We sit at the banquet table of life. We have only to sit and eat.

References

Buechner, F., 1982, *The Sacred Journey: A Memoir of Early Days*, New York: Harper and Row.

Burghardt, W. J., 1987, *Preaching: The Art and the Craft*, New York: Paulist Press.

Florence, A. Carter, 2007, *Preaching as Testimony*, London: Westminster John Knox Press.

14

Forming Future Preachers

GEOFFREY STEVENSON

It is one thing to learn the technique and mechanics of preaching, it is quite another to preach a sermon that will draw back the veil and make the barriers fall that hide the face of God. (Stewart, 1946, pp. 100–1)

Introduction

The purpose of this chapter is to discuss how preachers may be nurtured and educated to serve God's purposes in the churches of the twenty-first century. The American homiletician, Fred Craddock wrote:

> Preaching is the concerted engagement of one's faculties of body, mind and spirit. It is then, *skilled activity*. But preaching has to do with a particular content, a certain message conveyed . . . And since the basic content is not a creation of, but a gift to, the speaker, *preaching is both learned and given* . . . for the active presence of the spirit of God transforms the occasion into what biblical scholars have referred to as an 'event'. (1985, p. 17)

Craddock's observation pinpoints the dilemma that faces preachers as well as those charged with their ministerial formation. God's servants are called, tested and nourished in church structures, and yet they are forged in furnaces of holy fire, and in ways that are sometimes hidden from all, including themselves. Examining the human agency of the preacher and his or her ability to prepare and deliver sermons must always be accompanied by theological understandings of God's actions in revealing the Word to the Church. But seeing the preacher as some kind of 'divinely called, scripturally fluent, auto-didact' can miss important elements vital for a description of the process of learning preaching. There are a range of factors at work in the relationships between the preacher and the communities and social constructs of which she or he is a part. In this chapter I ask how much theories of education can contribute to our understanding of how preachers learn, and I propose a concept of social learning theory to enrich the development of our future preachers.

Traditional approaches

Arguably the first textbook written for Christian preachers is Book 4 of Augustine's *De Doctrina Christiana*. Michael Pasquarello, 'taking *doctrina* in the active rather than passive sense', translates this as 'Teaching Christianity' (2005, p. 20). Augustine is concerned with conversion and Christian formation, and reveals 'his strong commitment to the life-shaping wisdom of Scripture for the church and especially its preachers' (p. 20). His aim is the transformation of the preacher through teaching in order that the preacher may teach in a way that leads to transformation.

Where the Church as a forming, educating and nurturing body has developed strategies for growing preachers, the focus has often been on what the individual preacher learns. It has been content-driven, with the stress on orthodoxy, that is, having the right set of beliefs and being able to express them in oral delivery. This makes particular sense when viewing preaching as principally a form of teaching, concerned with Christian education. Even when and where the Church calls preachers to evangelize, to articulate and promulgate its Good News, the primary requirement is often that the preacher be schooled in the Scriptures and right doctrine.

When and where that has seemed to be the preoccupation of a minister's schooling, a reaction against that approach has turned the focus on the character of the preacher, his or her spirituality, piety and integrity, as well as demeanour, composure and self-control. One of the most commonly quoted definitions of preaching today was first given by the late-nineteenth-century American Episcopal preacher and writer Phillips Brooks. He said in his Yale lectures on preaching: 'Truth through personality is our description of real preaching' ([1887] 1989, p. 25). The great nineteenth-century Scottish preacher Robert Murray McCheyne said, 'My people's greatest need is my personal holiness' (Bonar and McCheyne, 1960). Forming a preacher then becomes a pastoral and spiritual, rather than educational, concern.

More recently, research work of the VOX Project at the Centre for Christian Communication, involving teachers of preaching from institutions across the UK and virtually all of the denominations, identified four subject areas as particularly important in the training of preachers. These were the theology of preaching, handling the biblical text, sermon construction and sermon communication (Stevenson and Wilkinson, 2003). It is assumed – though naively, some would say – that the student preacher is *already* being thoroughly grounded in systematics, ethics, church history, biblical interpretation and spirituality as part of their preparation for wider ministry, and without which homiletics is meaningless.

Learning to preach goes far beyond learning *what* to preach. Being certifiably orthodox and exegetically skilful does not guarantee being hermeneutically astute, pastorally wise, nor rhetorically effective. The significance of the preaching event is not to be found solely in the theological content of the sermon, but must include the meaning-making process in the interaction between God, the text, the preacher and the listeners. Before exploring this idea for its implications for developing our future preachers, it is worth considering how educational theory can contribute to our understanding of the enterprise.

Learning theory

The educational psychologist Mark Tennant points out that psychological theories of education fall broadly into two camps, depending on whether they begin with the individual or with the social environment (1997, p. 3). When they take the person as the starting-point, the emphasis is on the internal make-up, the motivations and conceptions in that person. When the environment is the starting-point or ground for understanding learning, the learner is viewed principally in relation to his or her social context, and learning is one aspect among many of the dynamic relationship between the person and society. Approaching learning from the individual point of view, among the descriptions of how people learn, there have been attempts to analyse individual learning patterns and to discern discrete and objective (if not quantifiable) learning aptitudes. In some schools of thought these aptitudes or learning styles are seen as relating to cognitive styles, or the different ways individuals characteristically or habitually organize and process mental phenomena.

There have been numerous classifications of cognitive styles, such as Howard Gardner's theory of Multiple Intelligences, first outlined in his 1982 work, *Frames of Mind*, and more recently strongly presented by Thomas Armstrong. Multi-dimensional instruments for measuring such styles include Myers-Briggs Type Indicator (MBTI), Riding's Cognitive Style Analysis (CSA), Witkin's field dependence–independence model, the Allinson–Hayes Cognitive Style Index (CSI), the Kirton Adaption–Innovation Inventory (KAI) and the Kolb and Fry Learning Style Inventory (LSI). For the homiletical educator, there are some promising avenues to be explored. One might ask how, for example, do 'adapters' and 'innovators' (Kirton) differ when as preachers they encounter extreme dissonance between time-honoured and institutionally enshrined dogma and the real and immediate pastoral problems such as suffering or gender orientation?

How does the conceptions-of-learning idea contribute to our understanding of the process of learning to preach? Some of these theories do show points of connection, but the concept of learning styles has been shown to lack theoretical coherence and empirical verification. There are also significant methodological limitations in the practical world of classroom instruction. The learning styles concept is not without merit, however, when students are invited to reflect and gain insight into their own preferred mode of learning. This can in turn give them opportunities to control their own learning. It can also help them to become more effective and sympathetic teachers themselves, recognizing the varieties of learning styles in congregations they face, and taking steps to ensure that their preaching is richly formulated to serve these differences. This is indeed explored especially in Leslie Francis's SIFT approach to preaching, outlined elsewhere in this book.

But what helps the preacher as a teacher does not necessarily help the preacher as learner. Traditional attitudes and practices persist, in which knowledge is treated as something that may be poured into the student, if you find the right pitcher and funnel. The concept of learning styles may be most useful if it feeds into the action–reflection cycle of learning, and builds on the self-regulation of adult learners. This draws most importantly on the learning cycle as described by Peter Honey and Alan Mumford and based on the work of D. A. Kolb and Donald A. Schön. Theological educators and those recently ordained will recognize this as Theological and Practical Reflection.

Learning to preach . . . socially?

In contrast to individualistic approaches, social learning theories attempt to describe a whole nexus or web of relationships that are significant in the learner's development. A useful concept is that of communities of practice as initially proposed by educational theorists Jean Lave and Etienne Wenger and developed by Wenger in later works. They asked what it was about apprenticeship in a range of professions that was so significant to the learning process. They considered studies carried out by several social anthropologists into the learning processes that operated in five apprentice-like situations: Yucatec Mayan midwives in Mexico, US Navy quartermasters, tailors in Liberia, butchers in US supermarkets, and 'non-drinking alcoholics' in Alcoholics Anonymous. They observed that apprenticeship as usually understood (that is, a master–novice relationship where craft instruction and wisdom are imparted over time) did not fully account for the ways in which novices learned. More important to learning than imitation, instruction and oversight was the cluster of social and interpersonal factors, a dynamic which they named 'legitimate peripheral participation'. 'Legitimate' here encompasses the idea that a group has an understanding of membership and belonging, and that an ability to perform a task (for example, butchering meat) or to hold in common the corpus of professional knowledge (as in midwifery) is a feature of membership in that group. Learning is not only a matter of technique and knowledge, and mastering a skill set, but it is involvement in a process in which the learner comes to understand their identity and their place or membership in the community of practice. The newcomer's participation, peripheral at first, is an acknowledged locus for appropriate forms of learning, but Lave and Wenger's thesis is that moving through such peripheral or outsider status to become a fully-fledged member is not just a place for learning, it *is* learning. Identity is as important as skills acquisition in an analysis of learning. Learning the jargon, swapping 'war stories' that extend the ability to handle non-textbook situations, being given responsibility before demonstrating competence, as well as in reward for achievement, are all part of learning processes that tend to escape the cognitive theorist, as well as the institutional educator.

An obvious objection to the application of this concept to preaching is that very, very rarely are preachers trained in an apprentice-like situation. To conform to the model, there should be newcomers who have just been ordained or licensed as well as 'old timers' who have been preaching for many years, and who carry higher status. Yet it seems true that the preacher often ploughs a lonely furrow. The minister, priest or pastor is frequently the primary occupant of the pulpit in his or her church, with little contact with or experience of the preaching and sermons of others. Trial and error puts a lot of preachers, and their congregations, through unnecessary pain. Where are there communities of practice to help?

The concept may yet be of value. We can ask if preaching can be seen as a shared enterprise involving a community in a close and/or formal, functional relationship with a preacher. In this respect it seemed fair to say that individual preaching acts are judged according to criteria shared by the worshipping congregation and variously expressed over centuries of theological tradition. There are questions demanded of a sermon that arise from the shared understanding and shared traditions of the community. Does the sermon reveal God? Is the soteriological kerygma of Jesus explicated in a way that touches the listeners? Does the sermon engage with or amplify or contradict the meaning of Scripture? Does it sound like a sermon, that is, is the preacher speaking with authority, or as an expert, or as a compassionate pastor, or as a wise philosopher or theologian?[1]

I maintain, then, that there are significant aspects of socially mediated training that make an exploration of such a concept worthwhile. These are:

1 The membership of the learner in a community with its deposits of knowledge and tradition;
2 Imitation and skills development through observation of role models;
3 Situated learning with mentors or coaches and one-on-one instruction;
4 Learning through and with peers;
5 The effect of the local community on the learner and vice versa.

I will explore these through a theologically charged version of Lave and Wenger's concept that I term 'communities of agreed sermonic enterprise'.

The CASE concept

I have substituted 'enterprise' for 'practice' because it brings with it teleological and purposive connotations present in words such as 'venture' and 'project' and 'endeavours' with quite definite and identifiable aims in view. 'Sermonic' includes not just the preaching event but also the preparation leading to that event and the follow-on from that event along with subsequent sermon events involving the same participants. Finally, it is an 'agreed' enterprise. There exists a shared understanding of the value, of the purpose, and of at least some of the means to achieve that purpose. This small term betrays a stumbling-block, for even preachers are by no means all agreed on the nature of what they are doing. For the preacher caught in the cross-fire, the expectations of listeners, the instruction of mentors, and examples of immensely diverse practices may together make even a lowest common denominator impossible to find. We cannot always take for granted a *high* level of agreement in the sermonic enterprise, but it is reasonable to believe that the enterprise will include a joint pursuit of truth and light and a (perhaps limited) understanding of what is a sermon, what it is for and what it sounds and feels like.

To aid this pursuit I am proposing five frames through which a community of agreed sermonic enterprise (CASE) may be viewed. These are different ways of exploring, of expanding and of testing the concept against what happens in practice and by which we may begin to name our vision for the forming of future preachers.

The educational frame

The first frame brings into focus the traditions of the community, particularly as passed on through the teaching and the accumulated, expressed wisdom about preaching that the novice preacher can receive didactically. This happens in various ways and settings in the larger Christian community of which she or he is a part. Admittedly, books and treatises on preaching, lectures and other forms of verbal instruction are primarily an aspect of cognitive forms of learning, as mentioned earlier. They may be received in quite individualistic, not social, ways. But it is important to recognize that, in the 'thick' description of social learning that I have attempted, such forms of instruction are also properly speaking one way in which the 'company of preachers' extends and replicates itself over time. Teaching preaching is a community enterprise, extended over time and geographically dispersed, yet binding the individual in loose webs of connections and influences, through publishing, through conferences, through distribution of audio, and increasingly video, sermons and lectures, as well as course lectures, essays and assigned reading.

The 'Cloud of Witnesses'

The American Episcopal homiletician David Schlafer wrote about the 'Ghosts and Graces of Your Preaching Parents':

> Anyone who has gone to church with any regularity has preaching ancestors – preachers who have modelled, for good or ill, what a sermon is supposed to sound like: how long, how loud, how laced with Scripture references, how esoteric, or how heart-rending it should be. Whenever you stand up to begin a sermon, there is a cloud of unseen witnesses behind you . . . They are present. And they are not silent. (1995, p. 33)

The second frame of the CASE concept is the 'cloud of witnesses', or in other words the traditional examples of preaching and Christian witness and exemplars from the past as well as the present. Preachers heard and/or seen in action, live or on video, sermons read or listened to through audio recordings will have an impact, often through imitative mechanisms.

Teachers of preaching from Augustine to the present have recognized and recommended imitation as of prima facie value to the preacher who desires to learn from others. But copying and mere behavioural imitation are discouraged, lest in the words of Fred Craddock (1985, p. 20) it produces 'caricatures in the pulpit'. Instead writers speak of paying attention in order to 'catch the spirit' of great preachers (Hale, 1913, p. 362) or of having their 'attitudes, philosophy, and style of preaching' (Shea, 2006, pp. 62–3) formed by modelling themselves on preachers heard in younger years. I suggest that imitative aspects of learning to preach may be seen in three areas that contribute to the identity and functioning of the preacher: skills development, character formation and theological standpoint.

It is clear from Paul's urging in Philippians 2.5, for example, that imitation is, as it were, woven into the fabric of discipleship. The development of the preacher's character is bound to be a matter of striving and/or unconsciously desiring to be like close and admired role models – models who themselves are evidently and earnestly engaged in *imitatio Christi*.

The student preacher is also subject to the dynamic of character formation and transformation during and following encounters, as the meaning of the sermons heard become the means of God's graceful work on the listening preacher-to-be. A social aspect of this formational dynamic is noted by James Nieman as 'the way social character formation occurs among those who engage a particular practice within its governing domain' (Nieman, 2008, p. 22). This frame is thus concerned with both role models and their effect on the learner preacher.

Mentors

This frame encourages us to consider the relationships between preachers and their mentors. Here we examine both positive and negative effects, the affirming as well as discouraging impact that a mentor can have on a preacher. Do schemes for mentoring that impose or assign mentors fall far short of the beneficial effects of a mentor freely chosen by the preacher and coming at a time that the student preacher chooses? Again, the matter of character formation, of being moulded by the attention and influence of another, is implicit in this frame.

Mentoring and forms of coaching are in some senses structurally established in denominational training schemes such as those provided by the Methodist Church in the UK (the On Trial and On Note process) and the Church of England system of training curacies. A primary weakness or point of compromise can occur when the mentor is expected also to provide and/or evaluate reports that materially affect the student's career progress. This is the teacher-as-gatekeeper problem.

Peer learning

The only set of relationships that seem free of the gatekeeper's oversight are within the peer group. One implicit condition of the trust peers put in one another is that they do not have the institutional assessor's power over one another. The potential of learning from and through peer groups and that of peer-assisted learning is supported by a body of educational literature, although the particularities of Christian ministers learning to preach together are only just beginning to be addressed (Long and Tisdale, 2008). When the developmental practice of preaching is conducted in the context of a peer group, it finds favour with students and teachers. The fact remains that it is less common to find this kind of educational practice in homiletics in UK than in US seminaries.

Giving feedback following a sermon is an activity where peer involvement may be of significant value in a preacher's development. This requires the careful construction of a safe environment, a shared understanding of the parameters of the craft, and the limits of criticism, as well as showing sensitivity for the emotional stress and personal involvement experienced in preaching a sermon. Under such conditions peer feedback can be intelligent, focused and helpful to the whole peer group. Barbara K. Lundblad, Professor of Preaching at Union Theological Seminary in New York, writes:

> The practicum group is the locus for the most intensive practicing . . . The small group may be the best place for students to discuss their theologies of preaching and learn to honor differences among them. Students can practice communal interpretation of texts, receive feedback on sermon theme or focus, or practice a possible sermon introduction. (Lundblad, 2008, p. 218)

In my own teaching of preaching I have found particular value in the construction of a practical learning environment where students are given the opportunity, structure and guidelines to discuss one another's sermons. This has been marked by strong student engagement, fruitful exchanges and positive evaluations. The benefits can be intellectual. As Christine Blair points out in her study of adult learning in theological education, 'reflection is strengthened when adults can return to the subject matter several times in different ways' (Blair, 1997, p. 15). But the benefit – and the learning – can go deeper than levels of conceptual understanding for some students.

One student wrote to me:

> One of the most helpful learning experiences for preaching has been an optional group for preaching practice, as part of our homiletics class . . . A key part to this learning was being part of a group that learned to grow in trust of each other and thereby be able to listen and learn from the criticisms made . . . The group was able to go to a deeper level of trust than perhaps in a parish setting might, because everyone was in a position of learning. It also felt like the criticism was part of our act of worship – all working together to build the kingdom of God.

Congregational learning

Finally the CASE concept may be framed by viewing the congregation not only as listener but also as teacher and as learner. A minister or priest arriving in a church or parish will encounter a set of expectations about the sermons preached as part of worship. There will be more-or-less precisely expressed customs regarding a sermon's length and its place in the service, the position of delivery, and the homiletical nature of the sermon, that is, whether it is teaching on Christian living and discipleship, or exposition of Scripture, or topical, sacramental, etc. Less explicit, but still discernible, will be the thematic relationship of the sermon to Scripture, to Christian tradition and doctrine, and to the rest of the service or liturgy. There will also be congregational expectations and understandings for the minister to discover about the rhetoric of the sermon, its intellectual level, the style of public speaking and the degree of self-revelation allowed. Of course this is a two-way process: the congregation has things to learn from most preachers about listening to sermons and hearing the word of God. All of these are part of the negotiation that takes place as a preacher and a congregation learn to create together that sermon event.

This is not entirely new. In their 1989 book on learning preaching, Wardlaw and Baumer note:

> We purposely involve the students in teaching methods that model a congregation's participation in the sermon formation process. (1989, p. 12)

Here the institutional setting being referred to consciously and strategically looks forward to the future setting of learning preaching that happens (most often) after training (in the USA). Feedback and reflection on practice, facilitated and provided by select congregational members, allows the preacher to learn and to develop sermons that are not only better sermons but also better for the community. Such a feedback context can be as intimate as one or two trusted church members providing criticism and assessment, or as broad as a web-based 'blog' where reactions to and discussions of a sermon can give the preacher considerable guidance on the effectiveness of his or her communication strategy.[2]

Less widely used, but not without strong advocates in the field of homiletics, is the creation of sermon planning groups to facilitate the creation of sermons that reflect more accurately the concerns and issues facing the intended listeners. This can take a variety of forms, and internet-based communication will extend the possibilities here as well.

Guidelines and recommendations

> If elephants can be trained to dance, lions to play, and leopards to hunt, surely preachers can be taught to preach. (Desiderius Erasmus: Bainton, 1970, p. 323)

The frames of the CASE along with my earlier remarks should enable us to evaluate courses, programmes, training schemes and the environments and contexts in which future preachers must learn. For the rest of this chapter I want to consider notable characteristics that will mark the forming of future preachers.

Homiletics and theologies of preaching

The first frame of the CASE, recognizing the teaching of preaching, also recognizes the pedagogical limitation of most seminary instruction in preaching.[3] Nevertheless, clear theologies of preaching will enable intelligent vocational commitments. Such theologies consider what preaching is for, why it is necessary, how God's word is heard through preaching, and what are the energies and stimuli available to the minister faced with weekly preaching commitments. That is homiletical theology, and is a vital companion to systematic, doctrinal, biblical and ethical theology shaping (it is hoped) the content of a student's sermons. In future, students in training for ministry will be able to articulate a personal theology of preaching in order to demonstrate engagement with the calling to preach, and to do so with respect to the culture as well as the denomination in which they are being called to serve.

Recognizing role models

Role models, the 'cloud of witnesses' shaping and influencing the learner preacher, are a prominent part of the second frame of the CASE. Candidates for ministry in training will be encouraged as early as possible to consider consciously their attitudes and receptivity towards role models and towards those who can give them wise and sound mentoring and coaching. This will overlap with other aspects of the spiritual formation of the minister and other ministerial roles being developed. In particular they will be encouraged and helped to recognize their preaching role models, not only in recent experience but also particularly during early periods of their formation as Christians. Prescribed forms of imitation, as in Donald Schön's theories of the reflective practitioner (1983), should be developed and encouraged. They will also benefit from being shielded somewhat from the prevailing individualism that pressures a preacher to be original before they can have the experience and maturity to develop their own authentic 'preaching voice'.

Mentoring to induct

Within the third frame of the CASE, there will be value in mentors giving not only coaching instruction and enabling reflection on practice but also induction into the more subtle values, expectations and codes of preaching conduct. Communities of practice that are educationally beneficial will provide mentors who are able to impart wisdom and constructive criticism. In my view it would be preferable (though it may be impractical) to separate these mentoring roles from evaluative assessment designed to have a bearing on the student's professional progress and future ministerial appointments. The degree to which a positive mentoring experience depends on 'personal chemistry' will be recognized and allowances made for this in institutional pedagogic structures.

For younger adults learning preaching, learning will include being given responsibility *before* demonstrating competence. This will be realized in active apprentice-like situations, where there are leaders who are prepared to 'take the heat' when things go wrong. Only in such ways can they safely move from stages of 'legitimate peripheral participation' to full membership in the 'company of preachers'.

Following on from this, where institutions must organize the provision of mentoring, many supervisory ministers will benefit from induction into mentoring preaching students. Some will benefit from explicit training in best practices of current homiletics. Promulgating theories of psychological type and particularly the work of Leslie Francis, as outlined in his chapter earlier, could be of great benefit to candidates and the supervisory ministers with whom they are placed. Sermon evaluation strategies taught in homiletics class are immensely enhanced when shared with an experienced mentor, and will become a standard feature of ministerial reflection on practice during placements and later supervised ministry. Supervising ministers during placements will both model and teach skills in exegeting congregation and culture.

Peer-assisted learning

As emphasized by the fourth frame of the CASE, there will be the recognition of the value of peer-oriented structures in theological education and ministerial development, and establishment of systems to encourage their organic growth. Natural and deep peer relationships are of course harder to form outside of the residential training model that is becoming increasingly outmoded and expensive. Therefore in the best homiletics courses a particular effort will be made to incorporate practical workshops giving primacy to delivery of sermons with a small group of students as a congregation. This will involve feedback from other students that is both structured and elicited for wise counsel and compassionate encouragement as well as for the sake of academic commitment and fair criticism given to the student preacher. Collaborative working experiences, such as worship and sermon pre-planning groups, will be introduced during pre-ordination training even as they are becoming – for UK Anglicans, at any rate – more and more a feature of team ministry situations and lay-led services of worship. This can even lead to understanding and experiencing preaching as a collaborative project, in which guise it can also become normative for the relationship between preacher and congregation.

Congregations as educators

I believe that in future there will be a greater appreciation among new ministers of the role of the congregation in inducting the preacher into the CASE. This will recognize the ways in which approval and disapproval, responses and non-responses can (and should) shape a preacher's theological standpoint, hermeneutic approaches and rhetorical strategies. Intentional ways of gaining congregational feedback will be taught in courses and modelled by supervisors. An important implication of this frame is that preachers entering parish or circuit ministry with regular preaching commitments will be much more aware of the process by which they and their congregations are *together* learning to preach the sermons that God has for that church at that time. This will happen if through programmes, schemes and strategic overtures placement congregations are taught sermon listening skills and become open to having their expectations raised about the sermon, whether it is a 50-minute teaching sermon or a 5-minute homily. In these ways congregations may be woven into the community of agreed sermonic enterprise.

Conclusion

The preachers of the future, as noted by other writers in this book, are enmeshed in a complex web of community expectations, liturgical traditions, technological developments, pluralistic cultures and changes to society. Even the most theologically conservative recognize that forms of preaching from the past are of limited value in the present, and are unlikely to fare any better in the future. But please do not assume I am advocating a slick accommodation to prevailing communication models, whether derived from the news anchor, the stand-up comedian, the electioneering politician, the doorstep salesman, or the internet blogger. Preaching in the future will only be preaching if it remembers that it is, *sui generis*, a unique activity in which the inexpressible wonder of the mercy of God in Christ Jesus miraculously and for brief, brilliant moments shines and takes shape in the clay of the faltering words of all-too-human preachers. This happens far more frequently than we have any right to expect, and encourages us to work with our preachers to train, to nurture and to develop them. The CASE concept attempts to recognize and extend the work that this entails, involving mentors, peers and congregations, as well as institutional structures that often hardly seem nimble enough to keep up with culture's jack-rabbit progress. The difficulties facing preachers over a course of lifelong learning are daunting, and many are the discouragements. Our confidence that there will be a future for these preachers is based on our confidence that God will continue to want to speak to us, embodying his Word again and again after the pattern of our Lord.

Notes

1. There are of course many different sermon types with different functions, and many of these are outlined most helpfully by David Schlafer (2004). His grid 'Preaching Parents: A Gallery of Caricatures' reminds us that for each sermon type (e.g. lecture, censure, legal defence, sales talk) there is a primary purpose (such as, respectively, to inform, correct, convince, or attract).

2. Such online reactions to sermons, as well as the recycling of sermons, in both text and video form (for example YouTube™) considerably extend the 'biography' of sermons. This new phenomenon is worthy of study, but I suggest that learning to preach 'cultural texts' that can or may be recycled in these ways is a further challenge to the developing preacher of the future.

3. As Joseph Sittler cautioned from the USA experience: 'the expectation must not be cherished that, save for modest and obvious instruction about voice, pace, organization and such matters, preaching as a lively art of the church can be taught at all. And therefore, seminary provisions for instructions in preaching, when these exist as separate curriculum items, should be re-examined' (1966, p. 7).

References

Armstrong, Thomas, 2000, *Multiple Intelligences in the Classroom*, 2nd edn, Alexandria, VA: Association for Supervision and Curriculum Development.

Bainton, Roland Herbert, 1970, *Erasmus of Christendom*, London: Collins.

Blair, Christine Eaton, 1997, 'Understanding Adult Learners: Challenges for Theological Education', *Theological Education* 34.1, pp. 11–24.

Bonar, Andrew Alexander, and Robert Murray McCheyne, 1960, *The Life of Robert Murray McCheyne*, London: Banner of Truth Trust.

Brooks, Phillips, 1989, *The Joy of Preaching* (1877), Foreword and Biographical Information by Warren Wiersbe, Grand Rapids, MI: Kregel.

Craddock, Fred B., 1985, *Preaching*, Nashville: Abingdon Press.

Hale, Edward, 1913, 'Recent books on preaching and preachers', *Harvard Theological Review* 6.3, pp. 360–6.

Honey, Peter, and Alan Mumford, 1992, *The Manual of Learning Styles*, 3rd edn, Maidenhead: Peter Honey.

Kirton, M. J., 1994, *Adaptors and Innovators: Styles of Creativity and Problem Solving*, rev. edn, London: Routledge.

Kolb, David A., 1984, *Experiential Learning: Experience as the Source of Learning and Development*, London: Prentice-Hall.

Lave, Jean, and Etienne Wenger, 1991, *Situated Learning: Legitimate Peripheral Participation*, Cambridge: Cambridge University Press.

Long, T. G., and Leonora Tubbs Tisdale (eds), 2008, *Teaching Preaching as a Christian Practice*, Louisville: Westminster John Knox Press.

Lundblad, Barbara K., 2008, 'Designing the introductory course in preaching', in T. G. Long and Leonora Tubbs Tisdale (eds), *Teaching Preaching as a Christian Practice*, Louisville: Westminster John Knox Press, pp. 207–22.

Nieman, James, 2008, 'Why the idea of practice matters', in T. G. Long and Leonora Tubbs Tisdale (eds), *Teaching Preaching as a Christian Practice*, Louisville: Westminster John Knox Press, pp. 18–40.

Pasquarello, Michael, 2005, *Sacred Rhetoric: Preaching as a Theological and Pastoral Practice of the Church*, Cambridge: Eerdmans.

Schlafer, David J., 1995, *Your Way with God's Word*, Cambridge, MA: Cowley Publications.

___, 2004, *Playing with Fire: Preaching Work as Kindling Art*, Cambridge, MA: Cowley Publications.

Schön, Donald A., 1983, *The Reflective Practitioner: How Professionals Think in Action*, Aldershot: Ashgate.

Shea, David J., 2006, 'Self-understanding in Catholic preaching: how the identity of the priest shapes his approach to preaching', dissertation, Aquinas Institute of Theology.

Sittler, Joseph, 1966, *The Anguish of Preaching*, Philadelphia: Fortress Press.

Stevenson, Geoffrey, and David Wilkinson, 2003, *The Vox Project on 21st Century Communication: A Research Report on the Provision of Training in Preaching, Apologetics and Media*, Durham: Centre for Christian Communication.

Stewart, James S., 1946, *Heralds of God*, London: Hodder & Stoughton.

Tennant, Mark, 1997, *Psychology and Adult Learning*, 2nd edn, London: Routledge.

Wardlaw, Don M., and Fred Baumer, 1989, *Learning Preaching: Understanding and Participating in the Process*, Lincoln, IL: Academy of Homiletics: printed by the Lincoln Christian College and Seminary Press.

Wenger, Etienne, 1998, *Communities of Practice: Learning, Meaning, and Identity*, Cambridge: Cambridge University Press.

Wenger, Etienne, and Richard A. McDermott, 2002, *Cultivating Communities of Practice: A Guide to Managing Knowledge*, Boston: Harvard Business School Press.

Witkin, H. A., et al., 1977, 'Field dependent and field independent cognitive styles and their educational implications', *Review of Educational Research* 47.1, pp. 1–64.

Afterword

Anticipating Unpredictable Resurrection

Preaching in the Hope of a God-Engendered Future

DAVID J. SCHLAFER

Any human enterprise hoping to *have* a future must *anticipate* it. To remain vital, businesses, governments, non-profits, interest groups and personal relationships all have to try their best to look ahead – to undertake exercises in anticipation.

This volume represents just such an exercise with respect to preaching. A company of colleagues – widely recognized as among 'the brightest and the best' of homiletical professionals in the United Kingdom – has been convened to articulate its reflections and insights, its concerns and cautions, its expectations and imaginings about the future of gospel proclamation within the context of Christian worship. The authors address a range of questions that, broadly speaking, are basic and standard in any 'future mapping' exercise:

1 What aspects of our history offer a perspective from which we can assess our present situation, and project our future prospects?
2 What patterns of current practice invite critique; and to what practices – long honoured but less than widely observed – might we need to be recalled?
3 What factors in current culture require fuller recognition; and what strategies ready-to-hand might we more effectively employ to engage these factors?
4 What new challenges face us; and what new resources and strategies might – if we discerningly appropriate them – foster fresh life?

All these questions are implicit in each of the foregoing chapters, yet certain chapters are especially helpful in focusing on one dimension in particular:

1 In the first section on Context, Roger Spiller, Duncan Macpherson, Ruthlyn Bradshaw, along with Ian Stackhouse (Chapter 4) analyse

the rich historical roots in the respective worship traditions they represent.

2 Trevor Pitt (Chapter 6) critiques the theological drift that has tended to de-centre preachers who feel driven (in the face of waning religious interest) to say whatever they hope will elicit a favourable response. Susan Durber (Chapter 13) calls preachers back to the earthy spiritual practice of attending to the everyday.

3 Roger Standing (Chapter 1) names contemporary cultural 'givens' that preachers must confront. Paul Johns (Chapter 8) urges more direct engagement with the daily news – as a source of continuing revelation, rather than merely as a means of illustrating revelation dispatched 'once upon a time'. Leslie Francis (Chapter 12) enjoins preachers to address the full range of psychological types that comprise most congregations. Margaret Withers (Chapter 9) commends simple strategies to foster community participation in worship with its younger members. And Ian Paul (Chapter 10) invites fresh attention to the possibilities inherent in careful exegesis and creative metaphor.

4 Stephen Wright (Chapter 7) and Richard Littledale (Chapter 11) perceptively explore aspects of recent communication technology – Wright in relation to how we hear God's word in Scripture, Littledale in connection with how we gain a hearing for God's word in preaching, in each case clearly evidencing that, judiciously employed, this technology can substantially contribute to the task of fitting preaching for the future.

Future mapping is always an exercise in educated guessing – and often a matter of debate. (The projections of experts were of little use in anticipating the recent worldwide economic downturn. Contention over the prospects of health care reform in the United States has been not just vigorous but vitriolic.) Notwithstanding the expertise and care evident in this disciplined attempt to anticipate the future of preaching in the UK, it is, therefore, not surprising (and certainly circumspect) for Geoffrey Stevenson, the volume's editor, to issue a caveat at the outset: 'Who would be so foolish as to try to predict the future of preaching?'

More is going on in this disclaimer, however, than a recognition that 'the best-laid plans' of any future-mapping exercise are always undermined by the advent of the unexpected. There is more going on here than what is entailed in a simple (and obvious) acknowledgement that 'things never turn out quite like we anticipated'.

This rhetorical question Stevenson poses is immediately preceded by two others – ones that are by no means merely rhetorical: 'What if [Christianity] always returns, as time and time again, to the resurrection form of the Lord? Would a resurrection in preaching be far behind?' Built into the framing of these two particularly theological questions is a clear distinction between future mapping generally and the attempt to undertake an exercise in anticipation with respect to preaching. In a word, it is the distinction between intellectual humility and spiritual reverence.

There is a dimension of unpredictability inherent in the affirmation of divine agency that far transcends the admission that 'our data are always incomplete and our projection models imperfect'. We worship a God whose 'ways are higher than [our] ways, and [whose] thoughts than [our] thoughts'; a God who is always doing 'a new thing' that we may not perceive – indeed, a God who 'is making all things new'.

Although there is a predictable rhythm in the liturgical life of the Church (one paralleling the regular seasonal cycles of nature in which 'flowers return in the Spring'), the point of liturgical predictability has to do precisely with enabling us better to perceive what is always unpredictable – and inevitably threatening. The move through Holy Week toward Easter is not simply an elaborate dramatic way of reassuring one another that, difficult and confusing though our circumstance may be, in the end we will all live 'happily ever after'. Death rears its head afresh every Holy Week. How it will be challenged is never, ever 'given in advance'. We can, in hope, anticipate resurrection; we can never predict its outbreak or its form.

The Holy Week during which I write these words from the United States is one fraught with raucous outpourings of venomous hate speech in the wake of the passage, at long last, of a clumsy, cobbled attempt to make health care available to those who cannot afford it. The anger being unleashed far exceeds the previous bounds of partisan, polarizing discourse. Elements of egoistic economic entitlement – and of racism raw and ill-concealed – suffuse the clamour. Racial and homophobic epithets have been hurled at legislators (and bricks thrown through the windows of some of their offices). One prominent legislator, en route to voting on the health care bill, has been spat upon. Threats of violence have been uttered in the mass media and in messages left on telephone answering machines. Attempts, through rational discourse, to achieve a measure of bipartisan consensus through respectful compromise have proven not only ineffective but even more incendiary.

Less dramatic, but perhaps more significant, is a gathering momentum of open hostility toward the proclamation of the gospel as 'good news to the poor' – in terms both practical and political. A widely acclaimed political pundit, with a 'gift' for oratory no less engaging than that of President Obama, is mounting an attack on all churches that affirm any commitment to social justice. Attempts by mainstream Christian advocates of social justice to engage in substantive, measured dialogue have been rejected.

Such forays into demagoguery, of course, are nothing new. What give them new and potent energy are the very technological factors to which this volume's contributors have alluded. A prime question, then, for the future of preaching (in my nation, at least), is this: what does it mean, in the midst of an increasingly life-squelching environment, to 'return to the resurrection form of the Lord'?

It will surely entail more than just preaching *about* Easter (or finding fresh preaching patterns and communication forms for doing so). 'New' life – resurrection life – if and when it comes – is likely to be as disorienting to those of us who are charged with preaching today as it was to those who were the initial witnesses to the resurrection. And such words – film clips, tweets – as we are able to craft may well be dismissed as 'an idle tale'.

As I reflect with sober realism in the midst of much uncertainty, I am reminded of earlier experience of uncertainty and loss – and of utterly unpredictable resurrection.

A movement known as 'The New Homiletic' was generating considerable energy in the United States, where the work of pioneers like Fred Craddock, David Buttrick, Thomas Long and Eugene Lowry was being widely embraced. Not restricted to (or rightly understood as) simply 'storytelling', the New Homiletic was (and is) an attempt to interpret texts of Scripture, and shape the form of sermons, not as didactic expositions (interspersed with inspiring illustrations and exhortations) but rather as 'narratives' of spiritual exploration, adventure and discovery. In a word (said the New Homiletic), rather than issuing informational reports about (and entreaties toward) transformation, sermons should shape and foster experiences of transformation akin to those witnessed to in the pages of Scripture.

I was invited by an English colleague to co-lead a conference, in which this way of preaching was presented to clergy in the Church of England. It was an invitation I accepted with a mixture of delight and dread. ('What, among those whom I've never met, can I say that will be at all helpful?'). I entered the conference venue – Sarum College on the close of Salisbury Cathedral. The atmosphere was sombre – even funereal – for the venerable theological college of Salisbury and Wells was ceasing operation.

We began the conference. At the first break for afternoon tea, one of the participants came up to me and said: 'My training in preaching at theological college consisted in being told, "Your vicar will help you with that when you get into your first parish."' The reception my training colleague and I received from the participants was quite cordial – and decidedly non-committal. This way of preaching we were trying to introduce seemed to sound in the ears of many as though it were an unknown tongue. There was clearly great interest and high expectation (generated in advance primarily due to the publicity efforts of a competent and dedicated group of Continuing Ministerial Education Officers who were sponsoring the event). But it was far from clear, as we approached the middle of a four-day event, that the conference was going to live up to its billing.

Conspicuous by their intense attention, but very silent presence, were 8 women in the group of 35, all of whom had recently been ordained to the Anglican priesthood, following the denomination's final ratification of the ordering of women as priests.

Among the features of the conference was the opportunity for participants to visit one-on-one with a conference leader, and to discuss a sermon text that they had submitted in advance. In my prior preparation for this series of individual conferences, an awareness began to dawn in me that, in most cases, the sermons I was reading from the female preachers were, by and large, significantly stronger, both theologically and homiletically, than those of their male counterparts. Noting the fact, I did not know what to make of it.

In the individual interviews, one woman after another, each in her own way, told me, in effect, 'We knew there was a more effective way to preach than the expository model set forth by our venerable male preaching instructors. What you have done in this conference is simply give us words for that which we have intuitively known, and been trying to practise.'

Encouraged in their individual coaching sessions, the women began to find their voices in the process of the conference. Their participation gently, deftly turned the tide. Other participants began to 'catch on', to experiment, to risk, to venture, to grow. One very nervous American homiletician (in addition to being profoundly grateful and more than a little relieved) heard sounds of resurrection he could never have begun to predict. (Though, in retrospect, I found myself thinking of those first women witnesses to the resurrection depicted by the Gospel Storytellers.)

'The New Homiletic' is no longer new. And, while research and reflection continue, no new paradigm for preaching has emerged on either side of the Atlantic (at least as far as I can tell). Furthermore, it is not clear to me, as American society becomes more akin to the secular culture in which Europe has been immersed for decades, that simply doing a New Homiletic upgrade will be sufficient for the preaching task ahead. This seems especially evident in the wake of a baseline of social interchange that is becoming not just more partisan but also more viral – words selected with specific intent for employment not as bridge-builders but as battering-rams.

Important though each dimension of the future mapping undertaken in this book quite clearly is, it does not yet appear (at least to me) how a God-engendered resurrection in preaching will be effected through them, individually or together. But having experienced resurrection in preaching (in my own, and in that of others), I am quietly confident that, when it comes, its features will, in retrospect, be as discernible as they are now unpredictable. And that the gathered wisdom comprising this book will come to be regarded as faithful waiting.

Meanwhile, how can we, here and now, preach toward such a resurrection with creative anticipation? I am much taken by Geoffrey Stevenson's proposal for the fostering of communities of preaching practice – especially insofar as this involves mentors (who are not also supervisors), peers and congregations. The notion of preaching as community practice has begun to gain some traction in the United States, primarily through the recent publication of *Teaching Preaching as a Christian Practice* (Long and Tisdale, 2008).

The authors of this volume affirm the importance of communities of practice in the process of learning preaching, and offer various teaching strategies and student exercises that they deem conducive to this vision. In large measure, however (or so it seems to me), the chapters consist primarily in *recasting* strategies for learning preaching rather than *revisioning* them – in taking the topics that comprise a standard homiletics curriculum and rendering them 'preaching lab friendly' – amenable to collegial group process. This is a worthy project, but does not, I think, get to the heart of what Stevenson is seeking to describe, substantiate with reference to other disciplines, and elicit in 'communities of agreed sermonic enterprise'.

How can preachers and listeners convene in mutual support to discern the evolving trajectories of one another's learning in the practice of preaching? Some years ago, an opportunity came to me as an extraordinary and priceless gift. After the election of its rector as a bishop, the lay leaders of a very large congregation in suburban Northern Virginia decided to offer support to the remaining four clergy staff members by underwriting for them a weekly continuing education experience in preaching growth. These four priests were, at first, somewhat guarded. ('Are they telling us they don't think our preaching is any good?') After an interview with those with whom I might be working, I was invited to serve as their consultant.

The four preachers were as different as they could be: (1) an intuitive, allusive, middle-aged man with a pronounced Jungian orientation; (2) a barrel-chested, thick-necked fellow with the raspy voice of a military drill sergeant who marched concepts with rigour from one end of his sermon to the other; (3) a middle-aged woman with keen sensory awareness who filled her sermons with artful image after image; and (4) an elderly gentleman, somewhat absent-minded, with a story – well, several – available for recounting at the drop of any opportunity.

These four worked together well as pastoral colleagues, but were very reticent (not surprisingly) to offer any commentary on one another's sermons. The difficulty (from the vantage point of this homiletical consultant) was that the sermons of the Jungian were like flying kites with no strings attached; the drill sergeant's sermons rolled over listeners like army tanks; the imagistic artist's sermons tended to foster either sensory overload or Attention Deficit Disorder; and the storyteller's endless anecdotes hopped about the Scripture lessons in ever-shifting, overlapping rabbit trails.

Tuesday mornings were designated as staff meetings, held in the church library. While the clergy processed parish business with other members of the church staff, I would listen to a tape of the sermon preached on the previous Sunday by one of the four. At mid-morning, the other staff were excused, I was invited in. All phone calls and other interruptions were held; and the five of us would spend well over an hour together in spirited professional conversation. First we reviewed the sermon offered by the previous week's preacher; then we listened to the texts appointed for the following week, and listened the following week's preacher into articulate speech by engaging his or her initial impressions, questions and insights-in-the-raw about a sermon in process.

It would be a serious misrepresentation to describe the two years we spent together as my 'teaching them preaching', or 'remediating, ameliorating and improving their preaching skills'. In truth, I served primarily as a discussion convener, a place holder, a sacred space keeper. A sacred space it was, as a 'community of sermonic enterprise' came into being and developed a rich life of its own. I knew I had (as the saying goes) 'worked myself out of a job', when, one Sunday morning after the first of the three services, the Jungian grabbed the artist, pulled her into the library, and said with urgency: 'My sermon didn't work; help me fix it before the next service begins.' (And she did.)

Particularly fascinating was the fact that none of these preachers lost their distinctive voices. Rather, each clarified and enriched it. The Jungian still soared, but there was a tether on his sermon kites. The artist began to order her images in coherent, discernibly unfolding patterns. The old storyteller's anecdotes began to have a point – and at least some recognizable relation with each other. The drill sergeant's concepts still had sharp movement and strong cadence; yet, somehow they began to sparkle and dance.

Midway through the process, we invited the whole congregation for lunch in the parish hall. The room was filled with close to 200 people who first listened to a description of the process in mutual listening that we had undertaken and then offered their own hearings to one another of the sermon preached that day.

Need I tell you who 'learned' the most from this two-year experience?

A critical element in our listening was a clear, sequential process that elicited 'a thick description' of the sermons preached. Not 'I really liked *this*; but *that* was heresy!' Rather: (1st) 'This is what I am still hearing.' (2nd) 'Here is where that hearing led me.' (And 3rd) 'Here is how the sermon's theological focus and homiletical framing *fostered* what I heard and where I was led.' No one was allowed to offer more than one observation at a time. Each stage of description was explicitly explored by the entire group before we moved on to the next.[1] Is there a place in this kind of collegial discussion for what is usually called 'critique'? Yes, but only after everyone has listened deeply to the multi-layered 'hearings' of all listeners. (For my 'assessment' is likely to be modified in light of my hearing from others certain things that, on my own, I did not hear.) Furthermore, the assessment offered is not as 'a summary judgement', but a set of probing invitations for the preacher to consider (and adopt, decline or modify).

This process of Spirit-ed Conversation and preaching discernment can be introduced at the beginning of a course in preaching. It can be employed in the process of group mentoring (the third frame of the CASE concept that Stevenson proposes). It can be used in entirely peer-led communities convened around the nurturing of preaching practice (Stevenson's fourth frame). And (last, but far from least) in congregational groups who are willing to own their essential role in the ministry of preaching in their local church (the fifth frame of his Communities of Agreed Sermonic Enterprise).

To reiterate the obvious, this set of practice strategies is *not* proffered here as any prognostication regarding the 'future' of preaching. Nor is it put forward as a means of preserving or promoting any particular vision of what preaching is or should become. It may, however, be considered in light of the editor's initial questions: 'What if [Christianity] always returns, as time and time again, to the resurrection form of the Lord? Would a resurrection in preaching be far behind?'

This model for the operation of communities of preaching practice (a partial fleshing-out of some of what Stevenson gestures toward in his CASE vision) is itself a place holder, a sacred space keeper, for the advent of a preaching resurrection that is God-engendered. Who knows what might emerge, Spirit-sparked, in the conversations that both manifest and create communities of preaching practice?

In John's Gospel, it is the peace breath of the Risen Lord, plus his bestowal of the Spirit, that releases the disciples from behind doors that are locked down tight. Luke's perspective is interestingly different. The disciples are instructed to await the outpouring of the Holy Spirit – an instruction they observe by means of the protecting, nurturing, imagination-energizing practice patterns of community worship. Rather than being constrained and constricted by fear, they are convened and conjoined in anticipation.

Homiletician that I am, I fantasize that they spend their time not just singing and praying, but also practising their preaching with one another. (Granted from whence they had just come, they are facing a rather steep learning curve.) The Spirit descends. Out they go to preach the resurrection – and in the process their preaching is resurrected. Yes the Spirit animates their discourse and opens the ears of the incredulous. But, I submit, the Spirit doesn't compose their sermons for them. The disciple preachers have to think with their minds, and articulate with their human tongues what the fiery tongues have energized from heaven. The result of their preaching mission? Their Community of Agreed Sermonic Enterprise is dramatically enlarged.

The disciples repeat the process from one end of Acts to the other. (The book is, in fact, the first recorded anthology of sermons by followers of the Risen Lord.) Each sermon preached in the book of Acts is provoked by actions of those who are seriously disoriented by the resurrection. And each resurrection sermon sets off further shock waves. (Think of the sermons preached by Peter, John, Stephen, Philip, Paul – and don't leave out the critical brief homily preached by Rhoda – a sermon that gets the same response as that received by those women who first witnessed the resurrection.)

So . . . what if we preachers return, 'as time and time again', in disciplined anticipation for the resurrection form of the Lord? Would a resurrection in preaching be far behind?

Even so, Lord, quickly come, and make our preaching new!

Note

1. A full description of the process may be found in the Appendix. As you will see, it is designed primarily for use in extended settings where three sermons are offered in dialogue with one another. It can easily be adapted for reflection on a single sermon.

Reference

Long, Thomas G., and Lenora Tubbs Tisdale (eds), 2008, *Teaching Preaching as a Christian Practice: A New Approach to Homiletical Pedagogy*, Louisville and London: Westminster John Knox Press.

Appendix

Spirit-ed Conversation

Learning Preaching in Communities of Practice

The following preaching workshop outline is designed primarily for use in extended settings where three sermons are offered in dialogue with one another. It can easily be adapted for reflection on a single sermon.

We gather as a Company of Preachers to share and sharpen our listening and preaching gifts. Inevitably, we bring with us default patterns of response imprinted by our culture – patterns of:

- **Fan Clubs** – who applaud their idols energetically but indiscriminately:

    You're so GOOD!

- **Town Hall Meeting Partisans** – who express passionate convictions in strident voices:

    I'm RIGHT; you're WRONG!

- **Focus Groups** – who record their preferences for polling purposes:

    I WOULD buy THIS; I WOULDN'T buy THAT!

- **Therapy or Support Groups** – who offer affirmation and support:

    Thanks so much for SHARING!

- **Contest Judges** – who render verdicts:

    You WIN – You LOSE! (Your rating is 2.587!)

- **Advisory committees** –who critique job performances:

    We'll FIX it for you!

In the setting of a community of preaching practice, however, we do not assemble in order

- to 'be nice' to the preacher
- to sniff out latent heresy

216

- to offer 'constructive criticism for the preacher's own good'
- to ascertain whether our own preaching is 'just as good' as that of others.

Rather, we convene as participants in *a spiritual exercise* of *multi-layered listening.* We seek:

- to apprehend 'the word of the Lord', as it comes to us through one another's words;
- to discover – through listening to one another – how our own preaching gifts might become more effective still;
- to 'listen' our preaching colleagues into clearer, richer, deeper speech.

In a word: *We undertake Spirit-ed Conversation in Covenant Community.*
What practices can we employ to embody this covenant commitment?

- Each session will commence with centring silence, or common prayer.
- No one will take notes during sermon delivery.
- Three preachers, one after another, will offer their sermons to the community.
- A period of silence will follow *each* sermon, so everyone can take notes (to assist them in 'holding' what they have heard – and remind them of questions they wish to pose, or issues they would like the community to address).
- At the conclusion of the three sermons, the group will take a short break.
- The company reconvenes. Each preacher will be invited *briefly* to express immediate feelings, and to request specific feedback (*not* to offer explanation, justification or elaboration).
- The community will then engage the offerings of each preacher, responding to the following four questions – *in sequence*:

1. **What are we still *hearing*?**

A descriptive naming of sermon content and listener awareness only. Not an evaluative assessment of theological competence or homiletical skill.

2. **Where are these sermons *leading*?**

An expression of where and how listeners experience the *dynamic focus* of each sermon – where it invites and empowers listeners, individually and corporately, to take a *next step* in the adventure of faith.

3. How did these sermons *play*?

An explicit naming of the theological and rhetorical elements employed in each sermon – what has fostered the 'hearings' that listeners have just experienced.

A discussion of *hermeneutical stances* and *homiletical strategies* – *NOT* an assessment of (or a debate about) *EITHER*.

4. How might these sermons *grow*?

A collegial conversation regarding possible *advantages and disadvantages* in the various strategies and techniques employed. (Any sermon strategy or technique comes with benefits and costs.)

A consideration of potential *modifications, additions, deletions, other directions* that might further sharpen and enrich the vision and direction of each sermon. (Respecting each preacher's own hearing, listeners pose the question: 'What would happen IF . . . ?')

At the end of the session all preachers will be invited to respond to what their sermons have evoked.

To summarize:

- We are not engaged in 'critiquing the speeches' but in 'continuing the conversation'. The primary question is not: 'What did I think about that sermon? but: 'What do we hear; and how might God speak through that?'
- If we approach with the narrowly focused objective of 'helping the preacher out', we may miss much of what we can learn of God by listening to each other. (And we may not be of much help to the preachers either!)
- If we approach with the broader, deeper objective of preaching – not as 'religious monologue' but as '*Spirit*-ed Conversation', we will (in all likelihood) offer nurture to each other, and enhance our own preaching vocation as well.

Responding to a sermon

Responses to these five questions can unfold in a wide variety of ways:

Appendix

1. **What are we still *hearing*?**

(What do we continue to hear, see, smell, taste and touch – immediately and reflectively?)

- **Point** ('The sermon *said* . . . ')
- **Picture** ('What I *saw* was . . . ')
- **Phrase** ('The words that keep *ringing* in my ear are . . . ')
- **Feeling** ('What I continue to *sense* is . . . ')
- **Free Association** ('What the preacher said makes me *think of* . . . ')
- **Question** ('But what if . . . ?' 'I was left wondering about . . . ')
- **Insight** ('I said to myself "AH HA!"')
- **Energy Pulse** ('I found myself saying: "YES!" "NO!" "WHAT!" "WHY!"')
- **Centring Focus** ('For me, what all this comes down to is . . . ')

2. **Where might this be *leading*?**

(Where in God's name are we going? What is the sermon's dynamic direction for us? What are we moved to do?)

- To offer thanks, praise, or petition
- To confess doubt, wound, or misdirected behaviour
- To think further upon, or differently about
- To talk things over with others
- To plan, undertake action, enlist the action of others
- To agree, disagree, or press the issue.

3. **How does this sermon *work*?**

- Hermeneutical *Stances*

   o What theological vision or orientation serves as a lens for the preacher?
   o How is Scripture understood and employed?
   o How do Christian doctrines and/or practices inform the sermon?

- Homiletical *Strategies*

   o How are the 'voices' that speak – in the *Scriptures*, in *society and culture*, in *faith communities (near and far)*, in the *liturgical/worship setting*, and in the *preacher's own experience* – *individually engaged* and *invited into dialogue* in this sermon?

o How are elements of *image, argument* and *story employed* and *integrated*?

o How is the sermon 'shaped' and 'plotted'?

  • How does it unfold through a discernible *trajectory* toward a clear *telos*?

  • How do *sequence, pacing* and *proportion* foster listener *attention* and *discovery*?

o Does the sermon *Instruct – Explain – Implore* or – *Engage – Evoke – Empower*?

4. How might this sermon *grow*?

(How can the good work begun in the sermon be even more effectively performed?)

• What costs and benefits are involved in these patterns of sermon play?
There are no cost-free sermon strategies. What is gained/lost by the strategies used?
• Question posed to the preacher: 'What would happen IF . . . ?'
How might this sermon look and sound when it 'grows up'?

Index

Index